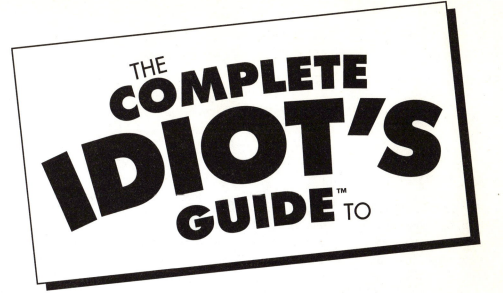

Netscape® Communicator 4

by Joe Kraynak

que®

A Division of Macmillian Publishing
201 W. 103rd Street, Indianapolis, IN 46290 USA

To Marc Andreessen, Netscape founder, for demonstrating how easy it is to work your way through college.

©1997 Que Books

All rights reserved. No part of this book shall be reproduced, stored in a retrieval system, or transmitted by any means, electronic, mechanical, photocopying, recording, or otherwise, without written permission from the publisher. No patent liability is assumed with respect to the use of the information contained herein. Although every precaution has been taken in the preparation of this book, the publisher and author assume no responsibility for errors or omissions. Neither is any liability assumed for damages resulting from the use of the information contained herein. For information, address Que, 201 W. 103rd Street, Indianapolis, IN 46290. You may reach Que's direct sales line by calling 1-800-428-5331.

International Standard Book Number: 0-7897-1029-3
Library of Congress Catalog Card Number: 96-72223

99 98 97   8 7 6 5 4 3 2 1

Interpretation of the printing code: the rightmost number of the first series of numbers is the year of the book's printing; the rightmost number of the second series of numbers is the number of the book's printing. For example, a printing code of 97-1 shows that the first printing of the book occurred in 1997.

Screen reproductions in this book were created by means of the program Collage Complete from Inner Media, Inc., Hollis, NH.

Printed in the United States of America

President
Roland Elgey

Senior Vice President
Don Fowley

Publisher
Joseph B. Wikert

Publishing Manager
Jim Minatel

General Manager
Joe Muldoon

Editorial Services Director
Elizabeth Keaffaber

Managing Editor
Thomas F. Hayes

Acquisitions Editor
Martha O'Sullivan

Product Development Specialist
John Gosney

Production Editor
Mark Enochs

Product Marketing Manager
Kristine R. Ankney

Cover Designers
Dan Armstrong
Barbara Kordesh

Designer
Kim Scott

Illustrations
Judd Winick

Technical Specialist
Nadeem Muhammed

Media Development Specialist
David Garratt

Indexer
Tim Tate

Production Team
Bryan Flores
Jessica Ford
Julie Geeting
Laura A. Knox
Tim Neville

*Special thanks to Christy Gleeson for ensuring
the technical accuracy of this book.
"Frumpy the Clown" was used by permission of Creator's Syndicate.*

We'd Like to Hear from You!

Que Corporation has a long-standing reputation for high-quality books and products. To ensure your continued satisfaction, we also understand the importance of customer service and support.

Tech Support

If you need assistance with the information in this book or with a CD/disk accompanying the book, please access Macmillan Computer Publishing's online Knowledge Base at:

http://www.superlibrary.com/general/support

Our most Frequently Asked Questions are answered there. If you do not find the answer to your questions on our Web site, you may contact Macmillan Technical Support by phone at 317/581-3833 or via e-mail at support@mcp.com.

Also be sure to visit Que's Desktop Applications and Operating Systems team Web resource center for all the latest information, enhancements, errata, downloads, and more:

http://www.quecorp.com/desktop_os/

Orders, Catalogs, and Customer Service

To order other Que or Macmillan Computer Publishing books, catalogs, or products, please contact our Customer Service Department:

Phone: 800/428-5331

Fax: 800/835-3202

International Fax: 317/228-4400

Or visit our online bookstore:

http://www.mcp.com/

Comments and Suggestions

We want you to let us know what you like or dislike most about this book or other Que products. Your comments will help us to continue publishing the best books available on computer topics in today's market.

> John Gosney
> Product Director
> Que Corporation
> 201 West 103rd Street, 4B
> Indianapolis, Indiana 46290 USA
>
> Fax: 317/581-4663
>
> CompuServe: **10436,2300**
>
> E-mail: **jgosney@que.mcp.com**

Please be sure to include the book's title and author as well as your name and phone or fax number.

We will carefully review your comments and share them with the author. Please note that due to the high volume of mail we receive, we may not be able to reply to every message.

Thank you for choosing Que!

Contents at a Glance

Part 1: Getting Wired with Netscape Communicator — 1

1. What Is Netscape Communicator? — 3
   The five programs that make up Communicator.
2. Installing, Connecting, and Exploring — 13
   In one chapter, you're up and running on the Web!

Part Deux: Mastering Netscape Navigator — 23

3. Weaving Through the World Wide Web — 25
   High-powered navigational tools.
4. Finding Information and Other Resources — 37
   Ten search tools you can't live without, and how to use them.
5. What Could Possibly Go Wrong? — 51
   Decipher error messages and regain your footing.
6. Revisiting Your Favorite Haunts — 57
   Tag your favorite Web pages with bookmarks.
7. Tuning into the Web with Netcaster — 71
   High-powered navigational tools.
8. Saving and Printing Your Finds — 83
   Haul off truckloads of goodies, and print them.
9. Driving Off-Road to FTP and Gopher Sites — 93
   When you need something that's not on the Web.
10. Customizing Navigator to Make It Your Own — 103
    Change Navigator's look, feel, and performance.
11. Digital Certificates, Cookies, and Other Security Issues — 113
    Make the Internet safe for you and your kids.

Part 3: Playing Video, Sound, and Interactive Worlds — 125

12. Going Multimedia with Plug-Ins and ActiveX Controls — 127
    Play sounds, pictures, and video clips.
13. Beefing Up Navigator with Helper Applications — 139
    Make Navigator more capable than it already is.
14. Exploring Java, Shockwave, and Virtual Worlds — 149
    Go three-dimensional and interactive with Navigator.

Part 4: Talking to Other People — 163

15 Corresponding with Electronic Mail — 165
Use Netscape Messenger to send and receive missives.

16 Managing Your E-Mail Messages — 181
Keep your inbox organized and uncluttered.

17 Creating and Using an Address Book — 191
Keep track of your friends, relatives, and colleagues.

18 Reading and Posting Newsgroup Messages — 199
Special interest bulletin boards.

19 Free Long Distance with Conference — 213
Meet, chat, and even write on a chalkboard.

Part 5: Publishing Your Own Web Pages — 227

20 Making a Simple Web Page — 229
Express yourself on the Web!

21 All You Need to Know About Links — 243
Link your page to other files and pages on the Web.

22 Working with Tables and Frames — 253
Learn the fancy Web page layout tools.

23 Formatting and Publishing Your Page — 267
Now that it's created, place your page on the Web.

Speak Like a Geek: The Complete Archive — 281
A glossary for Internet nerd wannabees.

Index — 293
Find (and refind) information in this book.

Contents

Part 1: Getting Wired with Netscape Communicator   1

1 What Is Netscape Communicator?   3

Netscape Navigator Center Stage 4
Netscape Netcaster (Subscribing to Your Favorite Sites) 6
Netscape Messenger (the E-Mail Postal Worker) 6
Netscape Collabra (News for Groupies) 7
Netscape Composer Does Web Pages 8
Netscape Conference (Free Long-Distance Calls) 9
How Communicator's Components Work Together 10
What Else Can Communicator Do? 11
The Least You Need to Know 11

2 Installing, Connecting, and Exploring   13

Where Can You Find Communicator? 14
Snatching Communicator Off the Internet 14
    FTPing with Your Web Browser 15
    Nabbing Communicator with an FTP Program 17
Installing Communicator 19
Day Tripping with Netscape Communicator 20
    Juggling Communicator Components with the
    Component Bar 21
The Least You Need to Know 22

Part Deux: Mastering Netscape Navigator   23

3 Weaving Through the World Wide Web   25

Moseying Around the Navigator Screen 26
Navigational Tools of the Trade 27
    Toolbar Basics 27
    What's with the Red Links? 28
    Going Home 30
    Recovering from Interrupted Transfers 30
    Going Back to Places You've Been 30
    The History Log of Your Journeys 30

Touring the Web with URLs 31
  URLs Dissected 31
  Hitting the URL Trail 32
  More Location Text Box Tricks 33
  Keyboard Navigation (Look, Ma, No Mouse!) 33
This Page Has No Links! 34
Juggling Two or More Web Documents 35
Working with Window Frames 35
The Least You Need to Know 36

4 Finding Information and Other Resources   37

It's Easy When You Have the Right Form 38
  The Warning Dialog Box: Do You Care? 38
  Composing a Unique Search String 39
  Using Boolean Operators (AND, NOT, and OR) 39
  Other Options Available with Some Search Tools 40
Using Navigator's Search Button 40
Various Search Tools in Action 42
  Yahoo!: Doing the Web by Category 42
  AltaVista: When the Other Search Tools Fail 43
  Macmillan's SuperSeek: Frames Gone Wild 44
  WebCrawler: It's Worth a Try 45
  Excite!: Great for Refining Your Search 45
  InfoSeek: The Newsgroup Search Standout 45
  Lycos: Just Don't Do the Default Search 46
Looking for People 47
  Using Netscape's People Finder Links 47
  Using Web Phone Directories 48
  Tracking Down Your Friends with Finger 48
Finding Tech Support on the Web 50
The Least You Need to Know 50

5 What Could Possibly Go Wrong?   51

Why the Web Is Soooo Buggy 52
Failed DNS Lookup 52
Navigator Can't Find the Document 53
File Contains No Data 54
Does It Seem S...L...O...W? 54
The Least You Need to Know 55

6 Revisiting Your Favorite Haunts   57

Going Back in History (Lists) 58
Making Shortcuts in Windows 95 59
Marking a Page with a Bookmark 59
Giving Your Bookmark List a Makeover 61
    Renaming and Deleting Bookmarks 62
    Shuffling Your Bookmarks 62
    Grouping Bookmarks with Separators and Submenus 63
    When You Add Bookmarks Later… 65
    Ugh! Adding Bookmarks Manually 65
    The Page Moved! 66
Creating and Saving Additional Bookmark Lists 66
Trading Bookmark Lists with Your Friends 67
Create Your Own Toolbar 68
The Least You Need to Know 69

7 Tuning into the Web with Netcaster   71

What's All This Push Content Nonsense? 72
Starting Netcaster: What Is This Thing? 73
Channel-Surfing with Netcaster 74
    Finding High-Profile Web Channels 74
    Adding and Viewing Channels from Channel Finder 75
    Updating Page Content Manually 77
    Adding Any Web Site as a Channel 77
    Tuning Out: Deleting a Channel 77
Placing Live Content Right on Your Desktop 78
Taking Control of the Netcaster Window 79
Browsing Offline to Save Time and Money 81
The Least You Need to Know 81

8 Saving and Printing Your Finds   83

Saving and Playing Clips and Pictures 84
What About Web Pages? 85
Taking a Peek at the Locals 87
Making Paper—Printing 88
    Entering Your Page Preferences 88
    Previewing Pages Before You Print 89
Hanging Wallpaper on the Windows Background 90
The Least You Need to Know 91

xi

9 Driving Off-Road to FTP and Gopher Sites — 93

FTP and Gopher: What They're All About 94
Connecting to an FTP Server 95
   Public (Anonymous) Servers 95
   Connecting to a Private FTP Server 96
   Navigating an FTP Server 97
   Downloading (Copying) Files from an FTP Server 98
   ZIP, TAR, and Other Compressed Files 98
Uploading Files 99
Navigating the Internet with Gopher Menus 100
   Searching Gopherspace with Veronica 100
The Least You Need to Know 102

10 Customizing Navigator to Make It Your Own — 103

Turning Toolbars On and Off 104
Speeding Up Page Loading 105
Giving Navigator a Makeover 106
   A Peek at the Appearance Options 106
   Dressing Your Text in the Right Font 107
   Taking Your Crayolas to the Screen 108
Changing the Navigator Settings 109
Working Offline to Save Time and Money 109
Tinkering with Some Additional Settings 110
   Establishing a Strong Cache Flow 110
   A Word About the Proxies Category 111
The Least You Need to Know 112

11 Digital Certificates, Cookies, and Other Security Issues — 113

Transferring Information Securely on the Net 114
Setting Navigator's Security Options 114
   Turning Security Warnings On and Off 115
   Is This Site Secure? 116
Grabbing Some Cookies 117
Using Digital Certificates 118
   Obtaining and Using Digital Certificates 119
   Protecting Your Certificates 120
   Using Site Certificates 120
Preventing Viruses from Entering Your System 121
Censoring Naughty Net Sites 122
The Least You Need to Know 123

Part 3: Playing Video, Sound, and Interactive Worlds — 125

12 Going Multimedia with Plug-Ins and ActiveX Controls — 127

Helper Applications, Plug-Ins, and ActiveX Controls 128
File Types that Navigator Can Play 128
Grabbing Plug-Ins the Easy Way 129
Visiting the Plug-In Warehouse 130
   Downloading from Stroud's 132
   Before You Download 133
   Downloading Files with Navigator 133
Installing and Uninstalling Plug-Ins 134
   Installing a Plug-In 134
   Uninstalling Plug-Ins 134
Playing ActiveX Controls 136
The Least You Need to Know 137

13 Beefing Up Navigator with Helper Applications — 139

How Do Helper Applications Help? 140
Decompressing and Installing the Software 140
Mapping Files to Their Helper Applications 141
Playing Multimedia Links 145
Do It! Cinema, Sounds, and Photos 145
A Word About Sound and Video Quality 146
The Least You Need to Know 146

14 Exploring Java, Shockwave, and Virtual Worlds — 149

What Is Java? 150
Can These Applets Hurt Me? 150
Playing Java Applets 151
Getting Shocked! 154
   Downloading and Installing Shockwave 154
   Playing with Shockwave 155
What Is VRML? 155
Using Netscape's Cosmo Player 156
Navigating with Cosmo Player 157
Exploring Some Worlds 159
Other VRML Browsers 160
The Least You Need to Know 161

Part 4: Talking to Other People — 163

15 Corresponding with Electronic Mail — 165

Running Netscape Messenger 166
You Have to Set It Up First 166
Writing (and Sending) an E-Mail Message 168
    Attaching Files to E-Mail Messages 169
    Getting Fancy with Formatting Tools and Graphics ... 170
    Sending a Copy of the Message to Another Person 172
    Entering Other Message Options 173
Reading and Responding to Incoming Mail 175
    Retrieving and Reading Your Mail 175
    Viewing and Saving Attachments 176
    Responding to Messages 176
    Quoting the Previous Message in Your Reply 177
Configuring Netscape Messenger 178
    Changing the Way Messages Are Displayed 179
    Changing Options for Outgoing Mail 179
The Least You Need to Know 180

16 Managing Your E-Mail Messages — 181

Using the Message Window and Message Center 182
    Taking Control of the Message Window 182
    Nickel Tour of the Message Center 183
Organizing Messages with Folders 184
Selecting, Moving, Copying, and Deleting Messages 184
Telling Messenger Where to Place Incoming Messages ... 186
Sorting Your Messages 187
Making Messenger Check for Mail Automatically 189
The Least You Need to Know 190

17 Creating and Using an Address Book — 191

Adding E-Mail Addresses to Messenger's Address Book ... 192
    Lifting E-Mail Addresses from Messages 193
    Adding Addresses from Online E-Mail Directories 193
    Importing an Address Book 194
Inserting Addresses from the Address Book 194
Doing Mass Mailings with Mailing Lists 196
Making and Using Your Own Electronic Business Card .. 197
The Least You Need to Know 197

18 Reading and Posting Newsgroup Messages — 199

Starting Netscape Collabra 200
Before You Can Read Newsgroups… 201
Doing Newsgroups from Navigator and Collabra 202
    Grabbing a (Long) List of Newsgroups 203
    Subscribing to a Newsgroup 204
Reading Newsgroup Messages 205
    Viewing Replies to Posted Messages 207
    Sorting and Searching for Messages 207
Replying to Newsgroup Messages 208
    Starting a New Discussion 210
Receiving and Sending Files in Newsgroups 210
Reading Newsgroups Offline 211
The Least You Need to Know 212

19 Free Long Distance with Conference — 213

What You (and the Person You're Calling)
Need to Get Started 214
Setting Up Netscape Conference 215
Placing a Call and Hanging Up 217
    Finding a Person in the Web Phonebook 218
    Using Your Address Book to Place Calls 219
    Creating Speed Dial Buttons 220
    No Answer? Leave a Voicemail Message 221
No Sound? 221
Answering Incoming Calls 222
Typing Messages with the Chat Tool 222
Collaborating with Whiteboard 223
    Here We Go! Using the Whiteboard 223
Team Web Browsing 225
Sending Files 225
The Least You Need to Know 226

Part 5: Publishing Your Own Web Pages — 227

20 Making a Simple Web Page — 229

Webtop Publishing with Composer 230
Running Composer 231
Step-by-Step Web Pages with the Wizard 233

Creating Your Own Web Page Using a Template 235
Starting with Your Bookmarks 237
Making Some Quick Adjustments 237
    Deleting and Adding Text 237
    Basic Formatting Options 238
    Inserting Graphics and Lines 239
    Checking for Misspellings and Typos 241
The Least You Need to Know 242

21 All You Need to Know About Links   243

Creating a Simple Link 244
    Editing and Removing Links 244
    Understanding Absolute and Relative Links 245
Linking Your Page to Other Pages at Your Site 246
Linking to a Specific Place on a Page 247
Inserting a Link for Your E-Mail Address 249
Drag-and-Drop Web Page Creation 249
Testing Your Links 250
The Least You Need to Know 251

22 Working with Tables and Frames   253

Inserting a Table 255
    Typing Entries into Cells 257
    Restructuring Your Table 257
    Adding and Deleting Rows, Columns, and Cells 259
    Page Formatting with Tables 259
    Framing Your Masterpiece 260
    Composer Doesn't Do Frames 261
    Entering the Frame Codes 262
    Holding Your Index Steady in the Left Frame 264
The Least You Need to Know 264

23 Formatting and Publishing Your Page   267

Fancy Text Formatting 268
Changing the Look of Your Graphics 269
Coloring Your Page 270

Using a Background Image 271
    Adding a Background Image to Your Page 272
Adding a Title, Description, and Keywords 273
Getting Your Page Out on the Web 274
    Finding a Home for Your Page 274
    Configuring Composer's Publisher 275
    Publishing Your Pages 276
Publicizing Your Page 278
The Least You Need to Know 279

Speak Like a Geek: The Complete Archive — 281

Index — 293

Introduction

When it began, the Internet was little more than a hangout for computer nerds, defense workers, and a handful of university students and professors. Internet connections allowed them to share computer resources and data, swap files, and exchange messages electronically. The Internet didn't offer much to excite the populace. It just couldn't compete with cable TV.

In a few short years, however, the Internet has made millions of people trade in their TV controls for mice. Baby boomers, retirees, high-school students, and even kindergarten kids are flocking to the Internet to channel-surf through a sea of multimedia pages offering music and movie clips, financial data, vacation information, shopping malls, electronic mailboxes, bulletin boards, game rooms, and much, much more.

With a local Internet connection and a copy of a Netscape Communicator, you can join in this mass migration to the Internet. Communicator comes complete with the Web browser you need to display and navigate through the billions of multimedia pages that make up the World Wide Web. Communicator also comes with an e-mail program (for sending and receiving messages), a newsreader (for posting and reading messages in newsgroups), a conference program (for virtual meetings and free long-distance "phone" calls), and a Web page creation tool (so you can publish your own multimedia pages on the Web).

But You'd Have to Be a Genius...!

Nah! You don't have to be a genius to wander the World Wide Web or use Netscape Communicator. You don't have to know how the Internet works, or even how the text, pretty pictures, sounds, and movie clips travel from computers all around the world to your computer. You have more important things to learn, like:

- Where to get the latest version of Netscape Communicator.
- How to install, run, and configure Netscape Communicator (or Communicator, for short).
- How to use Communicator's Web browser (Netscape Navigator) to bounce around the World Wide Web.
- How to make a list of your favorite Web documents.
- How to get pictures and video clips… and look at them.
- How to send e-mail messages, and read incoming messages.
- How to read messages in newsgroups and post your own replies and messages.
- How to create and publish your own pages on the Web.

In this book, you'll be up and running with Navigator in two—count 'em, two—chapters. In the remaining chapters, you'll learn how to use Communicator to fly around in the Web and plunder its resources. You'll be surprised at how little you *need to know* in order to use Communicator… and how much you *can know* to cruise the Internet like a master.

And You Are...?

In writing this book, I came up with a few generalizations about you. First, I figure you have some computer savvy. You know how to work with directories (folders), save and open files, and run programs. You've managed to set up your modem and establish an Internet connection (or you've suckered a friend into doing it for you). You may not sleep with your computer, but you feel pretty comfortable with it.

However, I could be wrong. If your knowledge of computers and modems is limited to what you've seen on *Good Morning, America*, maybe you should start with a more general computer book. I suggest *The Complete Idiot's Guide to PCs* (for general computer knowledge) and *The Complete Idiot's Guide to the Internet, Third Edition* (if you're not wired to the Internet yet, you can get some free "online time" with the purchase of this book).

How We Do Things in This Part of the Country

There are several conventions in this book to make it easier to use. Here's a list:

➤ Any text you type or items you select appear **bold**. For example, you click the **Start** button or type **Help!**.

➤ If you have to press two or more keys to enter a command, the keys are separated with plus signs. For example, you might press **Ctrl+C** to copy a selected item. To enter the command, hold down the first key while pressing the second one.

➤ Finally, any text you might see on your screen is shown in a funny-looking type like this: `OK`. For example, you might see a `Login:` prompt asking you to type your username.

If you want to understand more about the Internet, the World Wide Web, Navigator, and the commands you're told to enter, you'll find some background information in boxes. I put this sideline information in boxes so you can skip the gory details. But, just in case you're interested, look for the following icons:

Check This Out ...

These boxes contain notes, tips, warnings, and other information about the Web, the Internet, and Navigator. Some of these boxes contain only snide comments and quips.

Technical Twaddle

These boxes contain high-tech fluff that I promised not to inflict on you, but I would feel guilty if I didn't include it. You can skip this background fodder (technical twaddle) unless you're truly interested.

Frequently Asked Questions

Look to the FAQ (*Frequently Asked Questions*) box for answers to common questions about Netscape Communicator and other Internet topics.

Common Trademark Courtesy

As a courtesy to all the computer and program manufacturers who have complicated our lives, we have decided to list their trademarks or service marks here (so you'll know who's responsible). In addition, if we suspected a term of being a trademark or service mark (you just can't trust anyone these days), we capitalized it. We at Que cannot attest to the accuracy of this information, so don't expect any of this information to hold up in court.

Netscape Communications, Netscape, and Mozilla (Netscape's old mascot) are trademarks of Netscape Communications Corporation. (Although Netscape Navigator is a take-off of Mosaic, another Web Browser, Netscape Communications Corporation lives under the illusion that Navigator is an original idea.)

Microsoft Windows 95 is a registered trademark of Microsoft Corporation, and you can bet that you'll be sued if you try to use it.

Que Corporation, an imprint of Macmillan Publishing USA, is a Simon and Schuster Company.

Part 1
Getting Wired with Netscape Communicator

The vast ribbon of electronic highway we call the Internet is winding through networks, cables, and satellites as we speak. However, before you can start cruising this highway, you need to find a connection (an on-ramp) and you need an appropriate vehicle (a program to help you navigate).

In this part, I'll show you just what to do. I'll introduce you to the six programs that make up the Netscape Communicator suite, where to get the latest version of Communicator, and how to install it. I'll give you a sneak peek at Communicator's Web browser, Netscape Navigator, revealing its many navigational tools. I'll even take you on a quick tour of the Web to give you a little hands-on practice at the controls.

Chapter 1

What Is Netscape Communicator?

In This Chapter

- ➤ Name Netscape Communicator's six components
- ➤ Recognize Navigator when it pops up on your screen
- ➤ Tell the difference between Messenger and Collabra
- ➤ Find out what Composer composes
- ➤ Figure out whether you will ever need Netscape Conference

Netscape Communicator is essentially an all-in-one Internet gadget, sort of like that watch that Dick Tracy used to wear. Communicator provides you with a single window from which you can access the most common Internet features, including the World Wide Web, e-mail, and newsgroups. You simply point and click on what you want; Communicator figures out which tool to use to get you there.

In addition, many of Communicator's components work together to provide you with even more powerful tools. For example, Composer (the tool for creating Web pages) allows you to create multimedia e-mail messages, which you can then send with Messenger (the e-mail component). Because Communicator's components work together so seamlessly, you may never realize that you're actually using six different components!

This chapter introduces you to Netscape Communicator's six components and shows you how they work together.

Netscape Communicator Professional Edition

Netscape offers a "Professional" version of Communicator that offers three extra components: Calendar, AutoAdmin, and IBM Host-On-Demand. Calendar is a personal information manager. If you've ever used one of these PIMs, you've probably already sworn them off. AutoAdmin lets network administrators poke around in your private business on the Internet. And IBM Host-On-Demand is for eggheads who want to create their own Web applications. In short, this book doesn't cover any of these professional components.

Netscape Navigator Center Stage

At the core of Netscape Communicator is Netscape Navigator, Netscape's award-winning *Web browser*. To understand Navigator, you first need to know a little about the World Wide Web (the Web, for short). The Web is a collection of interconnected, multimedia pages. Think of it as a multimedia CD-ROM encyclopedia whose pages are stored on thousands of computers all over the world.

A Web browser is a program that can open and display these multimedia pages and carry you from one page to another, anywhere in the world. These pages may contain text, pictures, video clips, three-dimensional worlds, interactive programs, music and audio clips, and anything else that can be digitized and placed on a computer.

When you start Navigator, it automatically opens Netscape's home page. You can then use Navigator to open other pages, either by entering the address of a specific page, or by clicking on *links*. Links are pictures, icons, or highlighted text that point you to other locations and pages on the Web or to other resources on the Internet.

Internet versus Web

The Internet is a vast collection of interconnected computers that allows users to exchange e-mail, exchange files, post and read messages, open multimedia pages, and perform other tasks using remote computers. The Web is a subset of the Internet. The Web is in charge of serving up special Web pages that contain text, graphics, audio and video clips, interactive programs, and links to other pages.

Chapter 1 ➤ What Is Netscape Communicator?

Although I compare the Web to a multimedia encyclopedia, it is much more than that. The Web contains online versions of popular (and not so popular) magazines, such as *Time* and *PC Computing*, travel bureaus, government agencies, music labels, movie studios, classrooms, game rooms, museums, and much more. The Web is sort of like a big city, offering the best, and the worst, of what most real cities have to offer.

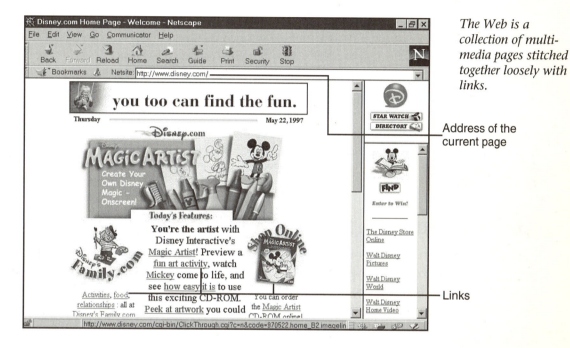

The Web is a collection of multimedia pages stitched together loosely with links.

Address of the current page

Links

You will learn much more about Netscape Navigator in Part Deux, "Mastering Netscape Navigator," and in Part 3, "Playing Video, Sound, and Interactive Worlds."

A Brief History

When it first started in 1994, Netscape Corporation had a single product called Netscape, a program for navigating the World Wide Web and opening multimedia Web pages. When Netscape started to acquire and develop additional Web tools (such as Mail and News), it renamed its Web browser Netscape Navigator to distinguish it from the other tools. With Navigator's support for the latest Web technology and its superior navigational tools, it soon commanded over 85 percent of the Web browser market. With Communicator, Netscape has assembled several of its most popular Internet tools into a single package, providing a suite of integrated programs.

Netscape Netcaster (Subscribing to Your Favorite Sites)

One of the latest breakthroughs on the Web is the concept of *push content*. The idea behind push content is that instead of using a browser to *pull* pages to your computer, you subscribe to your favorite Web sites, and have those sites *push* the latest information to you during off-hours or when your Web browser is not actively transferring other data. You can then open the pages and view them at your convenience. Because the pages are already on your hard drive, you can open and view them much more quickly.

Netscape Netcaster allows you to set up subscriptions to your favorite sites and control the frequency at which those sites send you updated information. For instance, you can subscribe to CNN for up-to-the-minute news, weather, and sports. Netcaster also transforms your Windows desktop into a Webtop that makes your desktop act like a Web page, and displays icons for all your subscriptions, giving you quick access to the information you need. To learn more about Netscape Netcaster, see Chapter 7, "Tuning into the Web with Netcaster."

Netscape Messenger (the E-Mail Postal Worker)

Netscape Messenger (formerly known as Netscape Mail) is Communicator's e-mail program. E-mail is one of the most popular features offered on the Internet, allowing users to have heated arguments with people they barely know. With an e-mail program, you can exchange e-mail messages and attached files with anyone in the world who has an Internet connection. This mail is postage-free (as long as you pay your monthly Internet membership fee), and the mail typically reaches its destination in a matter of seconds.

Netscape Messenger makes it easy to address and send messages to your friends, relatives, and colleagues. You enter a command to send a new message, and then you complete the dialog box that appears, entering the recipient's e-mail address, a description of the message, and the message itself. You can also attach and send a file that's on your hard disk. After the message arrives in the recipient's e-mail box, the recipient can use his or her e-mail program to display the message and retrieve any attached files. Messenger also offers an address book to help you keep track of e-mail addresses.

When you are on the receiving end of an e-mail message, Messenger doubles as an e-mail reader, allowing you to check your electronic mailbox, read incoming messages, and retrieve any attached files. Messenger provides high-powered organizational tools to help you sort messages, group them in folders, and delete old messages. (Chapters 15, "Corresponding with Electronic Mail," 16, "Managing Your E-Mail Messages," and 17, "Creating and Using an Address Book," show you how to use Messenger to send and receive messages and files, keep your inbox and outbox organized, and create and use an address book.)

Chapter 1 ➤ *What Is Netscape Communicator?*

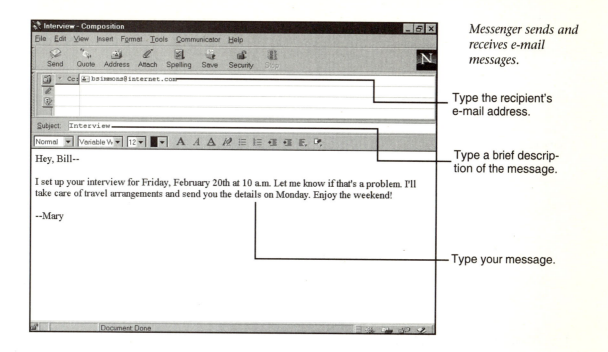

Messenger sends and receives e-mail messages.

— Type the recipient's e-mail address.

— Type a brief description of the message.

— Type your message.

Netscape Collabra (News for Groupies)

Netscape Collabra is a revamped version of Netscape News, Netscape's news reader. In case you're wondering, a *news reader* is a program that lets you read and post messages in a *newsgroup*, an electronic bulletin board where people with similar interests can post announcements, questions, concerns, opinions, and files. The Internet has thousands of newsgroups covering just about every topic you can imagine: caring for roses, lifting weights, debugging programs, fixing cars, refinishing furniture, and so on.

Although Collabra still allows you to read and post messages in Internet newsgroups, Netscape has added features to make Collabra more of a corporate tool. Instead of collaborating on projects by sending e-mail messages back and forth, colleagues can create discussion groups on the company intranet, where they can share information, ask questions, post updated material, and exchange ideas.

Intranet Hype

Intranets are local versions of the global Internet. An intranet is essentially a network (in a company or university, for instance) that uses intranet technology for exchanging e-mail messages and files, sharing computer resources, and distributing information.

7

As you work with Collabra, you will notice that it has the same look and feel as Netscape Messenger. This consistent look enables you to learn how to perform tasks in Collabra much more quickly.

Collabra lets you read and post messages in newsgroups.

When you access a newsgroup, Collabra displays a list of posted messages and replies.

Netscape Composer Does Web Pages

After you stumble around the Web for a couple hours and you see how cool it is, you will inevitably start to think that you would like to place your own page on the Web. The problem is that Web pages have a lot of complicated codes that tell the Web browser how to display the text, insert pictures, and link to other Web pages. In the past, you had to type these codes manually, using a text editor (such as Windows' Notepad).

Fortunately, Netscape Composer can handle the codes for you. You simply type the text, and then use Composer's formatting tools to change the look and layout of the text. Composer also has commands for inserting pictures, sounds, and video clips; adding a page background; inserting links to other pages; and adding tables. You create the page just as if you were typing a document in a word processing program. Composer adds the codes behind-the-scenes, so you don't have to mess with them.

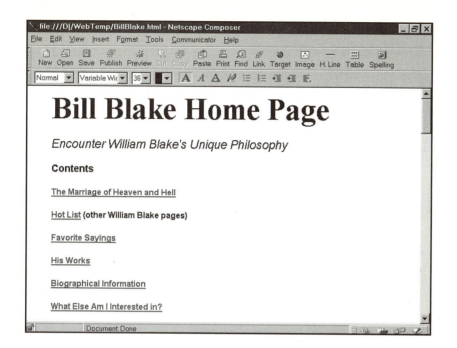

Netscape Composer helps you create and publish your own Web pages.

Netscape Conference (Free Long-Distance Calls)

Netscape used to offer a program called CoolTalk, which allowed you to place long-distance phone calls over the Internet. With CoolTalk, a sound card (with microphone), and an Internet connection, you could place a phone call to anyone, anywhere in the world, who had a copy of CoolTalk, a sound card (with microphone), and an Internet connection. The sound quality was lousy, and the person you called had to wait at the computer for your call—but hey, it was free!

Well, Netscape Conference is CoolTalk with a focus more on teleconferencing. You can still use Conference to place long-distance phone calls over the Internet, but Conference now focuses more on collaborating over the Internet. With Conference, you can type messages and transmit them to anyone who is currently sitting in on the meeting. You can exchange files, and surf the Web collaboratively. You can also display documents on a whiteboard, write comments on the document, and even have a doodling contest with your fellow workers.

You could do most of that in CoolTalk, too, but Conference offers several improvements, especially in regards to holding virtual meetings. For details on using Conference, see Chapter 19, "Free Long Distance with Conference."

Why Use Netscape Conference?

Over a slow modem connection (slower than 28.8Kbps), Netscape Conference is useless. Sound doesn't travel all that fast over a modem connection. However, over a network connection, Conference can be a valuable tool, allowing fellow workers to quickly call each other, examine documents and data, tour the Web together, and much more.

How Communicator's Components Work Together

Although Communicator's components perform separate tasks, they are designed to work together as an integrated unit. When you run Navigator, you'll notice that it now has a floating toolbar (a toolbar you can drag around on your screen) that lets you quickly switch to Navigator, Messenger, Collabra, or Composer with a simple click of a button. (You can also switch from one component to another, including Netcaster and Conference, by selecting the desired component from the Communicator menu of any of the other components.)

But simple task-switching is not what makes Communicator an integrated powerhouse. Many of the components support each other, making them even more powerful:

➤ Netcaster works closely with Navigator. Whenever you click a channel in Netcaster, Navigator loads and displays the selected page.

➤ If you click on an e-mail address link on a Web page displayed in Navigator, Messenger runs automatically, and displays the window you need to create and send a message.

➤ Composer's Web page authoring tools are available in Messenger, allowing you to add fancy formatting, graphics, and links to your e-mail messages.

➤ If you receive an e-mail message that contains a link to a Web page, you can click on the link to load the Web page in Navigator.

➤ In Conference, you can cruise the Internet with everyone else who is involved in the virtual meeting by using Navigator to pull up Web pages.

➤ Because Navigator lets you copy files to a remote computer on the Internet, you can save the Web pages you create in Composer to the Web, making them immediately available.

What Else Can Communicator Do?

Netscape Corporation has designed Netscape Communicator to work along with your other applications. You can use Communicator along with Corel's WordPerfect Suite 8 and Office Professional 8 to send e-mail messages directly from WordPerfect, and transform your existing documents into Web pages.

Communicator also provides enhanced support for data and file sharing through ActiveX. With an ActiveX plug-in (a program that adds capability to Communicator), Communicator can open files created in applications that support ActiveX, including the Microsoft Office 97 applications (Word, Excel, and PowerPoint). Communicator can also run ActiveX components, applications you will inevitably encounter on the Internet.

For more information about ActiveX, including instructions on how to obtain and install the ActiveX plug-in, see Chapter 12, "Going Multimedia with Plug-Ins and ActiveX Controls."

> **Techno Talk**
>
> **What Is ActiveX?** ActiveX is a relatively new technology that makes it easy to embed animated objects, data, and computer code on Web pages. With ActiveX controls and the right plug-in, Navigator can play ActiveX components and open documents that support ActiveX.

The Least You Need to Know

This chapter gave you the lowdown on Netscape's new Internet suite. When you first start to use it, keep the following points in mind:

- Communicator consists of six components: Navigator, Netcaster, Messenger, Collabra, Composer, and Conference.
- Navigator opens and displays pages on the World Wide Web.
- Netcaster makes your Windows desktop behave more like a Web page, and lets you subscribe to your favorite Web pages and information services.
- Messenger, formerly Netscape Mail, allows you to send and receive messages on electronically on the Internet.
- Collabra, formerly Netscape News, allows you to read and post messages electronic discussion boards (Internet newsgroups and intranet discussion groups).

- Composer helps you create your own Web pages without having to worry about the complex coding that's involved.
- Conference is a combination Internet phone/chat/whiteboard program that lets you have virtual meetings when you're telecommuting due to downsizing.
- Communicator's components help each other out in some incestuous, synergistic relationship that makes each component more powerful than it already is.

Chapter 2

Installing, Connecting, and Exploring

In This Chapter

➤ Grab the latest version of Communicator off the Internet

➤ Put Communicator on your hard drive

➤ Run Communicator

➤ Take Communicator for a day trip on the Internet

Before you can tap into the power of Communicator, you have to snatch a copy and get it up and running. This chapter provides everything you need to know to get started. You'll learn where Communicator hangs out, where to score the latest version, and how to install and run it. You'll even get to pull down a few menus and click a few buttons on a trial run!

Where Can You Find Communicator?

In the old days, Netscape products were like the Gideon Bibles of the Internet. You could find Netscape products everywhere—at the local computer store, on the inside back covers of some Internet books, and even on the Internet. Now that Netscape Communications is actually trying to make money off its Web browser (unlike the famous philanthropist Bill Gates), sales of Netscape products are a little more controlled.

Now, Netscape products have two favorite hangouts—computer stores and the Netscape Communications Internet site. Purchasing the product at a computer store is a no-brainer; you walk in, grab a box off the shelf, and hand over your Visa card. Nabbing a copy off the Internet is a little more complicated, but you don't have to leave your home, and you can probably save a little money in the process. The following section explains the details of downloading Netscape Communicator from the Internet.

Snatching Communicator Off the Internet

When I started working on this book, Netscape offered for free the beta (in-development) version of Netscape Communicator to anyone who wanted to test it or write about it. All you had to do was click on a link for it, save the installation file to your hard drive, and run it. If you're lucky, the beta version is still available; you can grab it and use it legally (and free) for the specified trial period.

Is Netscape Communicator Free? Many people have a strange notion that everything on the Internet is free. Although many Internet offerings are free, you must pay for commercial software. Software companies use the Internet to distribute their products to save you money, make it more convenient, and allow you to quickly update programs—not so they can be ripped off.

However, even if the beta version is not available, you can still download Communicator from Netscape's Internet site. (Netscape does expect you to pay for it, though).

When you download a file from the Internet, you use something called *FTP (File Transfer Protocol)*. This FTP thing is just a file transfer standard that ensures the sending and receiving computers are speaking the same language.

As with most Internet procedures, you can FTP in a number of ways. The easiest way is to use your current Web browser (a different Web browser, such as Internet Explorer, an older version of Navigator, or your online service). The next simplest way to FTP is to use an FTP program, such as WS_FTP, which you should have obtained from your Internet service provider. The following sections explain how to grab a copy of Communicator using either of these methods.

Chapter 2 ➤ *Installing, Connecting, and Exploring*

FTPing with Your Web Browser

You'll learn all about using Communicator to perform FTP file transfers in Chapter 9, "Driving Off-Road to FTP and Gopher Sites," but you have to get Communicator before you can use Communicator to get Communicator. (Sorry, I studied metaphysics in college.) However, if you have a Web browser (Mosaic, Internet Explorer, an old version of Navigator), you can use the browser to quickly download the latest version of Communicator. Here's what you do:

1. Do whatever you have to do to establish your Internet connection. (For example, if you have a modem, you have to run your TCP/IP program to dial into your service provider's computer.)

2. Run your Web browser, and look for an Address, URL, or Location text box or command. Most Web browsers display such a text box at the top of the Window, but others might require you to select the URL or Location command (usually from the File menu).

3. Drag over any text that might be in the URL or Location text box, type **http:// home.netscape.com** and press **Enter**. After a moment, you should be connected to Netscape Corporation's home page.

4. Click on the trail of links until you arrive at the Download Netscape Communicator Software page. Scroll down the page to display a form asking you to pick the product you want and the operating system you use.

5. From the drop-down lists, select the version of Netscape Communicator you want, the operating system you use (for example, Windows 95, Windows 3.1, UNIX, or Macintosh), the language (for example, U.S. English), and your geographical location (for example, North America).

6. Click on the **Click to Display Download Sites** button. Scroll down the page for a list of download sites.

7. Click on the link for the download site nearest you. For example, if you live in the Midwest, you might click on the **Download** link for Washington University in St. Louis. What happens next depends on which Web browser you're using.

8. Take the required steps to download the file using your Web browser.

9. With an old version of Navigator, you simply click the link, and then follow the dialog boxes to nab the file.

10. With Mosaic, hold down the **Shift** key while clicking on the link, and then follow the dialog boxes to complete the task.

15

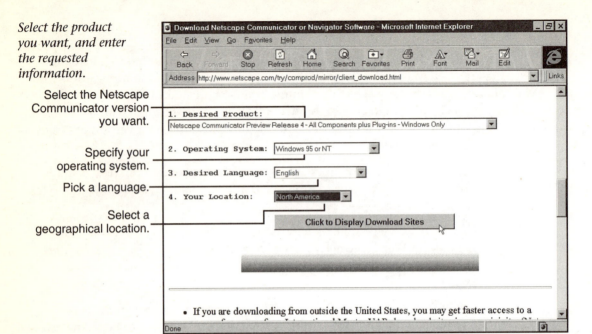

Select the product you want, and enter the requested information.

Select the Netscape Communicator version you want.

Specify your operating system.

Pick a language.

Select a geographical location.

With Internet Explorer, right-click on the link, and select **Save Target As**. Use the dialog boxes to save the file.

11. Wait until the file transfer is complete (you may have to wait quite a while, depending on the speed of your Internet connection).

12. Close your Web browser, and then disconnect from your service provider by using your TCP/IP program.

The easiest, and least expensive, way to pay for a legal copy of Communicator is to purchase an upgrade certificate, using your Visa card. This certificate entitles you to download the current version of Netscape Communicator and any updated versions for a complete year. Netscape then gives you access to a special subscriber's download area. If Netscape updates Communicator, you can download the updates from this area using your certificate.

You can purchase a subscription to Netscape Communicator or other Netscape Products by returning to the Netscape Communicator home page and clicking on the link for purchasing the latest version of Netscape Navigator or Netscape Communicator (or by selecting the subscription option from a drop-down list). This displays a form asking you to specify the type of license (and quantity of licenses) you want. Make the desired selections, and then click on the **Click here to place your order** button.

Chapter 2 ➤ *Installing, Connecting, and Exploring*

A dialog box appears, indicating that you are about to enter a secure Web site (a place where you can safely enter billing and credit card information). Click on the **Continue** button. Netscape presents you with a form asking you to enter billing information. Complete the form by clicking inside each text box, and typing the required entry.

Nabbing Communicator with an FTP Program

Poke around in your program groups to see if you have a Windows FTP program (your service provider may have slipped you an FTP program). One of the more popular Windows FTP programs is called *Ws_ftp*. If you have it, your job is going to be a lot easier. In fact, transferring files with a Windows FTP program is almost as easy as copying and moving files using the Windows Explorer or File Manager. Here's what you do:

1. Make a directory or folder on your hard disk called TEMP, if you don't already have one. (You'll store your files temporarily in this directory or folder.)

2. Run your FTP program. (You may have to run your TCP/IP program to connect to your service provider before you can run the FTP program.)

3. Enter the **Connect** command, and type **ftp2.netscape.com** in the **Host Name** text box. (This is the address of the remote FTP site where you'll get your files.)

   Netscape Corporation has several FTP servers you can try if the first one you try is busy. If you have trouble connecting to ftp2.netscape.com, try reconnecting at **ftp3.netscape.com**, **ftp4.netscape.com**, or another ftp number up to 20.

4. Type **anonymous** in the **User ID** text box.

5. In the **Password** text box, type your e-mail address. For example, you might type **jsmith@iway.com**. If you don't have an e-mail address, try typing your name.

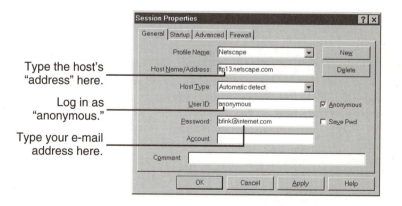

Enter your connect information up front.

Type the host's "address" here.

Log in as "anonymous."

Type your e-mail address here.

17

Part 1 ➤ *Getting Wired with Netscape Communicator*

6. Click the **OK** or **Connect** button. If all goes right, the FTP program connects you to the remote server.

7. Select **Binary** as the Transfer option.

8. Use the **Remote System** list to find the file you need: **c32e40.exe** (for Windows 95) or **c16e40.exe** (for Windows 3.1). (Netscape Corporation is constantly updating Communicator, so the file names you see might differ slightly.)

9. If you have Windows 95, make sure you get the file that has "32" in its name (meaning it is the 32-bit version). If you're still using Windows 3.1, make sure you get the file with "16" in its name.

10. The "40" represents the version number (version 4.0).

Poke Around

At the time this book was published, the Netscape Communicator 4.0 file for Windows 95 was in the /pub/communicator/4.0/4.0b4/windows/ directory. Some joker may have moved the files since then. If you don't find the files in one directory, switch to another directory that looks promising.

11. Use the Local System to change to the TEMP directory on your hard disk.

12. Click the name of the Netscape Communicator file (for example, **c32e40.exe**) to highlight it.

13. Click the arrow button to copy the files from the host computer to your PC.

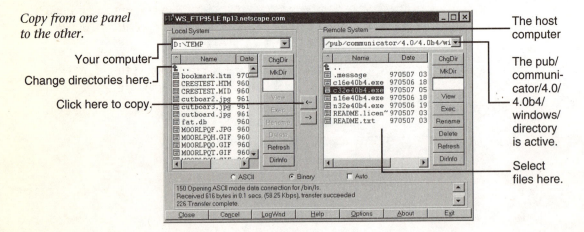

Copy from one panel to the other.

- Your computer
- Change directories here.
- Click here to copy.
- The host computer
- The pub/communicator/4.0/4.0b4/windows/ directory is active.
- Select files here.

14. Wait until the copying is complete.
15. Exit your FTP program.
16. Disconnect from your service provider.

Now you have a self-extracting compressed file on your computer. This file contains all the files that comprise Communicator. Skip ahead to one of the "Installing" sections later in this chapter for instructions on how to proceed.

Installing Communicator

Installing Communicator is a no-brainer. The file you just grabbed is a self-extracting zip file, so all you have to do to unzip it is run the program file. Simply run Windows Explorer (or File Manager, if you're using Windows 3.1), change to the folder or directory that contains the file you just downloaded (for example, c32e40.exe), and then double-click the file.

The Netscape Communicator Installation dialog box appears, telling you that the file you've just chosen to run will install Netscape Communicator. Click **Yes** to proceed. The compressed file extracts itself, placing the Netscape Communicator installation files on your hard drive. The Installation utility starts, and displays the Netscape Communicator Setup window with the Welcome dialog box in front.

In Windows 95, running the file automatically starts the installation utility. In Windows 3.1, running the file merely extracts its contents to the current folder. You must then double-click the **setup.exe** file to run the installation.

The installation utility will lead you through the installation process by displaying a series of dialog boxes, asking you questions, such as "Where do you want us to put the files?" Respond to the dialog box questions to the best of your ability, or just keep clicking on the **Next** button until no more dialog boxes appear. At this point, Communicator is on your computer.

At the end of the installation, you may be asked if you want to look at the Readme file, which contains a bunch of information, such as system requirements. You might also be asked if you want to connect to Netscape's Web site to register. Either of these steps is optional.

Part 1 ➤ *Getting Wired with Netscape Communicator*

The Communicator Installation program installs Communicator for you.

Follow the on-screen instructions to complete the installation.

The Mac Edition...

The Macintosh version of Netscape Communicator comes as an HQX file. When you download an HQX file using an FTP program, the FTP program automatically decompresses the file, and you can run the setup utility. However, if you downloaded the file using a Web browser, the Web browser does not perform this important step. To use the HQX file, you'll first have to decompress it using a program such as StuffIt Expander. Ask your Internet service provider for details.

Day Tripping with Netscape Communicator

After you install Communicator, you should have a Netscape Communicator submenu on the Windows 95 Start, Programs menu and a Netscape Communicator icon on the desktop. If you're using Windows 3.1, check the Netscape Communicator program group for the icons you need to run Communicator's various components. To run Navigator (the Web browser), first establish your Internet connection, and then double-click on the **Netscape Communicator** icon (on the Windows 95 desktop), or select Netscape Navigator from the Netscape Communicator program group. Navigator runs and displays Netscape's Home Page.

Chapter 2 ➤ *Installing, Connecting, and Exploring*

Juggling Communicator Components with the Component Bar

You should also see a floating toolbar, called the *Component bar*, in the upper right corner of the screen. If the Component bar is not displayed, open the **Communicator** menu and select **Show Component Bar**. (You can "dock" this bar to the status bar by opening the **Communicator** menu and selecting **Dock Component Bar**. Docking shrinks the toolbar and anchors it to the lower right corner of the window.)

When undocked, the Component bar floats on the desktop, and allows you to quickly switch to the other Netscape Communicator components. The Component bar offers the following buttons:

➤ **Navigator** for running Navigator.

➤ **Mailbox** for displaying a Netscape Messenger window that shows a list of e-mail messages you have received.

➤ **Discussion Groups** for running Collabra, Communicator's news reader.

➤ **Composer** for creating and publishing your own Web pages.

Just click on the button for the Communicator component you want to use. You can right-click on the toolbar's title bar to display a menu for controlling and customizing the Component bar, or you can drag the title bar to move the toolbar. You'll learn more about this toolbar in Chapter 10, "Customizing Navigator to Make It Your Own."

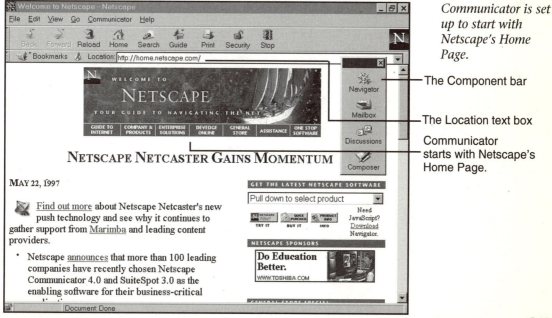

Communicator is set up to start with Netscape's Home Page.

— The Component bar

— The Location text box

Communicator starts with Netscape's Home Page.

The Least You Need to Know

Netscape Communicator is out there, just waiting for you to grab a copy and start cruising the Internet. All you need to know is right here:

- If you have a copy of any Web browser, use it to download a copy of Communicator from **http://home.netscape.com**.

- If you don't have a Web browser, use an FTP program, such as WS_ftp to download Communicator from **ftp2.netscape.com**.

- Once you have the Netscape Communicator installation file, double-click on the file's icon to run the program. Follow the on-screen installation instructions.

- After installing Netscape Communicator in Windows 95, the Netscape Communicator icon appears on the Windows desktop. Double-click on it to run Netscape Navigator and display the toolbar that lets you switch to the other Communicator components.

- To go to a specific Web page, type its address in the Location text box at the top of the Navigator window, and press **Enter**.

- Most Web pages contain highlighted text, called links, which you can click on to jump to other pages and sites on the Web.

- Communicator is not free. The cheapest way to obtain a legal copy of the latest version is to purchase a software subscription from Netscape.

Part Deux
Mastering Netscape Navigator

Anyone can fire up Navigator, plunge into the Web, and click link after link in a frenzied spree, but only masters of the Web and Navigator can get where they're going in a hurry. If you're interested in government, maybe you want to visit the White House. Or maybe you're a movie buff, and you want to see trailers for the latest Hollywood flicks. Or perhaps you just need a recipe for tonight's dinner. Whatever the case, this wandering business isn't going to get you where you want to be in a hurry.

In this part, you're going to learn how to take control of Navigator and the Web. You'll learn how to find information; return to your favorite places; copy, save, and print pages; and even flip Web channels with Netcaster! By the end of this part, you'll know everything you need to know to master Navigator and the Web.

Chapter 3

Weaving Through the World Wide Web

In This Chapter

- Cruise the Web like a pro
- Pick a page that opens automatically when you run Navigator
- Use a URL to "dial into" a specific Web page
- Flip back and forth with Back and Forward Buttons
- Pick a page from a list of pages you visited

Wandering the Web is as stimulating as wandering through downtown Chicago. You find museums, shops, peep shows, and cultural havens tucked into the most unlikely places. However, you'll eventually want to visit a specific site on the Web, to do research, or to find a cool picture or game that one of your friends has told you about.

When you need to get somewhere in a hurry, links may not be the most efficient way to reach your destination. They'll just pull you deeper into the Web, and take you off on some fruitless journey. In this chapter, you'll learn how to take control of the Web. You'll learn how to go to specific Web sites, search for information, and quickly backtrack when you get stuck.

Moseying Around the Navigator Screen

The overall Navigator screen should look pretty familiar… like all Windows applications, Navigator displays a standard application window. It has a menu bar, a couple toolbars, scroll bars, controls for resizing and closing the window, and a status bar at the bottom that displays informative messages.

How Can I Tell if Something Is a Link? Sometimes it's difficult to distinguish a link from other text, graphics, and icons on a page. If you're not sure whether something is a link, rest the mouse pointer on it. If the pointer turns into a hand, it's a link.

What makes the Navigator window so different from other application windows are its contents. Notice that the page displayed here has one or more underlined, highlighted words or phrases. These are *links* that point to other pages or Web sites. Click a link, and Navigator loads the appropriate page, no matter where that page is stored (on the current server or on a server in Alaska, Sweden, or anywhere else). Links can come in all shapes and sizes; they can be text, icons, or even small graphics, but they all work the same way.

One other unique element on the Navigator window is the big **N** with the flying comets. Look in the upper right corner of the Navigator window. This little eye-catcher isn't just for decoration. Comets fly across the **N** as your connection transfers data. This shows you when Navigator is busy fetching information for you. (You can click on the **N** to quickly return to Netscape's home page at any time.)

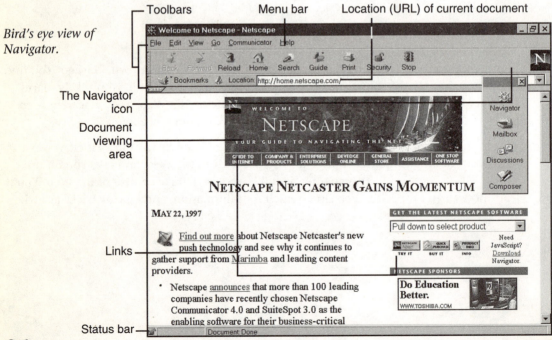

Bird's eye view of Navigator.

Navigational Tools of the Trade

You took a day trip on the Web in Chapter 2. Maybe you clicked one or two links, clicked the **Back** button to return to a site, and used the **Forward** button to pick up where you left off. Using these basic navigational tools is like trying to use your keyboard to steer and shoot in your favorite arcade game. They're just not designed for the quick turns and turbocharged movement you want on the Web.

The following sections show you some of the more advanced navigational tools that Navigator offers. Once you master these tools, you'll be skipping along the Web like a spider on speed.

Check This Out...

Back and Forward

If you enter a URL in the Location text box, Navigator assumes that you're taking off on an entirely new journey, and it loses track of the trail of links you clicked. You may not be able to use the Back and Forward buttons to step back through previous pages. However, the name of the page you want may be at the bottom of the Go menu.

Toolbar Basics

Navigator 4.0 offers new, improved toolbars. Netscape removed the Open button, which nobody used, and introduced *smart buttons*—buttons whose name and function changes depending on the available options. The following list describes some of the improvements to the toolbar, and explains the basics of how to use the toolbar:

➤ Each toolbar has a tab that allows you to move or turn off the toolbar. Click the tab to tuck the toolbar out of the way or bring it into view. Drag the tab to move the toolbar.

➤ To view a name and description of a button in the toolbar, rest the mouse pointer on it. A pop-up text box displays the name of the button, and a description of the button's function appears in the status bar (at the bottom of the window).

➤ In Navigator 4.0, Netscape has removed the Open button, which nobody ever used. (It's easier to open a page by typing the page's address in the Location text box and pressing Enter.)

➤ Navigator offers a Personal toolbar to which you can add buttons for your favorite sites. Click the tab below the Location toolbar to display the Personal toolbar. To place a button on the toolbar, drag the desired link over the toolbar. You will learn more about this toolbar in Chapter 10, "Customizing Navigator to Make It Your Own."

- The Navigator 4.0 toolbar now offers *smart buttons*. Smart buttons appear only when you turn on an option for which the button is required. For instance, if you enter an option telling Navigator not to automatically load graphics on a page, the Images button appears. You can click Images to view graphics that were not loaded.

- The Back and Forward buttons double as drop-down lists that contain the names of pages you have visited. Point to one of the buttons and hold down the mouse pointer to display the list. Click on the name of the page you want to revisit.

- The new Guide button displays a menu that contains links to the Internet (a categorical guide to the Internet), Yellow Pages (to locate businesses), People (a helpful search tool for tracking down people online and offline), What's New (for links to the latest Web sites), and What's Cool (for links to the pages that Netscape thinks are the coolest).

What's with the Red Links?

You've encountered the blue, underlined links that take you places, but have you encountered any red links yet? The red indicates that you've already visited the page. By default, Navigator keeps track of the links you've visited for up to nine days. This allows you to see which pages you've visited, so you can avoid unnecessary return trips to those pages. After nine days, Navigator returns the links to their original blue.

You can tell Navigator to return the links to their original color. Open the **Edit** menu, and select **Preferences**. Under **Category**, click on **Navigator**. Under **History**, click the **Clear History** button. You can also change the number of days Navigator keeps track of the links.

You can also change the color used for links you've explored. Click the plus sign next to **Appearance**, and select **Colors**. Next to **Visited Links**, click the color button, and select the color you want to use. (Some documents have codes that specify a color for links. To have Navigator override these color codes, make sure there's a check in the **Always Use My Colors, Overriding Document** box.)

Chapter 3 ➤ *Weaving Through the World Wide Web*

Click a tab to turn a toolbar on or off.

When you rest the mouse pointer on the Forward or Back a box appears, displaying the name of the page that this button will open.

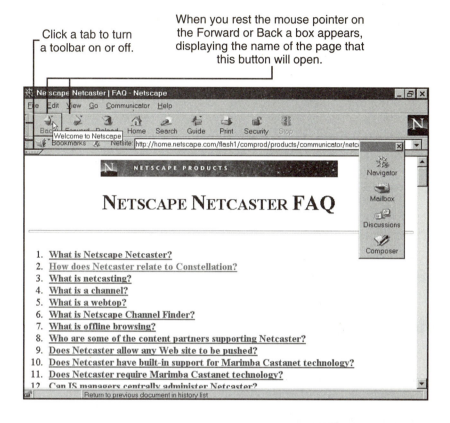

Know your toolbar.

Navigator keeps track of all the pages you've visited.

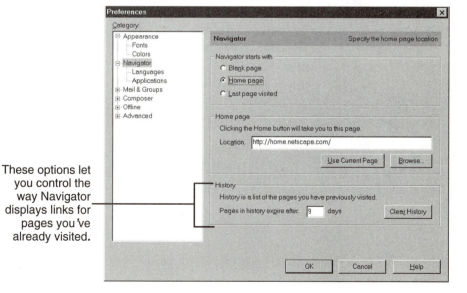

These options let you control the way Navigator displays links for pages you've already visited.

29

Going Home

Although you can use the Back button to step page-by-page back to the first page Navigator loaded, there's a quicker way. Simply open the **Go** menu and select **Home**. An even faster way to go home is to click the **Home** button in the toolbar. To go to Netscape's Home Page, click the **N** in the upper right corner of the Navigator window.

Recovering from Interrupted Transfers

Occasionally, you'll skip through pages before Navigator is done loading them. While Navigator is busy loading some huge image or a bunch of tiny ones, you see the link you want, and you click it. This terminates the transfer of the current page. If you go back to that page, only a portion of it is loaded, and you might see a message at the bottom of the page indicating that the transfer has been terminated.

To have Navigator nab the rest of the page, simply click the **Reload** button in the toolbar, or open the **View** menu and select **Reload** (or press **Ctrl+R**). Navigator uses the URL to find the page and reload its contents.

Going Back to Places You've Been

Navigator lists the most recently loaded pages near the top of the Go menu. To quickly return to a page, open the **Go** menu, and click the name of the page. When you exit Navigator, it erases the page names from the Go menu.

The History Log of Your Journeys

In addition to keeping track of pages on the Go menu, Navigator keeps a history list of the pages you visit. You can display this list by opening the **Communicator** menu and selecting **History**.

The Go menu contains the names of the most recently loaded pages.

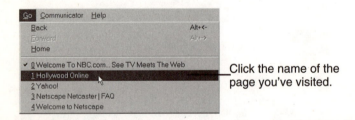

Click the name of the page you've visited.

Touring the Web with URLs

So far, you've managed to avoid all the behind-the-scenes wizardry that enables you to jump from document to document. You click a link, and you're swept away to Switzerland. Three links later, and you're in a Cajun recipe database in Louisiana. You might start to wonder what's going on behind the scenes. More importantly, you might wonder how you can take more control of your wanderings.

The secret is to use *URLs (Uniform Resource Locators)*. URLs are addresses that specify the locations of the millions of pages and files that make up the Web. Each link you select (each starting point you choose) has a corresponding URL that kicks you out to the linked document.

What does this have to do with you? You'll learn later in this chapter how to enter URLs to load specific hyperdocuments... assuming, of course, you know the document's URL.

URLs Dissected

Each URL indicates the type of server, the server's unique *domain* (name), the directory in which the Web page is stored, and the document's name. Let's look at a sample URL to see how it's made. Here's the URL for a Web page that deals with the Beat Generation author, Jack Kerouac:

> http://www.charm.net/~brooklyn/People/JackKerouac.html

Let's dissect it. First, there's **http**. This stands for *HyperText Transfer Protocol*, which is a set of rules that govern the exchange of data on the Web. Every URL for Web servers starts with http (or https if you are at a secure site). If you see a URL that starts with different letters (for example, ftp or gopher), the URL is for a different type of server: Gopher (gopher), FTP (ftp), WAIS (wais), USENET (news), or Telnet (telnet).

The next part of the URL (**www.charm.net**) is called the *domain name*. Each computer on the Internet has a unique domain name that distinguishes it from other computers on the Internet. That way, when the phone rings, all the computers don't answer at the same time. Domain names usually provide some vague indication of the establishment that runs the server. For example, guess who runs this one: **www.whitehouse.gov**. As you work with URLs, look for these common abbreviations: com (commercial), www (World Wide Web), edu (educational), pub (public), gov (government), and net (network). The URL might also specify the country (for example, jp for Japan).

Next comes the directory path (**/~brooklyn/People**) that shows the location of the file. Following that is the name of the document (**JackKerouac.html**). The **.html** is a file name extension that stands for *HyperText Markup Language*, a simple set of commands that tells Navigator (or whatever Web browser you use) how to display the document. You'll work with HTML when you create your own home page in Part 5, "Publishing Your Own Web Pages."

To complicate matters, some URLs do not end in a document name. For example, **http://www.yahoo.com** does not specify a directory or a file name. However, when you connect to the Yahoo! Web server, it loads the Yahoo! home page by default. Many Web servers are set up to automatically load a home page.

Hitting the URL Trail

Opening an HTML document is like... well... opening a document. You select the **File, Open Page** command, type the directory path and file name of the document, and then click **Open**. The only difference in opening an HTML document is that the "directory path" is a URL.

Practice entering URLs by taking the following guided tour of the Web:

1. Open the **File** menu and select **Open Page** (or press **Ctrl+O**). The Open Page dialog box appears, prompting you to type the URL of the page you want to load.

The Open Page dialog box lets you type the location and name of a document.

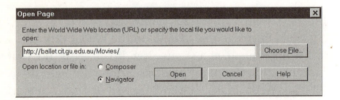

2. Type the following URL: **http://ballet.cit.gu.edu.au/Movies/**. (Always type a URL exactly as shown. If you type **movies** instead of **Movies**, the domain name server won't know which page you want.)

3. Make sure **Navigator** is selected, and then click the **Open** button. Assuming all goes as planned, you should now see The Internet Movie Database Browser at Griffith University in Australia.

Bypass the Open Page Dialog Box

A quicker way to enter a URL is to click inside the **Location** text box, type the URL, and press **Enter**. When you click inside the text box, the existing entry is highlighted (if the entry is not highlighted, double-click inside the text box again). As you start typing, **Location** changes to **Go to**, and the characters you type replace the existing entry.

4. Repeat steps 1-3 for the following URLs:

   http://www.pointcom.com/   Displays the Lycos' Top 5% Web Sites list.

   http://www.nasa.gov/   Connects you to NASA's (yes, the space program people's) Web server.

   http://www.w3.org/pub/DataSources/bySubject/Overview.html   Displays The WWW Virtual Library, an index of topics ranging from Aboriginal Studies to Zoos.

   http://www.ufoic.com   Connects you with the UFO Information Center.

In most cases, you can omit the **http://** at the beginning of a URL. Like most browsers, Navigator inserts the **http://** for you. For simple URLs, such as www.microsoft.com, you can even leave off the **www** and the **com**. Just type **microsoft** and press **Enter**. Try it!

More Location Text Box Tricks

The Location text box moonlights as an abbreviated history list. As you enter URLs and click on links to jump from page to page, the URLs of those pages are added to the Location drop-down list. To quickly return to a page, click on the arrow to the right of the Location text box. This displays a list of pages you have recently visited. Click on the URL for a page to return to it.

Keyboard Navigation (Look, Ma, No Mouse!)

The mouse makes it easy to work the Web; you just point and click like a kid in a candy store. However, if you don't like taking your hands off the keyboard, Navigator does offer some keyboard alternatives:

➤ **Tab** from one link to another on a page, and press **Enter**.

➤ Use the arrow keys to move up or down a page.

- Press **Page Up** or **Page Down** to scroll.
- Press **Ctrl+Home** to go to the top of a page or **Ctrl+End** to drop to the bottom.

Also, don't forget the shortcut key combinations, such as **Ctrl+O** to open a page, **Esc** to stop loading, **Alt+Left Arrow** to move back to the previous page, and **Alt+Right Arrow** to move ahead to the next page.

This Page Has No Links!

Occasionally, you'll come across a Web page that does not use the standard blue text links. Instead, the page displays a Web navigational tool called a *map*, which uses graphics instead of text for its links. Below is a picture of a map on the Kids' Space home page.

If you happen upon a map, but you're not sure what it is, roll the mouse pointer to different areas of the map, while keeping an eye on the status bar. The URL displayed in the status bar changes as you move the mouse pointer over different areas. If you click an area, Navigator loads the corresponding Web page.

Sometimes, a simple graphic might look like a map. Don't let it fool you. If the URL in the status bar remains the same no matter which part of the picture you point to, the graphic is merely a picture, not a map.

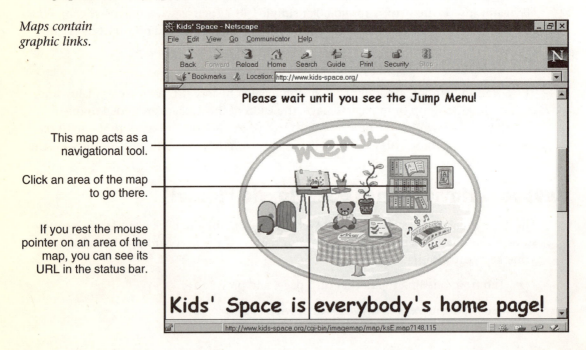

Maps contain graphic links.

This map acts as a navigational tool.

Click an area of the map to go there.

If you rest the mouse pointer on an area of the map, you can see its URL in the status bar.

Juggling Two or More Web Documents

You're surfin' now, but if you really want to hang ten on the Web, you can load several Web documents. Navigator is set up to allow you to open several Web documents at the same time—each in its own separate window.

To open another Navigator window, open the **File**, **New** menu and select **Navigator Window** (or press **Ctrl+N**). A new window opens and loads the starting page. You can now use this window to open another Web document, by clicking links, or by entering the URL of the document you want to open. To change from one window to another, open the **Communicator** menu, and click the name of the window you want to go to (listed at the bottom of the menu). (You can also switch windows by pressing **Ctrl+Tab** or using the Windows 95 taskbar.)

You can arrange the windows by resizing or moving them, minimizing one window while you work in the other one, or using Windows to arrange the windows for you. In Windows 95, you can quickly arrange windows by right-clicking a blank area of the taskbar and selecting **Cascade**, **Tile Horizontally**, or **Tile Vertically**. In Windows 3.1, these same commands are on the Program Manager's Window menu.

Right-Click a Link

Right-click a link inside the current Web document, and then select **Open in New Window**. This opens the Web document that the link points to and displays the document in a separate window.

Working with Window Frames

Occasionally, you'll come across a Web page that splits your Navigator window into two frames—an upper and lower frame. Each frame has its own scroll bar, so you can view two or more Web pages at the same time, as shown here. Frames are especially useful for helping you move around in a long Web document. For example, one of the panes may contain an outline of the document. Whenever you click a link in the outline, the other frame displays the page that contains detailed information about the topic.

You can't turn these frames on or off from your end. They're built into the Web page, and they tell Navigator to split the window in two. You can change the relative size and dimensions of the frames by dragging the borders that separate them. You can also move from one page to another by clicking a link in any of the frames.

Frames make it easier to move around on long Web pages.

Window frames

You can use the scroll bars to scan the page.

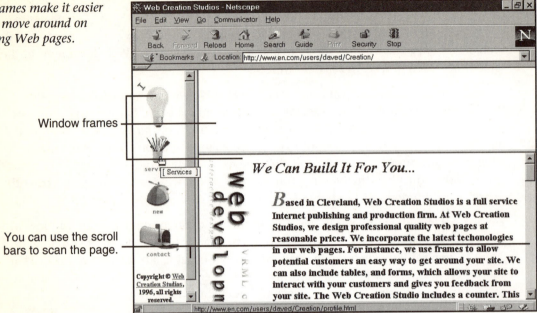

Reload a Frame

If the contents of a frame are not transferred completely, you can reload the frame. Click on a blank area inside the frame to select it. Open the **View** menu and select **Reload**.

The Least You Need to Know

Now that you know how to go places with URLs, you can skip to the back of this book for a list of nifty Web sites you can visit. While you're entering URLs and cruising, keep the following in mind:

➤ At the bottom of the **Go** menu is a list of the sites you most recently visited.

➤ Another way to go to recently visited sites is to open the **Location** drop-down list and then click the site's URL.

➤ The easiest way to open a Web page when you know its address is to type the address in the **Location** text box and press **Enter**.

➤ Type a URL *exactly* as it appears, or it won't take you where you want to go.

Chapter 4

Finding Information and Other Resources

In This Chapter

➤ Name the 10 most popular Internet search tools

➤ Search for Web pages by category

➤ Find a lost friend's phone number in a Web telephone directory

➤ Get technical support for your computer or applications

Wandering the Web appeals to the free-wheeling side of all of us. We like to stumble onto new sites that few have visited, take the road less traveled, ride the backroads, and check out the scenery.

That's great if you have an infinite amount of time, a patient disposition, and little concern for reaching a specific destination. However, if you need to research a topic, find out about a recent film release, or check on arrivals or destinations at the airport, wandering with links will just pull you deeper into the Web, and ditch you in some dark alley.

In this chapter, you'll learn how to fill out search forms at various Web sites to look for information, companies, phone numbers, games, software, and much more. You'll learn where these search forms are located and how they work.

It's Easy When You Have the Right Form

All Internet search tools have one thing in common: when you open the search tool page, a fill-in-the-blanks form greets you, asking you what you want to look for. You click inside the **Search** or **Find** text box (or whatever the page's creator decided to call it), type a word or phrase, and then click the **Search** or **Find** button, or press **Enter**.

The search tool finds a bunch of Web pages and other Internet resources that match your entry, and displays a list of links you can click to tap those resources.

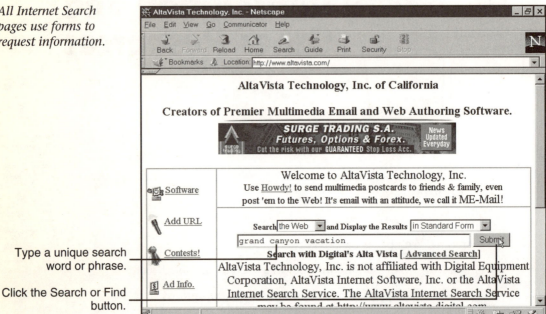

All Internet Search pages use forms to request information.

Type a unique search word or phrase.

Click the Search or Find button.

The Warning Dialog Box: Do You Care?

Because forms allow you to send information, including credit card numbers and personal data across the Internet, Navigator may display a warning when you use a form to enter data. You see, the information might bounce around several servers on the Internet, and someone could possibly read the information in transit. Not likely, but it could happen.

The warning appears whether you type entries into two or more text boxes on a form, whether that information is something sensitive (such as a credit card number) or a search term like **Mickey Mouse**. Read the warning dialog box, and if you don't really care if anyone reads the data you're about to send, click **Continue**. You can turn the warning off by selecting **Show This Alert Next Time**, before clicking Continue. (For more information about these and other security features, see Chapter 11, "Digital Certificates, Cookies, and Other Security Issues.")

Isn't It Dangerous to Turn the Warning Off?

These warnings are for people who call the Psychic Network and who really think they have a chance to win the Reader's Digest Sweepstakes, not for smart people like you. Just don't enter any sensitive information at a site that's not secure. How do you know if a site is secure? Read Chapter 11.

Composing a Unique Search String

If you can't think of anything more specific to search for than "recipes," "The New York Times," or "World Wide Web," don't waste your time filling out a search form. The search tools work by creating an index of Web pages from all over the world. As you can imagine, this index is huge, so the search tools try to limit their indexes by indexing only specific terms. If you search for "World Wide Web," it's likely that the search tool will respond with a message saying that it can't find any pages that match your entry, or that it found *too many* pages, and you should start over.

The moral of this story is to enter one or two unique words. Give it a little thought.

Uppercase or Lowercase?

Most search tools ignore capitalization. You can type your entry in all uppercase or all lowercase characters, or mix and match. It doesn't matter.

Using Boolean Operators (AND, NOT, and OR)

Most search tools (except Lycos) assume that you want to find pages that have **all** the search terms you type. So, for instance, if you type **bill clinton whitewater election**, the search tool inserts AND (or + or &) between the search terms for you. This focuses the search, which is what you usually want.

Some search forms contain options, which allow you to search for pages that contain *any* of the search terms you enter. In such a case, the search tool inserts OR between the terms you type.

To take more control of your search, you can type AND, OR, and NOT between search terms. These words, called *Boolean Operators*, are logic tools that were originally developed for mathematics to determine the state of an expression. (Yeah, it's more complicated than you need to know.)

For example, if you want to find all pages about Bill and Hillary Clinton that don't have anything to do with Whitewater, you might type **bill and hillary and clinton (not whitewater)**. Some search tools use + and - instead of AND and NOT. Be sure to read the instructions on the search page (you might have to click a link such as Search Tips to display the instructions) before attempting to type your own operators.

Other Options Available with Some Search Tools

Although most search tools display a single text box prompting you to enter your search words, some tools give you other options. For example, WebCrawler lets you specify the number of matching entries you want to display (10, 25, or 100) and allows you to view summaries for each match it finds (instead of displaying only the name of the link).

Other search tools might let you specify which area of the Internet you want to search. For example, you can search for Web pages, for information at this site, for newsgroup messages, or for e-mail addresses.

Using Navigator's Search Button

With Navigator and some help from one of Netscape's Web pages, you don't have to poke around on the Internet to find search pages. Netscape has a page that displays a form with links to four (maybe more by the time you read this) search pages. To display this page, click the **Search** button in Navigator's toolbar.

> **Check This Out...**
>
> **The Magical Location Text Box** Navigator's Location text box doubles as a Search text box. Type your search phrase (two or more words) into the Location text box, and press **Enter**. Navigator connects you to a Web search tool and inserts the search phrase for you. You must use two or more words, or Navigator will "think" that you typed the abbreviated address of a Web page.

Click the name of the search tool you want to use (Excite, Infoseek, Lycos, or Yahoo!). Type two or three unique terms in the **Search for** text, and click the **Search** button (the button's name varies depending on the search tool you select). Navigator connects you to the selected Search page and enters the terms you typed to tell the search tool what to find. If you did a good job of composing your search phrase, and if the information you're looking for is on the Internet, the search tool should display several links to pages that match your search phrase.

Chapter 4 ➤ *Finding Information and Other Resources*

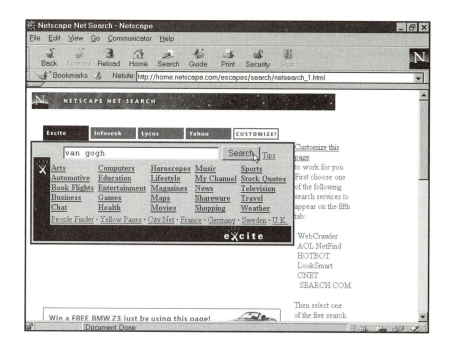

You can use any of several search tools from Netscape's Net Search page.

If the search tool does not return any links for matching pages or sites, click the **Back** button and try a different search phrase (or a different search tool).

Typically, a search tool ranks the resources it finds according to the number of *hits* (matches). For example, if you searched for **bill clinton whitewater**, the search tool might find one Web page that contains 10 occurrences of "Bill Clinton Whitewater" and another page with only 5 occurrences. The link to the page that has 10 occurrences is normally displayed at the top of the list, because it is more likely to contain the information you need.

Techno Talk: Spamdexing

Spamming is a marketing technique in which a company sends unsolicited messages to individuals, typically in a newsgroup (electronic message board). *Spamdexing* is a more sinister technique in which a Web page creator repeats dozens or hundreds of key terms in a document in order to make a search tool view the page as more important than it really is, and places the page first in a list of matching pages.

Various Search Tools in Action

You've used Netscape's Net Search page to connect to and use many popular search tools on the Web. But maybe you want to go directly to these search pages instead of through the Netscape middleman.

The following sections list the most popular and useful search tools on the Web. Each tool has its own benefits and drawbacks. For example, Yahoo! is the best at helping you zero in on a link by proceeding through a list of categories and subcategories, whereas InfoSeek is the most thorough search tool in the bunch. Each of the following sections provides the name of the search tool, its URL, and a brief (I promise) review of its strengths and weaknesses.

Yahoo!: Doing the Web by Category

Address: http://www.yahoo.com

Yahoo! is the most popular Web search tool—and my personal favorite. When you connect to Yahoo!, you get not only a text box into which you can type a search phrase, but you also get a long list of categories. To perform a less formal search, click a link for the category you want to explore. Follow the trail of links till you find something that interests you.

When you've selected a category or subcategory, Yahoo! displays an additional search option at the top of the page. You can type a search phrase in the text box, and then choose to **Search all of Yahoo** or **Search Only in** the current category or subcategory.

Search Tip
When typing search terms, consider dropping plurals, "ing" endings, and other text off the beginning or end of a search term to broaden the search. For example, instead of typing **telephone directories**, type **phone director**. The matches would then include *telephone directories* as well as *telephone directory* and *phone directory*.

At any time, you can click the **Options** button to the right of the Search button to display additional search options, as shown in the next figure. These options allow you to specify the number of items you want to find, whether you use Yahoo! to find pages that have all the words you typed or only one of them, and specify the number of years back you want Yahoo! to search (three years by default). Enter your preferences, and click **Search**.

One of the best features of Yahoo! is that it displays links to other search tools. If you can't find what you're looking for in Yahoo!, simply click a link at the bottom of the page. Yahoo! inserts the text you entered into the form for the search tool you linked to, so you don't have to retype it.

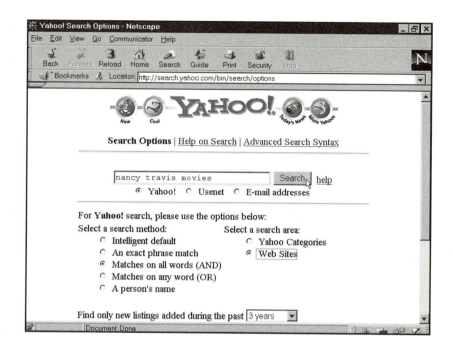

Yahoo! lets you take more control over the search.

AltaVista: When the Other Search Tools Fail

Address: http://www.altavista.digital.com/

Simple, fast, and comprehensive, AltaVista is the golden boy of Internet search tools. When all other search tools display a message saying that there are no Web pages that match your search instructions, AltaVista will usually prove them wrong, displaying a list of links a mile long.

When you connect to AltaVista, you're greeted by the usual text box into which you can type your words or phrases. In addition, you can use the two drop-down lists at the top of the page to choose whether you want to search the Web or Usenet newsgroups, and to specify how detailed you want the page listings to be. For example, **Compact** displays the page title, date, and a very brief description of the page, whereas **Detailed** displays a sentence or two about each page.

At the bottom of the list of matching pages, AltaVista displays a series of numbers. Click a number to view the next set of ten matching pages. You won't believe the number of pages AltaVista is capable of finding, even for the most off-beat search.

Macmillan's SuperSeek: Frames Gone Wild

Address: http://www.mcp.com/superseek

SuperSeek is unique in that it links you to several other search tools on the Web. When you enter a search string at SuperSeek, it searches Yahoo!, the WWW Yellow Pages, Lycos, InfoSeek, and several other search pages, and displays the results of each page in a separate frame.

SuperSeek, a frame for each search page.

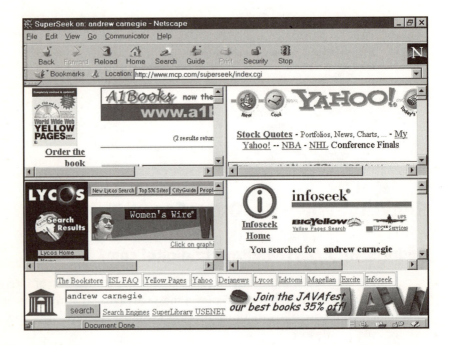

The feature that makes SuperSeek so unique is the same feature that can drive you crazy. As you can see from the figure, these frames clutter your screen, preventing you from viewing the search results. You have to use the scroll bars of each frame to bring the results into view.

Because of the clutter, I can't recommend this search tool. However, one of the search pages that SuperSeek links you to (WWW Yellow Pages, also from Macmillan) is an outstanding search tool. When you reach Macmillan's home page (at **www.mcp.com**), instead of clicking the SuperSeek icon, click the **Yellow Pages** icon. The Yellow Pages search form is shown in the first figure in this chapter.

WebCrawler: It's Worth a Try

Address: http://webcrawler.com

Like Yahoo!, WebCrawler lets you perform an informal search using categories; although its list of categories pales next to that of Yahoo!.

However, WebCrawler is a competent, simple search tool, offering you a couple options you won't find in Yahoo!. For example, in WebCrawler, you can choose to display only the titles of pages that match your search entry or the title and description of each page. For examples of effective search strings, click the **Hints** link.

Excite!: Great for Refining Your Search

Address: http://www.excite.com

Excite! may not be the best search tool around, but it does offer some unique features. For instance, if you click Search Options, Excite displays a list of Internet features you can search: The Web, Selected Web Sites (best of the Web), Current News, Newsgroups, or a Travel Guide. Excite also offers links for a People Finder, Yellow Pages directory, Stock Quotes, and Weather. For more information about refining a search, click the **Search Tips** beside the Search button.

InfoSeek: The Newsgroup Search Standout

Address: http://guide.infoseek.com/

InfoSeek's reputation is built on its capability to find newsgroup messages on just about any subject. (You'll learn more about newsgroups in Chapter 18, "Reading and Posting Newsgroup Messages.")

The InfoSeek search form contains a drop-down list that lets you search various Internet offerings: the Web, Usenet Newsgroups, News Wires, Premier News, E-mail Addresses, Company Profiles, and Web FAQs. Click the desired area, enter your search terms, and click the **seek** button. (For additional search options, click on the **Tips** link beside the seek button.)

Another cool feature of InfoSeek is that a search turns up not only a list of links to specific pages but also links to matching categories.

Matching categories are on the left; matching pages, on the right.

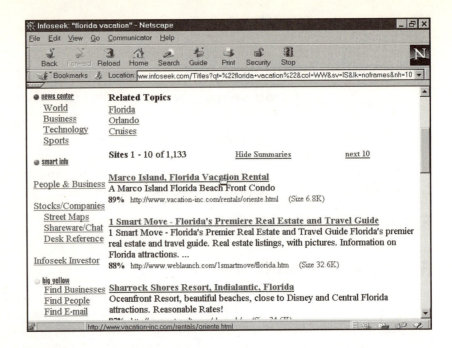

Lycos: Just Don't Do the Default Search

Address: http://www.lycos.com/

Lycos is one of the first search tools to become popular on the Web, and it keeps getting better. However, its default search settings are questionable. Most search forms will find pages that match *all* the terms you enter, performing a well-focused search. Lycos searches for pages that contain *any* of the search terms you enter, resulting in a long list of links that may not do you much good.

To work around this weakness, don't perform a standard search. After typing the search phrase, select **Match all words** before clicking the **Go Get It** button. You can set other search options as well, by clicking **Custom Search**. These options include setting the number of search terms you want Lycos to match (or all the search terms you type), specifying a loose or strong match, setting the number of matches you want Lycos to display on each page, and specifying whether you want only page names or page names and summaries of matching pages displayed.

Chapter 4 ➤ *Finding Information and Other Resources*

Looking for People

Most of the search tools described above won't help you find your long lost Grandma Sally, unless of course Grandma Sally has her own Web page. To find her or other people on the Internet, you can use a tool called *Finger* or any of several phone directories (assuming you know the person's last name and the state or city in which she lives).

Using Netscape's People Finder Links

Some of the best tools for finding people are right on the Web, and Navigator can help you find these tools. Click the **Guide** button on the Navigation toolbar, and click **People**. This displays a search form at Netscape, which allows you to use any of several people search tools.

Click on the link for the search tool you want to use. A form appears, prompting you to enter the person's first name, last name, and city and state of residence. Complete the form, and click the button to start the search. (There may be a couple search options; for example, you may be able to look for phone numbers, addresses, or e-mail addresses.)

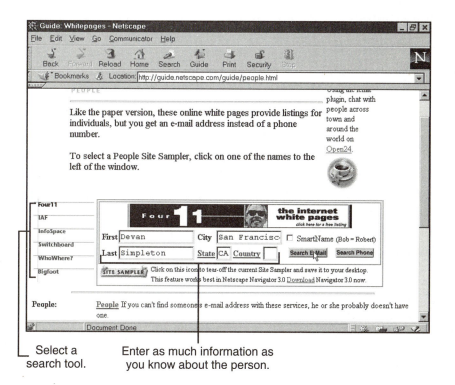

Netscape has a page that provides access to the most popular people finders.

Select a search tool.

Enter as much information as you know about the person.

47

Using Web Phone Directories

Several companies (mostly phone companies) have transformed their paper telephone directories into electronic versions and placed them on the Web. You can search for a person by last name if you know the city or state in which they live. Of course, you could also just dial the person's area code followed by 555-1212 and ask the operator, but that's no fun, and it can't help you track down a person's e-mail address.

I'm not going to bore you with details on how to fill out these search forms once you get there. It's just like filling out forms at the doctor's office—and almost as much fun. I'll just give you a list of addresses for phone directories that I've found useful (the first one provides links to other people search tools):

http://www.four11.com

http://www.infospace.com

http://www.bigfoot.com

http://www.nova.edu/Inter-Links/phone.html

http://www.switchboard.com/

http://www.yahoo.com/search/people/

http://iypn.com/

http://www.tollfree.att.net/

If your wife just cashed in your retirement account and ran off with the mailman, she'll probably have an unlisted number (or a new last name). There are several companies on the Internet whose specialty it is to track down missing persons. (It'll cost you, of course.) Try the following pages (good luck, by the way):

http://www.fpf.com/fpf_2.html

http://www.greatbasin.net/~windsong/pef.html

http://pages.prodigy.com/mikep/search.htm

Tracking Down Your Friends with Finger

Finger is a tool that allows you to find a person if you know the person's e-mail address and the server that the person uses (the company where the person works, the university where she studies, or the person's Internet service provider). Of course, if you knew all that information, you wouldn't really need to find the person, would you? The only good thing about Finger is that (if you're lucky) it can turn up the person's real address and phone number.

To Finger from Navigator, simply enter the URL of the Finger gateway you want to use. (A *gateway* is a bridge between two incompatible computer networks.) Type one of the following URLs in the **Location** text box, and press **Enter**:

http://www.nova.edu/Inter-Links/cgi-bin/finger.pl

http://www.cs.indiana.edu/finger/gateway

http://www.rickman.com/finger.html

In moments, Navigator displays a page with a text box on it. Click inside the text box and type the e-mail address of the person you're looking for (for example, type jsmith@iquest.com). Press **Enter**.

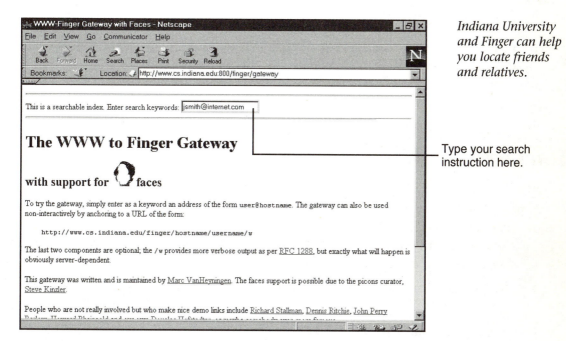

Indiana University and Finger can help you locate friends and relatives.

Type your search instruction here.

Assuming that Finger can find any information about the e-mail address you enter, Finger displays the information.

Using Whois

Whois is another Internet tool for people-searching which allows you to find a person's e-mail address and phone number if you know the person's last name. Type **gopher://sipb.mit.edu:70** in the **Address** text box, and press **Enter**. Now, click **Internet Whois Servers**. This displays a list of publicly accessible sites that allow Whois searches.

Finding Tech Support on the Web

Most computer manufacturers, mail-order companies, and software companies have their own Web pages. For example, you can go to IBM at **http://www.ibm.com** or Microsoft at **http://www.microsoft.com**. To find a computer or software company on the Internet, simply use any of the Web search tools described earlier in this chapter to search for the company by name. The Web page you pull up typically has a link for obtaining tech support, updated files, and answers to commonly asked questions.

If you'd rather call these companies and talk to a regular human-type person, you can usually get a phone number from the Web page. You can also view a comprehensive list of phone numbers (toll and toll-free) by entering the following URL:

> http://www.mtp.semi.harris.com/pc_info.html

The Least You Need to Know

Search pages are easy. You just pull one up, enter two or three terms, and click the **Search** button. As you search, keep the following in mind:

➤ Memorize the addresses of your favorite search pages, or just remember **www.altavista.com**. Add your favorite search pages to your Bookmarks menu, as explained in Chapter 6, "Revisiting Your Favorite Haunts."

➤ You can find people and businesses on the Web by searching any of several online phone books.

➤ When you connect to a search page, click the **Search Tips** link (if there is one). If the search tool is quirky, you'll learn about the quirks.

➤ If the search tool returns too few or too many pages, click the **Back** button and start over.

Chapter 5

What Could Possibly Go Wrong?

In This Chapter

➤ Translate an error message into plain English

➤ Determine what caused the error

➤ Find out the answer to the question, "Was it me?"

➤ Sidestep most connection problems

When I first ventured into the Web, I received all sorts of error messages:

Failed DNS Lookup

Connection timed out

Unable to Locate Document

I began to wonder. Was I doing something wrong? Did I inadvertently try to access classified Pentagon documents? Is my Internet service provider trying to tell me something?

You'll get many of these same error messages. I guarantee it. Just realize that it's usually *not* you, and you can't do much about most error messages. The purpose of this chapter is to desensitize you to these messages, and help you fix any problems that you can solve on your end. As for problems that are out of your control, why worry?

Why the Web Is Soooo Buggy

It's amazing that the World Wide Web works as smoothly as it does. Think about it. People all over the world have stitched together documents that refer to other documents on other computers all over the world. Now, say somebody deletes one of the documents or moves it to another directory. Maybe the link you click has a typo, sending you to a page that doesn't exist. Or perhaps the network administrator on one of the Web servers decides to close down the network for maintenance. Any of these scenarios contains the formula for producing an error message.

But the Web is not the only thing under construction. The copy of Netscape Communicator you downloaded in Chapter 2, "Installing, Connecting, and Exploring," might also have a few bugs. Sure, it's a good program, and it'll get you around the Web, but the programmers who are developing it are constantly tweaking their creation to make it run more efficiently. Until the program is perfected, it's likely that you, too, will encounter at least one of these bugs.

And that's not all. Now add your own human error into the equation. You might mistype a URL, try to skip around the Web too fast for it to keep up, or try to view a link before you've installed the proper helper application. When you take all these variables into account, you begin to realize how amazing it is that you can navigate the Web at all.

Failed DNS Lookup

If you spend an hour on the Web and you *don't* get this error message, you're probably doing something wrong. This reigning king of Web error messages is ambiguous; it can have any of several meanings. First, it might mean that the DNS (Domain Name Server) is having trouble matching the domain name of the server you're trying to access to its IP (Internet Protocol) number. Huh? (That's what I say. Look at the Techno Nerd Teaches, if you're interested in learning about the DNS.)

When Navigator can't find a server, it displays this dialog box.

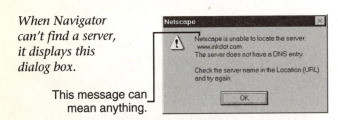

This message can mean anything.

More commonly, this error message *really* means that maybe you mistyped the URL of the desired server (or the person who created the Web page mistyped the URL for the link you clicked). Try any of the following tactics to pull up the desired Web page:

➤ Did you remember to run your TCP/IP program before running Navigator? If you forgot, Navigator can't find the page, because it's not even connected to the Internet. Establish your Internet connection, and try again.

➤ If you typed the URL (in the Location text box), check your typing. One minor typo (an uppercase letter that should be lowercase, a slash mark that points the wrong way, or even a misplaced period) can cause the problem. Retype the URL and press **Enter**.

➤ If you received the error after clicking a link, the URL behind the link may have a typo. Rest the mouse pointer on the problem link, and look at the URL in the status bar. If you see an obvious typo, retype the URL in the Location text box, and press **Enter**.

➤ This error message might also mean that you lost your connection with the service provider. In other words, your TCP/IP program hung up on you. Try some other links to make sure you're connected. If you keep getting this message no matter which link you click, you've probably been disconnected. Go back to your TCP/IP program, and log in again.

➤ If you're connected all right, but you keep getting this error message no matter which Web page you try to load, maybe your service provider's DNS server is down, or you have the wrong address for it. Contact your service provider to find out the correct address for the DNS server.

Navigator Can't Find the Document

Say you type a long URL or click a link for a long URL that looks something like this...

http://www.yahoo.com/Entertainment/Movies/

...and you get a screen that says something like **Document Not Found**, then you're connected to the right Web server, but somebody moved or deleted the Web page you want to pull up. Try chopping the end off the right side of the URL, and enter the shortened URL into the Location text box. For instance, in the previous example, you might try typing:

http://www.yahoo.com/Entertainment

If you still have trouble connecting, try chopping another portion off the right side of the URL (for example, type the URL without **/Entertainment**). You can chop all the way down to the domain name (for example, **www.yahoo.com**). This gets you in the general vicinity of the Web page you're looking for. You can then click links to search for the specific Web page.

File Contains No Data

Another ambiguous error message, this one usually means that the end is chopped off the URL. URLs typically end with a file name, telling Navigator which page, graphic, video, or sound file to open. For example, **http://home.netscape.com/newsref/ref/index.html** opens a Web page document file called index.html. Sometimes, if the file name is chopped off (as in **http://home.netscape.com/newsref/ref/**), Navigator might tell you that the document contains no data.

Because you do not know the name of the file, you can't just type it into the URL and press **Enter**. Instead, try chopping more off the right side of the URL. Type the chopped URL into the Location text box, and press **Enter**. Most Web servers display their home page whenever you connect to the server. You can then click the links on this page to find a specific page.

Of course, this error message might also mean that the page you pulled up really is blank. However, Web people rarely stick blank pages on the Web. It's just not fun (or annoying enough) to inspire such an act.

Does It Seem S...L...O...W?

Hyperdocuments can be packed with pictures called *inline images*, no relation to inline skates. These buggers take forever to transfer over the phone lines and can slow your Navigator sessions down to a mere crawl. There is, however, a trick to speeding up Navigator. Open the **Edit** menu, and select **Preferences**. Under **Category**, click on **Advanced**, and then click on **Automatically load images** to remove the check from its box. Click **OK**. In the next hyperdocument you load, standard icons will appear in place of the images. To view a single image, you can click it. To view all images on the page, click the **Images** button (below Navigator's menu bar).

You can always switch back to having all the images displayed by selecting **Edit, Preferences, Advanced, Automatically load images**. However, as you wander the Web, you'll discover that you can get around a lot quicker by turning Automatically Load Images off. When you find the page you were looking for, click the **Images** button.

Can I Stop Images from Loading Even if Automatically Load Images Is On?

Yes. If a page is taking much longer to load than you had expected, and you're losing patience, click the **Stop** button. Navigator will display as much of the page as it has loaded, usually displaying all the text. You can then click links or partially loaded graphics to move on.

The Least You Need to Know

As you cruise the Internet with Navigator, you will hit some potholes and drive into a good share of dead ends. Don't let it get to you. The following tips will free you from the most common traffic jams:

- ➤ If you hit a snag, simply click the **Stop** button and try a different link.
- ➤ When you get the Failed DNS Lookup message, retype the URL and try again.
- ➤ If you continue to receive a message saying that a document does not exist, try entering a shorter version of the URL.
- ➤ Many error messages result from the fact that the server you are trying to connect to is undergoing maintenance. Try the same URL later.
- ➤ If a page is taking a long time to load, it may be packed with graphics, or traffic at the site may be heavy. Be patient, especially during business hours.

Chapter 6

Revisiting Your Favorite Haunts

In This Chapter

- ➤ Jump back to a page you just visited
- ➤ Slap a bookmark on a page, so you can quickly return to it
- ➤ Create a list of hot Web pages
- ➤ Swap Web page lists with your friends

You just clicked on a trail of 35 links trying to find the Elle MacPherson home page, and you racked up an hour in Internet connect time charges. But now your eyes are getting droopy, and you don't have the energy to look at the 120 pictures of Elle you found. What do you do? Even if you could remember how to get back to this page, you wouldn't have the energy or desire to repeat the trip... well, maybe you would—it is Elle after all.

In this chapter, you'll learn how to go back to pages you've visited by selecting them from the history list and by creating bookmarks for your favorite pages. As a bonus, you'll also learn how to transform a list of bookmarks into a Web page, and how to trade bookmark lists with your friends, family, and colleagues.

Going Back in History (Lists)

As you carelessly click links and enter URLs, Navigator keeps track of the URLs for the pages you visited. It adds each URL to a *history list*. When you use the Back and Forward buttons, you are actually moving up and down the history list to return to the documents you viewed.

But what happens when you visit 10 sites and want to return to the fifth one? Clicking on the Back button 5 times is hardly the fastest way to return. To zip back, select the desired URL from the history list. The easiest way to do this is to open the **Location** drop-down list; then click the URL for the page you want to view, as shown here.

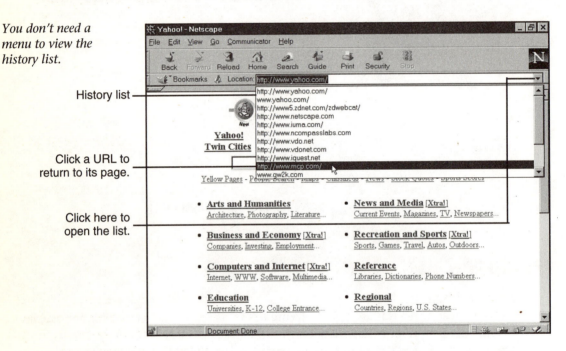

You don't need a menu to view the history list.

History list

Click a URL to return to its page.

Click here to open the list.

You can also get at the history list in a dialog box. To view the history list in this way, open the **Communicator** menu and select **History** (or just press **Ctrl+H**). This displays the History window. To return to a page, double-click on its name in the history list, or right-click on it and select **Go to Page**.

Another way to revisit a page is to open the Go menu, and select the page from the bottom of the menu. Unlike the Location drop-down list (which displays only URLs), the Go menu displays the actual page names, so they might make more sense to you. The History list that is displayed in the History window gives you the best of both systems, displaying the page name and URL.

Making Shortcuts in Windows 95

In Windows 95, you can make shortcuts to your favorite Web pages. (Shortcuts are icons that sit on the Windows desktop.) To create a shortcut, right-click on the link for which you want to make a shortcut, and then click on **Create Shortcut** to display the Create Internet Shortcut dialog box. Type a name for the shortcut in the **Description** text box, and click on **OK**.

The shortcut is placed on the Windows desktop, and appears as a Netscape Navigator icon. To load a page for which you've created a shortcut, double-click on the shortcut.

> **New Feature!**
> The **Back** and **Forward** buttons are more powerful in the new Navigator. They now double as drop-down lists. Point to the **Back** or **Forward** button and hold down the mouse button to open a list of pages you've visited. Drag over the name of the desired page and release the mouse button.

> **Make Navigator Your Default Browser**
> If you have more than one Web browser installed on your computer, you can use only one of them to create and use shortcuts. If you run Netscape Navigator, and a dialog box appears, telling you that this browser is not the default browser, click the **Yes** button to make Navigator the default browser; otherwise, you won't be able to use shortcuts.

Marking a Page with a Bookmark

You have this gargantuan book (the Web), over a million pages, and you find a page that has an interesting picture, or a mind-altering quote. You want to remember this page, and you'll probably want to return to it someday. What do you do? Create a bookmark for the page. A *bookmark* is an entry that you can select (from the Bookmarks menu) to quickly return to a page you visited.

The Bookmarks menu already contains nearly 100 bookmarks arranged in categories, including Finance, Business, Computers, and Entertainment. These bookmarks are grouped on submenus. To go to a bookmarked page, open the **Bookmarks** menu, point to the desired category, and click the page name.

You can quickly create bookmarks for any page that's displayed, and for any URL you have (even if you haven't yet visited the page). All the bookmarks are dumped at the bottom of the Bookmarks menu, but you can group the bookmarks, place them on submenus, and even juggle them to place them in some order that you can follow.

To create a bookmark for a page that's displayed, take the following steps:

1. Open the page you want to display.

2. Watch the flying comets and the status bar to make sure the document has been completely transferred. If the document is in the process of being transferred, you can't mark it.

3. Open the **Bookmarks** menu and click **Add Bookmark** (or press **Ctrl+D**).

The bookmark is added to the bottom of the Bookmarks menu. When you add a bookmark in this way, the page name appears on the Bookmarks menu, and the URL remains behind the scenes. However, if nobody gave the page a title, the page's URL may appear on the menu. In either case, you can quickly revisit a page you've marked by opening the Bookmarks menu and clicking on the name of the page, or on its URL.

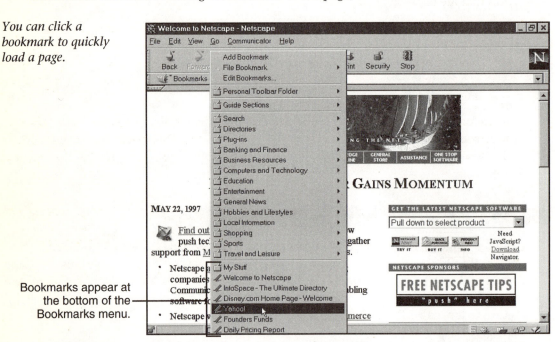

You can click a bookmark to quickly load a page.

Bookmarks appear at the bottom of the Bookmarks menu.

If you have more bookmarks than will fit on the Bookmarks menu, the menu expands to the left or right, showing another column of bookmarks. It's nearly impossible to test the capacity of this expanding menu.

Bookmarking a Link

If you see a link that you might like to visit later, you can create a bookmark for it without opening its page. Right-click the link to display a shortcut menu, and then click **Add Bookmark**.

Giving Your Bookmark List a Makeover

As you add bookmarks, they're dumped at the bottom of the Bookmarks menu and stuck with whatever name or complicated URL the Webmaster decided to use. As time passes, your Bookmarks menu becomes cluttered with all sorts of incomprehensible names and URLs that are listed in no logical order.

The good news is that you can take control of your bookmarks. In the following sections, you'll learn how to rename bookmarks, place them in logical groups, delete bookmarks you no longer need, and even create your own bookmark submenus. By the time you're done with these sections, you'll have a leaner, more efficient Bookmarks menu, one that even Al Gore would be proud of.

But, before we get into the nitty-gritty of remolding your Bookmarks menu, let's display the screen you use to edit the Bookmarks menu. Open the **Bookmarks** menu, and click **Edit Bookmarks** (or press **Ctrl+B**). The Bookmarks window appears, showing the existing structure of your bookmarks.

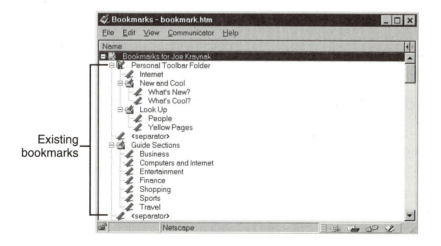

Use this window to restructure your Bookmarks menu.

Renaming and Deleting Bookmarks

The first step in restructuring your Bookmarks menu is to give your bookmarks names that you can easily recognize. This is especially important if you have raw URLs on your menu. The easiest way to rename a bookmark is to right-click it and choose **Bookmark Properties**. This displays the Bookmark Properties dialog box, with the Name entry highlighted. Type a new name for the bookmark, and click **OK**.

One word of caution: Don't change the **Location (URL)** entry. This is the URL that works behind the scenes to load the specific page. You can change the name of the bookmark, but changing the URL entry is the same as changing an address on a letter. If you give this bookmark the wrong address, Navigator won't be able to find the page.

You can give your bookmarks more recognizable names.

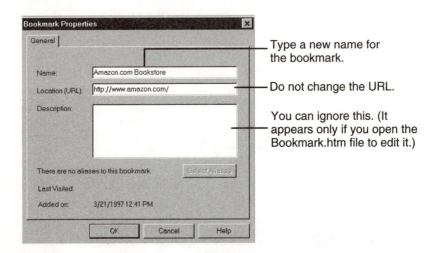

Type a new name for the bookmark.

Do not change the URL.

You can ignore this. (It appears only if you open the Bookmark.htm file to edit it.)

If your bookmark list is cluttered with bookmarks you no longer use, delete them. Simply click the bookmark, and then press the **Del** key (or select **Delete** from the **Edit** menu).

Shuffling Your Bookmarks

Once you've renamed any bookmarks that needed it, think about rearranging your bookmarks. For example, you might want to place the bookmarks for all the sports pages together, and stick the bookmarks for entertainment sites next to each other.

To move a bookmark, click it, and then drag it up or down in the list. A line appears, showing you where the bookmark you're dragging will be placed. When the line is where you want the bookmark moved, release the mouse button.

Grouping Bookmarks with Separators and Submenus

You've cleaned up your Bookmarks menu, deleted the fluff, and assigned names to faceless URLs. What more could you want? Well, if your list is still too long to fit on the Bookmarks menu, you might want to create some submenus and add separators to place your bookmarks in logical groups.

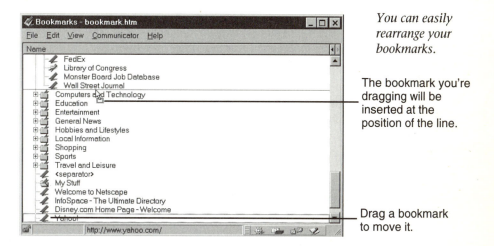

You can easily rearrange your bookmarks.

The bookmark you're dragging will be inserted at the position of the line.

Drag a bookmark to move it.

Separators are the lines that divide options on a menu into groups. If you open Navigator's View menu, you'll see three separators: one before Increase Font, one before Reload, and one before Page Source. You can add separators to your Bookmarks menu. In the Bookmarks window, click the bookmark below which you want to insert the separator; then open the **File** menu and click **New Separator**. Or, right-click on the bookmark below which you want to insert the separator, and click on **New Separator**.

Separators are great if you have only about 10 to 15 bookmarks, but if you have many more than that, you should consider creating submenus for related bookmarks. For example, you can create a submenu called Business that includes bookmarks for all your business-related Web pages. To create a submenu and place bookmarks on it, take the following steps:

1. Open the **Bookmarks** window, and click the bookmark below which you want the submenu to appear.

2. Open the **File** menu and click **New Folder**. The Bookmark Properties dialog box appears, prompting you to name the folder.

3. Type a name for the folder, and press **Enter** (or click **OK**). A folder appears in the list of bookmarks. You can now drag bookmarks into this folder to place them on the submenu.

Part Deux ➤ *Mastering Netscape Navigator*

4. To move a bookmark to your folder, simply drag the bookmark over the folder and release the mouse button. Repeat this step to move additional bookmarks to your folder.

5. If you end up creating a submenu of a submenu, you can move the submenu up one level in the tree by dragging it to the top of the tree. This moves the submenu and all its bookmarks.

In the Bookmarks window, if you see a folder that has a plus sign (+) next to it, you can click on the plus sign to *expand* the folder (display its contents). The plus sign is then replaced by a minus sign (-), which you can click to hide the contents of the folder.

Use submenus to group related bookmarks.

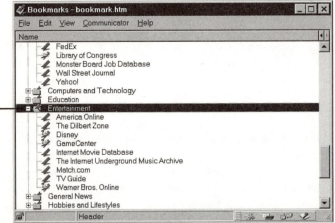

Bookmarks appear under the submenu you created.

When you are done editing your bookmark list, open the **File** menu and select **Close**, or click the **Close** button in the upper right corner of the window (or press **Ctrl+W**). Your Bookmarks menu is immediately updated to reflect your changes. To open a submenu, simply open the **Bookmarks** menu, and rest the mouse pointer on the submenu's name. You can then click a bookmark to select it.

Techno Talk

Your Bookmark List Is a Web Page!

Congratulations, you just created your first HTML (Web) document. You don't believe me? In the Navigator window, open the **File** menu and click on **Open File**. Use the resulting dialog box to open the file named Bookmark.htm (in Windows 95, the file is in the C:\Program Files\Netscape\Users\yourname\ folder). You can also set the Bookmark.htm file as your starting Web page; see "Trading Bookmark Lists with Your Friends," later in this chapter.

When You Add Bookmarks Later...

If you add bookmarks later, the bookmarks are placed at the bottom of the Bookmarks menu. You can move them to one of your submenus by displaying the Bookmarks window again and dragging the bookmark(s) over the submenu name.

Another way to add bookmarks to a submenu is to tell Navigator on which submenu you want the bookmarks placed. Open the **Bookmarks** menu and click **Edit Bookmarks**. Click on the name of the submenu on which you want the new bookmarks placed. Open the **View** menu and select **Set as New Bookmarks Folder**. Now, whenever you display a Web page and then enter the **Bookmarks/Add Bookmark** command, the bookmark is added to the specified submenu, instead of to the bottom of the Bookmarks menu.

You can also choose to use a submenu's bookmarks as your Bookmarks menu. Open the **Bookmarks** menu, and click **Edit Bookmarks**. Click on the name of the submenu you want to use as your Bookmarks menu, and then open the **View** menu and click on **Set as Bookmark Menu**. When you open the Bookmarks menu, you'll see only the bookmarks on the selected submenu.

To return your Bookmarks menu to its original condition, display the Bookmarks menu, and click on the folder icon at the top of the bookmarks list. Then, open the **View** menu and click on **Set as New Bookmarks Folder**. Open the **View** menu again, and click on **Set as Bookmark Menu**. Now, the Bookmarks menu will look and behave the way it used to.

Drag-and-Drop Bookmarks

One of the big improvements in Navigator 4.0 is that you can now add a bookmark to the Bookmarks menu or one of its submenus by dragging and dropping a link from a Web page. Simply drag the link over the Bookmarks menu and release the mouse button. To add a bookmark for the current page, drag the icon next to the Location text box over the Bookmarks menu, and release the mouse button. To add a bookmark to a submenu, drag the link over the Bookmarks menu, over the submenu name, and then onto the submenu. A line appears, showing where the bookmark will be placed. Release the mouse button.

Ugh! Adding Bookmarks Manually

By far, the easiest way to add a bookmark is to pull up a Web page, open the **Bookmarks** menu, and click **Add Bookmark**. If you're a masochist, however, you might like adding bookmarks yourself—by typing them in.

To insert a bookmark, first open the **Bookmarks** menu and click **Edit Bookmarks**. This opens the Navigator Bookmarks window. Click the bookmark (or submenu name) below which you want the bookmark to appear. Then, open the **File** menu, and click **New Bookmark**. A dialog box appears, prompting you to enter the name and location (URL) of the page. Type the page's name (or the name you want to give it), and then tab to the **Location (URL)** text box and type the URL for the page. Click **OK**.

The Page Moved!

If some joker on the Web moves a page, you may have to change the URL for one of your bookmarks. This is easy enough. Click the bookmark; then open the **Edit** menu and click **Bookmark Properties**. This displays the dialog box showing the bookmark's name and location. You can then edit the item, as necessary.

An easier way to check for an update on your bookmark URLs is to have Navigator do it for you. Display the **Bookmarks** window, and then open the **View** menu and click on **Update Bookmarks**. The What's New dialog box appears, asking if you want to check all your bookmarks or only the selected bookmarks. Click on the desired option, and then click on the **Start Checking** button. Navigator updates the URLs for any bookmark whose URL has changed. (This might take a while, depending on the number of bookmarks you have and how busy each Web page is.)

When Navigator is done updating the books, it displays a special icon next to bookmarks that have changed. Question marks appear next to any bookmarks that Navigator was unable to check.

Creating and Saving Additional Bookmark Lists

As you know, the bookmark list you created is a Web document file called bookmark.htm, but you can save the list under another name. For example, if you have hundreds of bookmarks, you might want to save them in separate files—one for entertainment, one for business, and one for research. Then, you can choose which bookmark file you want to use.

To save a bookmark file under another name, display the Navigator Bookmarks window (**Bookmarks/Edit Bookmarks**). Open the **File** menu, and select **Save As**. Type a name for the bookmark file (you can leave off the extension), and click **Save**.

To specify which bookmark file you want to use (so its bookmarks will appear on the Bookmarks menu), open **Bookmarks**, and select **Edit Bookmarks**. Open the **File** menu and click on **Open Bookmarks Folder**. Use the Open bookmarks file dialog box to select the drive, folder, and name of the bookmark file you want to use. Click **Open**. This opens the specified bookmark file. Now, when you close the Netscape Bookmarks window, the specified bookmark file is made active; its bookmarks appear on the Bookmarks menu.

Chapter 6 ➤ *Revisiting Your Favorite Haunts*

You can create and use any of the bookmark files you create.

Select the name of the bookmark file you want to use.

Trading Bookmark Lists with Your Friends

If you're reading all the little boxed tips throughout this chapter, you know that a bookmark list doubles as a Web page, which goes by the name of bookmark.html or bookmark.htm. You can open it in Navigator, and it even looks like a Web page. Because a bookmark is structured as a Web page, you can trade your bookmark lists with your friends and colleagues. You can send your bookmark file to a friend, who can then import it into her bookmark list or open it as a Web page. Or you can import a bookmark list you received from a friend. (You can also tell Navigator to use a specific bookmark file, as explained in the previous section.)

The bookmark.html or bookmark.htm file is in the C:\Program Files\Netscape\Users \yourname\ folder in Windows 95. You can copy the file to a floppy disk or send it via e-mail. If you receive a bookmark file, you can add its bookmarks to your Bookmarks menu by performing the following steps:

1. Make sure the bookmark file is on your hard disk or on a floppy disk inside one of your floppy disk drives.

2. Open Navigator's **Bookmarks** menu and click **Edit Bookmarks**. This displays the Navigator Bookmarks window.

3. Open the **File** menu and select **Import**. The Import bookmarks file dialog box appears, prompting you to select the bookmark file you want to import.

4. Change to the drive and folder that contains the bookmark file.

5. Click the name of the bookmark file you want to import, and then click the **Open** button. The bookmarks are appended (tacked on) to the end of your bookmarks list.

Here's a great tip that makes this book well worth the money you paid for it. You've created a Web page (your bookmarks file), so consider using it as your starting page.

Open the **Edit** menu, and select **Preferences**. Select the **Browser** category. Make sure **Home Page** is selected, and then type the path to your bookmark file in the **Location** text box, or click the **Browse** button, and select the file from the file list. For example, type

```
file:///C|/Program Files/Netscape/Users/yourname/Bookmark.htm
```

Notice that the "URL" starts with "file," indicating that the page is stored on your computer. There are three forward slashes after **file:**, followed by the drive letter and the pipe symbol (|), *not* a colon. Click **OK**.

Create Your Own Toolbar

Although bookmarks are fairly impressive, Navigator has one more trick tucked up its sleeve—a customizable button bar, called the Personal toolbar. To display this new toolbar, click on the tab below the Bookmarks toolbar. (If there is no tab, open the **View** menu and select **Show Personal Toolbar**.) You can quickly add shortcuts to your favorite Web pages by dragging links up to this toolbar.

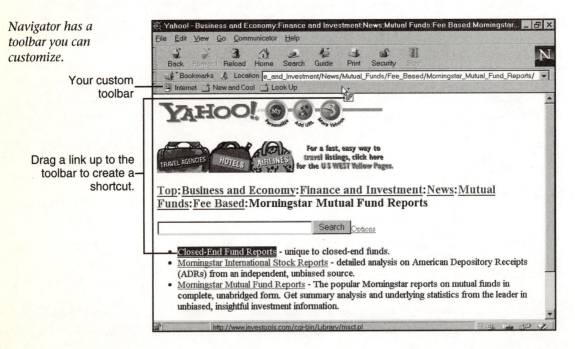

Navigator has a toolbar you can customize.

Your custom toolbar

Drag a link up to the toolbar to create a shortcut.

To edit the toolbar (add or remove buttons, change a button's name or appearance), open the **Bookmarks** menu and select **Edit Bookmarks**. The Personal Toolbar folder contains the bookmarks that appear as buttons on the Personal toolbar. You can delete and move buttons and change their names, just as if you were editing your bookmarks. In other words, these buttons are nothing more than bookmarks with fancy clothes. You can also move bookmark folders to the Personal Toolbar.

The Least You Need to Know

Okay, I admit that this chapter probably contains about three times as much information about bookmarks as you really wanted. Here are the points you should never forget:

- To add a bookmark for a page, first open the page. Then, open the **Bookmarks** menu and select **Add Bookmark**.

- Another quick way to add a bookmark is to drag a link up to the **Bookmarks** menu or one of its submenus.

- If you care to fiddle with your Bookmarks menu (no one says you have to), open the **Bookmarks** menu, and click **Edit Bookmarks**.

- Click on the tab below the Bookmarks toolbar to display the Personal toolbar. You can drag links up to this toolbar to create your own buttons.

- To edit the Personal toolbar, edit the bookmarks in the Personal Toolbar folder.

- You can drag a link over a blank area of the Windows desktop to create a shortcut to a Web page.

- You can open your bookmarks file as a Web page. Use the **File Open Page** command, click **Choose File**, and look in the C:/Program Files/Netscape/Users/yourname/ folder.

Chapter 7

Tuning into the Web with Netcaster

In This Chapter

➤ Understand why *push content* is your best friend

➤ Have updated Web pages delivered to your desktop while you work (or sleep)

➤ Stick a Web page right on the Windows desktop

➤ Program your own channel changer for the Web

In a concerted effort to transform your computer monitor into a TV set, Web developers have come up with some innovative tools. Netscape's entry into this wave of the future is Netcaster, a tool that enables you to subscribe to Web sites and have updated Web pages delivered to you while you are working on something else or just catching a few Zs. That way, you don't have to twiddle your mouse thumbs while waiting for pages to trickle through the cables.

Although Netcaster is fairly diminutive when viewed as part of the Communicator suite, it offers two features to cut down on your connect time, and to deliver the latest Web updates (for the sites you visit most) directly to you:

➤ *Channels* allow you to tune in to the best sites the Web has to offer. Netcaster comes with a channel finder that allows you to select from popular sites, such as *ABC News*, *CBS SportsLine*, *CNN*, and *Wired* magazine. You can also place your favorite sites on the channel changer.

➤ *The Webtop* is a new concept that provides you with a desktop overlay. You can set up any Web page as an automatically updating Webtop, which displays its latest content. The Webtop allows you to stay on top of the news as it happens.

In this chapter, you will learn all you need to know about selecting, viewing, and subscribing to channels, and how to take control of your new Webtop. (Although "subscribing" sounds as though this is going to cost money, it usually doesn't. "Subscribing" just means that you will tell Netcaster which pages you want and when to download them.)

What's All This Push Content Nonsense?

If you've been stranded on a deserted island in the Caribbean, you have probably missed the latest Web innovation: *push content*. The idea behind push content is that instead of using a Web browser to *pull* pages to your computer, you *subscribe* to Web sites that *push* their pages to you. This allows you to schedule page updates and have them sent to your computer while you are working on something else (or sleeping or daydreaming). You can then disconnect from the Internet and load the pages from your hard drive. Although it takes the same amount of time to download the page, you don't have to sit there waiting for it. You can then open the page from your hard drive, which serves it up quick.

Techno Talk

Push-Me-Pull-You

The term "push content" is a little misleading. Is the site really *pushing* pages to your little ol' computer? Heck no! All that's happening here is that instead of typing a page address or clicking on a link to open a page, you tell Netcaster ahead of time what you want and when to get it. Your computer, with Navigator's help, is still the one *pulling* the page to your computer. But if any of the industry big shots were to say any different, push content wouldn't seem such a big breakthrough now, would it?

Starting Netcaster: What Is This Thing?

So much for preliminaries—let's take a look at the beast. You can run Netcaster in any of several ways. You can select **Netcaster** from the **Communicator** menu in any of the Communicator component windows (Navigator, Messenger, Collabra, or Composer), or press **Ctrl+8**. You can also run it by opening the **Start** menu, pointing to **Programs**, **Netscape Communicator**, and selecting **Netscape Netcaster**. To have Netcaster run when you start Communicator, open Navigator's **Edit** menu, select **Preferences**, click **Appearance**, and make sure there is a check mark next to **Netcaster**. Click **OK**.

You have it running, right? And you just lost the right third of your screen. Fortunately, this is a temporary loss. On the left side of the Netcaster window is a tab with an N on it. Click the tab to hide the window; click the tab again to bring the window back into view. (The tab stays on top of your other windows.) To completely exit Netcaster, click **Exit** near the bottom of the window.

As you can see from the following figure, the Netcaster window is divided into the following four areas, listed from top to bottom:

➤ **Channel Finder** displays a list of popular channels that are registered with Netscape, including ABC News and CNET. You can click More Channels to view a list of additional channels. See "Channel Surfing with Netcaster," later in this chapter, for details.

➤ **My Channels** is a list of channels you have chosen to tune in. Click My Channels to hide Channel Finder, and display a list of your favorite channels. Netscape took the initiative of adding itself to your list as your first channel. To add channels to this list, see "Adding and Viewing Channels," later in this chapter. (You can click Channel Finder again to hide My Channels and display Channel Finder.)

➤ **Control Bar**, near the bottom of the window, provides options for adding a channel (to the My Channels list), configuring Netcaster (see "Taking Control of the Netcaster Window" later in this chapter), viewing online help, and exiting Netcaster.

➤ **Button Bar**, at the very bottom, allows you to use Netcaster to navigate your channels (flip forward and back, and print the current page), and to control your Webtop (hide it, move it to the front or back, or close it). You'll learn more about these buttons as you proceed through this chapter.

Part Deux ➤ Mastering Netscape Navigator

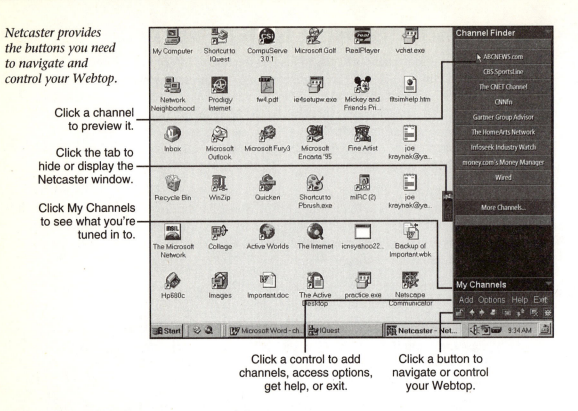

Netcaster provides the buttons you need to navigate and control your Webtop.

Click a channel to preview it.

Click the tab to hide or display the Netcaster window.

Click My Channels to see what you're tuned in to.

Click a control to add channels, access options, get help, or exit.

Click a button to navigate or control your Webtop.

Channel-Surfing with Netcaster

As you have probably guessed, Netcaster is basically a channel changer for the Web. You program in the channels you want to view, and then you can view those channels with a simple click of a button. But how do you program these channels? And what do you do if your favorite Web site isn't on Netcaster's Channel Finder list? The following sections provide answers to these questions and detailed instructions on how to program Netcaster.

Finding High-Profile Web Channels

Netcaster's Channel Finder lists over 100 popular Web sites that have taken it upon themselves to register their "stations" with Netscape. First, make sure Channel Finder is open by clicking **Channel Finder** in the Netcaster window. You can then preview a channel—click the channel's name, and the channel's title and logo appear on a *card*. In the lower left corner of the card is an Add Channel button, which you can click to view the page in Navigator and add the channel to your channel changer (see the next section for instructions).

If you don't see the channel you want, click **More Channels** at the bottom of the Channel Finder list. This connects you to Netscape's Web site, which contains a list of additional channels.

Adding and Viewing Channels from Channel Finder

You already have some idea of how this channel changer works, so let's go through the process of adding a channel step-by-step:

1. Click **Channel Finder** to display a list of popular channels.

2. Click the channel button for the channel you want to add to the My Channels list. The channel's card appears, letting you preview the channel.

3. Click the card. The ChannelFinder window appears, displaying the contents of the selected channel.

> **Check This Out...**
>
> **The Ever-Changing Channel Finder**
> As this Web-TV thing catches on, more and more companies will be registering their Web sites as channels, so be sure to check Netscape regularly for additional high-profile channels.

4. Click the **Add Channel** button in the upper left corner of the Channel Finder window. The Channel Properties dialog box appears, as shown in the following figure, displaying the channel name and its address.

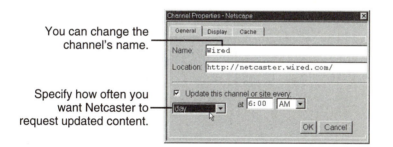

You can change the channel's name.

Specify how often you want Netcaster to request updated content.

Netcaster provides several options for controlling your channels.

5. (Optional) Double-click in the Name text box, and type a more descriptive name for the channel. Do NOT edit the entry in the Location text box.

6. Open the **Update this channel or site every:** drop-down list, and select how frequently you want Netcaster to download updates from this site. (If you choose Day or Week, specify the day and/or time that you want Netcaster to download the update.)

7. Click the **Display** tab, and select one of the following options:

    Default Window displays the page in a standard Navigator window, providing you with Navigator's navigational tools.

    Webtop Window lets the page take over all the real estate on your Windows desktop, and does not display the Navigator toolbars or menus. This makes the page nice and big but difficult to handle. See "Placing Live Content Right on Your Desktop," later in this chapter, for details.

8. Click the **Cache** tab, and enter the following preferences (each channel has its own default settings):

    Download ___ level(s) deep in site tells Netcaster to download pages that are linked to the main channel. Be careful with this option; if a page has many links, or you select to download more than two or three levels deep, you'll end up cramming your hard drive with Web pages.

    Don't store more than ___ KB of information tells Netcaster to stop downloading when it has received a certain measure of data. Again, keep this number below 1 megabyte (1000 KB), or you might find your hard drive full in the morning.

9. Click **OK**.

The channel is now added to you're My Channels list. To view the channel, click **My Channels**. If you see a red and gray bar below your channel, Netcaster is busy downloading the latest update. When Netcaster is finished downloading, the bar disappears. You can then disconnect and view the page offline. See "Browsing Offline to Save Time and Money," later in this chapter.

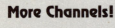

More Channels!

Remember, you can find additional channels by clicking **More Channels** at the bottom of the Channel Finder list. This displays a page of additional channels, each one having its own card. To view more channels, click the up arrow icon centered above the list, or the down arrow icon centered below the list. To preview a page, click its card. You can then click the **Add Channel** button to add the channel to the My Channels list.

Updating Page Content Manually

When adding channels, you have the option of telling Netcaster to retrieve page updates at a specified interval. However, if you set Netcaster to update a page on a weekly basis, you may be receiving old news. To find out if a channel has recently been updated, rest the mouse pointer on the channel name. A box pops up, displaying the date and time the page was last updated.

If the channel has not been updated for some time, you can manually request an update. Click Netcaster's **Options** button, click on the name of the page you want to update, and click the **Update Now** button. Netcaster fetches the most recent version of the page. Remember to wait for the red/gray progress line to disappear, indicating that the download is complete.

> **Check This Out...**
>
> **Right-Click on Your Channels**
> You can right-click on the name of a channel in the My Channels list to display a context menu, which allows you to update the channel, stop an update, change the channel properties, or delete the channel.

Adding Any Web Site as a Channel

Netcaster's Channel Finder is loads of fun and can open your eyes to popular sites you didn't know were popular (or didn't know existed). However, I'm sure you have your own list of favorite sites, perhaps sites that you have already bookmarked.

To add a site to the My Channels list, click the **Add** button in Netcaster's control bar. The Channel Properties dialog box appears, as shown in the previous figure, except the **Name** and **Location** text boxes are empty. Type a name for the channel, and then click in the Location text box, and type the URL that points to the page. Enter any additional options, as explained in the previous section, including how often you want Netscape to request updated content. Click **OK**.

Tuning Out: Deleting a Channel

Once you've set up a couple dozen channels, your list might become a little cluttered with channels you never "watch." To clean up your list, you can delete channels. Here's what you do:

1. Click the **Options** button in the control bar. The Options dialog box appears, with the Channels tab up front.
2. Click the name of the channel you want to remove.
3. Click the **Delete** button. A warning appears, prompting you for confirmation.
4. Click the **Yes** button.

Placing Live Content Right on Your Desktop

When you first add a channel, you can choose to have its Web page displayed in a standard Navigator window or as a Webtop. You can change this window setting for any channel at any time. Click the **Options** button, click the name of the page whose settings you want to change, and click the **Properties** button. This displays the same Properties dialog box you saw when you first set up the page as a channel. Click the **Display** tab, and select **Default Window** (to display the page in a standard Navigator window) or **Webtop Window** (to make the page overlays your current desktop).

When you choose to display a channel as a Webtop, it covers your current desktop, and blocks access to any of your desktop icons, as shown in the figure below. However, Netcaster does allow the Windows 95 taskbar to show through, and Netcaster displays the following Webtop controls:

- **Security** is the lock icon all the way on the left. If it's locked, you're viewing a secure page.

- **Go to previous page on webtop** displays the previous channel that you have chosen to display as a Webtop Window. If you chose to display the channel in the Default Window, this button will not bring it into view.

- **Go to next page on webtop** displays the next channel that you have chosen to display as a Webtop Window.

- **Print the webtop** prints the Webtop.

- **Show or hide the webtop** turns the Webtop on or off, so you can get at your desktop icons.

- **Send the webtop to the front or back** moves the Webtop to the top or bottom of a stack of windows. This works only if you have other application windows open that are not maximized. Any maximized window will cover the Webtop.

- **Close the webtop** turns off the Webtop and returns your desktop to normal.

- **Open a Navigator window** opens a Netscape Navigator window, so you can browse like in the good ol' days.

Chapter 7 ➤ *Tuning into the Web with Netcaster*

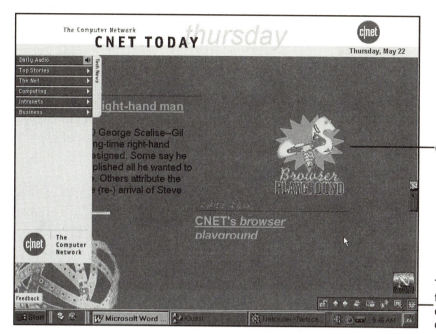

The Webtop provides the maximum viewing area for a Web page.

—Channel appears here.

Toolbar allows you to navigate Webtop channels and control the Webtop.

Right-Click on the Webtop

Although the Webtop offers little in the way of menus, you can still right-click on objects and links to display a context menu with the most common options.

Taking Control of the Netcaster Window

Until you get used to it, that Netcaster window can be a little intimidating. It just sits there, covering a third of your screen, and there seems to be no way to make it less intrusive. However, Netcaster does provide a few options to reposition and control the Netcaster window. To access these options, click the **Options** button, and then click the **Layout** tab. You can then change the following settings:

➤ **Attach Netcaster drawer to** lets you move the Netcaster window to the left or right side of the screen.

➤ **Attach Webtop to** lets you move the Webtop to the left or right side of the screen. (If you move the Netcaster window to the right, consider moving the Webtop to the left.)

79

- ➤ **Automatically hide Netcaster window** forces the Netcaster window to roll back whenever you select a channel. This gets it out of the way, so you can view the Web page.

- ➤ **Default Channel** allows you to pick any of your channels as the opening channel whenever you run Netcaster. Initially, Netcaster does not use a default channel. To use a channel as the default, select **Set default to**, and then pick a channel from the drop-down list.

You can reposition and configure the Netcaster window.

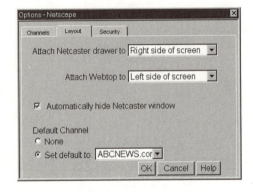

How Do I Know Which Channels Are Webtops?

If a small rectangle appears to the right of a channel name, that channel is set to display in Webtop mode. No rectangle means the channel will open in a standard window. Other than the difference in modes, a Webtop is nothing more than a channel—the process for deleting, updating, and changing their properties is the same.

Chapter 7 ➤ *Tuning into the Web with Netcaster*

Browsing Offline to Save Time and Money

Several companies, including Netscape, have been busy working on ways to speed up the Internet. Cable companies, modem manufacturers, and PC satellite developers have gone the hardware route, trying to solve the problem by increasing the speed at which data travels from the Internet to your PC. However, these solutions have an upper limit and cost users more time and money than they are willing to spend.

As a temporary solution, other companies have looked at the problem from a software standpoint, and have developed the clever notion of *push content*. With push content, instead of waiting for you to request pages, Web sites can broadcast updated content to your computer while you are busy working or counting sheep. You can then disconnect from the Internet and view your pages offline.

Viewing offline is very useful if you can't establish an Internet connection, if you are working offline with Navigator, or if you are on the road and don't have access to a phone line. With Netcaster, you have the perfect tool for viewing Web content offline. Here's what you do:

1. Make sure that Netcaster has downloaded the Web page at least once, preferably recently. If Netcaster hasn't downloaded the page, you can't view it offline.
2. Disconnect from the Internet.
3. Start Netcaster, if it is not already running.
4. Click **My Channels**, and click the button for the channel you want to view.

The Least You Need to Know

If all you get from this chapter is that the Web is going to replace your TV set, you have a pretty good grasp of Netcaster. However, in the event that that concept didn't come across, here's a list of important points to drive it home:

➤ To run Netcaster, choose it from the **Start**, **Programs**, **Netscape Communicator** menu or from the **Communicator** menu in any of the other Netscape components.

➤ To view a list of interesting channels, click **Channel Finder**.

➤ To add a channel from Channel Finder to My Channels, click a channel in the Channel Finder list, and click the **Add Channel** button.

81

➤ To make any Web page a channel, click the Add Channel button in the Netcaster window, type a name for the channel, and enter its address in the Location text box.

➤ To change the properties of a channel, click the **Options** button, click the channel whose properties you want to change, and click the **Properties** button.

➤ You can choose to display a channel in the Navigator window or as a Webtop by changing the channel's properties.

Chapter 8

Saving and Printing Your Finds

In This Chapter

- ➤ Save multimedia files to disk for your future enjoyment
- ➤ Save a Web page and open it later
- ➤ Print a Web page and make some minor page adjustments
- ➤ Take a behind-the-scenes look at a Web page

The Web is like some big computerized flea market. You snake through the aisles picking up interesting facts, stories, bits of poetry and fiction, movie clips, sound clips, and even the occasional picture of your favorite actor or actress. You pull this stuff up in Navigator or in a helper application, give it a quick look, and then, like some overstimulated kid at Christmas, you drop the item to hurry to another site.

But then it happens. You find it. A movie clip that sucks the breath right out of you. A document that answers your most profound questions. You gotta have it. What do you do? In this chapter, you'll learn various ways to preserve the treasures you discover on the Web. You'll learn how to save all your discoveries, print your favorite documents, and even see the skeletons that hang behind the HTML documents.

Saving and Playing Clips and Pictures

The method of choice on the Web is to grab the loot, disconnect, and then play with the newly acquired toys later. If you have an Internet service provider who charges by the hour, you don't want to waste precious time viewing clips while you're still connected. Besides, it's considered bad manners to loiter at Web sites; other users are trying to connect.

There are a couple ways to download files (copy files to your hard disk) on the Web. Here's my personal favorite: Right-click the link for the item you want (any item—text file, graphics, Web page, whatever), and then click the **Save Link As** or **Save Image As** option. This opens the Save As dialog box, which prompts you to select the drive and folder (or directory) in which you want to save the file. You can also give the file a new name. Make the appropriate selections, and then click **Save**. The reason I like this method is that it gives you the greatest flexibility: You can click to view, or right-click to download. You don't have to worry about setting any options.

The only trouble you'll run into using this technique is when you encounter a graphic that is used as a link to some other file type (for example, if the Web page contains an icon that acts as a link pointing to a text file). In such a case, you want to right-click on the link and select **Save Link As**. If you select Save Image As, Navigator will save the graphic (for instance, the icon) rather than saving the file that the link points to.

Right-click a link to display the shortcut menu.

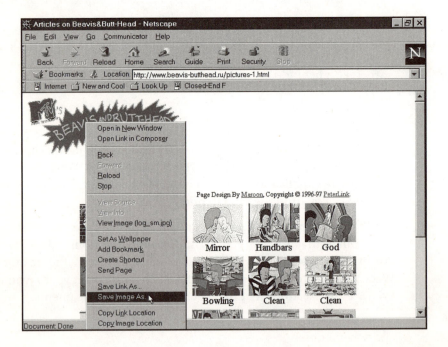

My second favorite method for saving clips and pictures is to use the *helper application* or *plug-in*. (You'll learn more about using helper applications and plug-ins in Part 3, "Playing Video, Sound, and Interactive Worlds.") Click the link to open the file in the helper application, and then use the helper application's **File/Save** command to save the file. With this method, you don't have to make any long-term commitments. You get to preview the clip before you save it to disk. Some helper applications, such as Navigator's audio player, save the file automatically in your TEMP folder or directory, and offer no **File/Save** option. Other applications will play the file, disappear, and dump the file.

If you become a serious download junkie, there's one more approach to downloading files that might appeal to you. You can set up Navigator to save a file whenever you click on a link for that file type. For example, you might set up Navigator to automatically save GIF and JPG (graphics) files. To do this, open the **Edit** menu and select **Preferences**. Click the plus sign next to **Browser**, and click **Applications**. Highlight the file type that you want Navigator to save to disk, click the **Edit** button, click on the **Save to Disk** option, and click **OK**. Now whenever you click a link for this file type, Navigator will display the Save As dialog box, prompting you to specify where you want the file saved. (For details on setting up file associations, see Chapter 13, "Beefing Up Navigator with Helper Applications.")

Reassociating File Types

If you turn on the **Save to Disk** option for a particular file type, you entirely foul up the association with the helper application. If you decide later that you want to associate a file type with its helper application, skip ahead to the section, "Mapping Files to Their Helper Applications," in Chapter 13.

Once you've saved a file to disk, you can open the file and play it in one of your helper applications. Run the helper application, and use its **File/Open** command as you would in any application. Then, if you have a sound or movie, use the application's controls (they'll vary, of course) to play the file.

What About Web Pages?

Ever wonder what's behind one of those Web pages? I'll show you. Load your favorite page. Now open the **View** menu and select **Page Source**. You should see something like the Web page pictured here. Not much to look at, eh? This is the original HTML document that's stored on the server. All those bracketed codes tell Navigator how to display the document without turning you to stone.

Behind the scenes with a Web page.

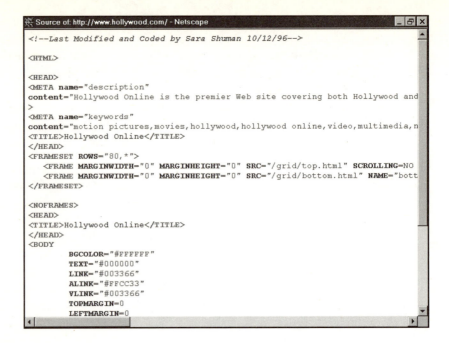

Why would anyone ever want to view one of these documents? Two reasons. First, sometimes, there's a rebel URL in the background (one with a typo in it). You click the link (which you can see), but the URL (which you can't see) isn't pointing to the page you want to go to. In such a case, you can enter the **View/Page Source** command to take a peek at the URL. You can even highlight the URL (by dragging over it), and then copy it (by pressing **Ctrl+C**). Then, close the View Source window, click inside the **Location** text box, and paste (**Ctrl+V**) the URL. You can then edit the URL to correct it (assuming it has an obvious typo).

The other reason you might want to view a source document is to learn how to code a Web page (which can come in handy when you design your own home page in Part 5).

You can also save Web pages as Web pages or as text files, but don't expect too much. In Navigator, you might see a Web page with a bunch of fancy graphics, but when you save the file, all you're getting are the text and/or codes that appear on the page. Now that you've been warned, you can take the following steps to save a Web page:

1. Display the Web document you want to save.
2. Open the **File** menu, and select **Save As** (or press **Ctrl+S**). The Save As dialog box appears, prompting you to specify a drive and folder or directory.
3. Select the drive and folder in which you want the file saved.

Chapter 8 ➤ *Saving and Printing Your Finds*

4. To change the name of the file (you don't have to), drag over the entry in the **File name** text box, and type the desired file name.

5. Open the **Save as type** drop-down list, and click the desired format in which you want the file saved:

    HTML Files retains all the Web page codes that were inserted in the file. You can then open the file in Navigator, and it will look something like a Web page (minus the cool graphics).

    Plain text (*.txt) strips out all the Web page codes and saves just the text. This is good if you find some text that you want to paste into a document you're creating (for example, to lift a quote).

6. Click **Save**. The file is saved in the specified format and is stored in the drive and folder you selected.

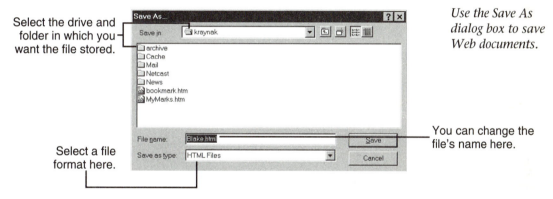

Use the Save As dialog box to save Web documents.

Select the drive and folder in which you want the file stored.

Select a file format here.

You can change the file's name here.

When saving a Web page, Navigator does not save the graphics. To save the graphics, use Navigator along with Composer. Open the page you want to save, and then open the **File** menu and select **Edit Page**. Use Composer's **File Save As** command to save the file. It's a good idea to save the page to its own directory to prevent its graphics files from becoming mixed up with other files on your hard drive.

Taking a Peek at the Locals

Your computer has files too, you know, and Navigator can open them for you... assuming they are HTML (Web) or text documents, or that you set up a file association for that file type. (This makes it convenient to view files that you downloaded earlier—again, see Chapter 13 for more information on associating files). To open a file that's on your hard disk, open the **File** menu and select **Open Page** (or press **Ctrl+O**). Click on the **Choose File** button, and use the Open dialog box to select the file.

87

If you select a file that's associated to another (helper) application, Navigator runs that application, which then loads and plays the selected file. If you select an HTML or text document, Navigator opens it just as if it were stored on a Web server. If the HTML document contains links, you can click those links to open them (assuming you are connected to the Internet with your TCP/IP software).

Making Paper—Printing

The World Wide Web is as close to paperless electronic publishing as you can get. However, you might encounter a document you want to print: maybe a Navigator help screen or an interesting quote or story. There's no trick to printing a document from Navigator. Simply display the Web document you want to print, and click the **Print** button.

If you want to get fancy about printing, however, you can do more. You can select some page setup options to specify how you want the document to be positioned on the page and to indicate the type of information you want printed (the page's URL, for example). You might also want to preview the page before you print it. The following sections explain all this in detail.

Entering Your Page Preferences

If you print a Web document now, you get a basic 8.5-by-11-inch page with a header and footer, and half-inch margins all around. However, you can change the page settings to reposition the text on the page or select the type of information you want printed in the header and footer.

To change the page settings, open the **File** menu and select **Page Setup**. The Page Setup dialog box appears. The settings are fairly self-explanatory, so I'm not going to bore you with the details. Just enter the desired settings, and then click **OK**.

More Control

If you want any more control over the printing, go into your Windows printers setup (in the Windows Control Panel), and enter the desired settings.

Chapter 8 ➤ *Saving and Printing Your Finds*

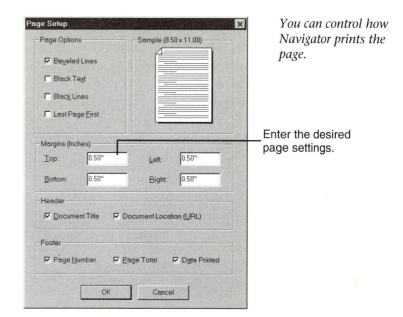

You can control how Navigator prints the page.

Enter the desired page settings.

Previewing Pages Before You Print

You can never be sure how a Web page will appear in print. Will the sparkling graphics you see on your screen transfer to paper? How will the lines and bulleted lists look? In Navigator, you can quickly see how a page will appear in print by opening the **File** menu and selecting **Print Preview**. This opens the Print Preview screen, which displays the first page of the current Web document. You can then click the following buttons to control the page display:

Print Opens the Print dialog box, which allows you to send the document to your printer. Enter your print settings, and then click **OK**.

Next Page Displays the next page of the document (assuming the Web document consists of more than one page).

Prev Page Opens the previous page of the document, if you clicked on the **Next Page** button.

Two Page Displays two pages of the document side-by-side.

Zoom In Makes the page bigger, showing more detail. You can also zoom in by moving the mouse pointer over the area you want to see in more detail and then clicking the mouse button.

89

Zoom Out Returns the page to its smaller view, giving you a bird's eye view of the page.

Close Closes this window and returns you to the Navigator window. Be sure to use this button rather than the Close (X) button in the title bar; otherwise, you'll close Navigator altogether.

You can preview a document before printing it.

Be sure you click this Close button to return to Navigator.

The mouse pointer lets you zoom in on an area of the page.

Hanging Wallpaper on the Windows Background

After hours of searching, you have finally found the Pamela Anderson home page. You've researched her entire career, from her early days on *Home Improvement* to her stellar performance in *Barb Wire*. You can't believe the number of Pamela Anderson pictures that are wasting away on the Web. If only you could grab a picture and place it on your Windows desktop. Wouldn't it be great to have Pamela lounging behind your word processor window while you worked?

Well, here's your chance. With two clicks of the mouse, you can transform that hot picture of Pamela into Windows wallpaper. Just right-click on Pamela's schnoz, and click on **Set As Wallpaper**. Yep, that's it.

Chapter 8 ➤ *Saving and Printing Your Finds*

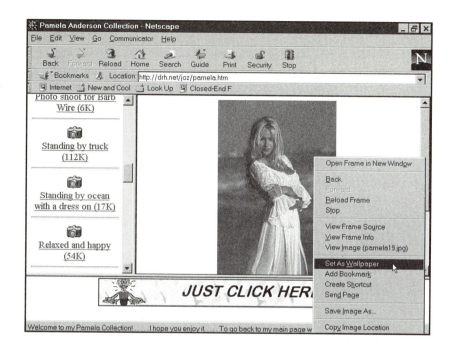

You can quickly transform a graphic image into wallpaper.

Now, I bet you're really embarrassed, afraid that someone will walk into your office and catch you ogling your screen. You want to strip the wallpaper (sorry about the pun). Right-click on a blank area of the Windows 95 desktop and select **Properties**. From the Wallpaper list, select **(None)**.

Why Is the Picture so Small?

When you use a small image as the wallpaper, it won't cover the entire background. You can enter settings in Windows to tile the background. In the Display Properties dialog box just below the list of wallpaper designs, click **Tile**. Better yet, find an image that's big enough to cover the entire screen.

The Least You Need to Know

As you ready yourself for a download binge, try to remember the following:

- ➤ To quickly download a file, right-click its link, and then click the **Save** option.

- ➤ If you plan on downloading several files, open the **Preferences** dialog box, select **Applications** (below Browser), and turn on **Save to Disk** for the file type you want to download (instead of view).

91

- To view a coded Web page, open the **View** menu and select **Page Source**.
- To open files stored on your hard disk, open the **File** menu and select **Open Page**.
- To print a Web page, click the **Print** button in the toolbar.

Chapter 9

Driving Off-Road to FTP and Gopher Sites

In This Chapter

➤ Explain "gopher" to a foreign exchange student

➤ Fake your way through a conversation about FTP

➤ Find specific files when you know their names

➤ Pilfer files off the Internet

When the Internet started out, it wasn't much more than a gigantic file warehouse. Businesses and universities stored files on various Internet servers, where other people could connect and copy (download) those files.

As the Internet grew and diversified, it had to assign specific jobs to different servers. World Wide Web servers were given the task of storing Web pages, newsgroups were set up to act as bulletin boards, mail servers were given the job of receiving and delivering e-mail, FTP servers became the file warehouses, and Gopher servers were set up to help users find their way through this megamaze we call the Internet.

In this chapter, you'll learn how to access Gopher and FTP servers, how to determine if you're connected to one of these special servers, and how to navigate when you get there.

FTP and Gopher

FTP stands for *File Transfer Protocol*, a set of rules that govern the transfer of files between computers. *Gopher* is named after the furry, burrowing critter, who moonlights as mascot for the University of Minnesota (where Gopher originated). Gopher is an index/menu system designed to help you find resources on the Internet.

FTP and Gopher: What They're All About

As you wandered with Navigator, you probably stumbled across a few FTP and Gopher sites. Unlike Web pages, which typically display graphics and some interesting text, FTP and Gopher sites display drab icons (if you're lucky) and lists. These sites aren't set up to dazzle and impress; they are there to list files and help you locate resources.

If you were to see a Gopher and FTP site placed side-by-side with their names covered, you probably wouldn't see much difference between the two. Navigator 4.0 displays both as lists of links. However, the purpose and function of each site differs greatly. An FTP site is designed to help you copy files, whereas Gopher is a menu system for locating resources.

Gopher and FTP side-by-side.

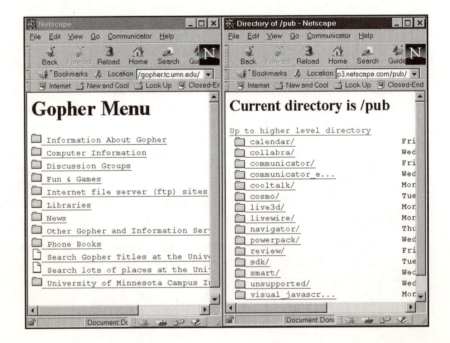

Connecting to an FTP Server

Earlier in this book, you learned how to copy and save files from the Internet. You right-click on the link for a file, click **Save Link As**, and fill out the Save As dialog box. When performing these steps, you were actually performing an FTP file transfer. However, you may not have been at a bona fide FTP site, and the site may have been fairly lax about giving you access to its files. When you hit a real, live FTP site, you may find that it's a little more difficult to get into it and to navigate it. The following sections will help.

Public (Anonymous) Servers

You'll encounter two types of FTP servers: those that let anyone transfer files (*anonymous* sites) and those that don't. To connect to an anonymous site, you usually log in as **anonymous**, and then use your e-mail address as your password.

Nonanonymous sites require you to enter a specific username and a password. To connect to one of these sites, you must contact the network supervisor of the site beforehand (usually by sending the supervisor an e-mail message or by calling that person on the phone). That person will provide you with a login name and password... assuming she agrees to give you access. (See the next section, "Connecting to a Private FTP Server," for details.)

To connect to an anonymous FTP server, you should make sure that Navigator is set up to send your e-mail address as a password. Open the **Edit** menu select **Preferences**, and click the **Advanced** category. Make sure **Send email address as anonymous FTP password** is checked, and then click **OK**.

You should also make sure that your e-mail address is specified under Mail and Discussions preferences. Open the **Edit** menu and select **Preferences**. Click the plus sign next to Mail & Groups, click **Identity**, and type your e-mail address in the **Email Address** text box (if it is not already entered). Click **OK**.

Know the Rules

If you ruffle the administrator at an anonymous FTP site, you will quickly lose your anonymity. The administrator can use your e-mail address to lock you out. You'll try to log on as anonymous, and you'll get an **access denied** message or something similar. When you first access a site, read its rules. On most anonymous FTP servers, the only rule is, "Don't connect during business hours."

Make sure you tell Navigator to send your e-mail address as the FTP password.

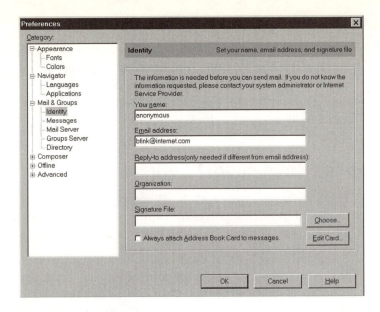

Connecting to a Private FTP Server

Some FTP sites are private. For example, your service provider probably has a private FTP server that you use (unknowingly) for e-mail and other data. The service provider doesn't want nonmembers to be messing with members' files, so it protects the server by requiring members to enter their username and password in order to access the server.

If you need to access files on a private server, you must obtain a username and password from the server's administrator. Once you have a username and password, you must enter it correctly into Navigator. To connect to a password-protected FTP server, enter your name and password into the **Location** text box in the following form:

ftp://*username:password@ftp.sitename.domain*

For example, you might enter:

ftp://bfink:x23qrtvg@ftp.internet.com

Chapter 9 ➤ *Driving Off-Road to FTP and Gopher Sites*

Navigating an FTP Server

Chances are you stumbled unknowingly into a couple of FTP sites already. If you looked in the Address text box, you would see that the URL started with **ftp://** rather than **http://**. You would also see something resembling a file list without file and folder icons. The list shows the date and time the file was posted (or the directory was updated), the size of the file (or simply "directory"), and the name of the directory or file.

To change to a directory, click on its link. You may see additional directories. Continue clicking on links until you find the desired file. Use the Back button to move back up the directory tree, if you move too far down it.

> **Don't Forget About Bookmarks** When you find a great FTP site, add it to the Bookmarks menu. Open the **Bookmarks** menu and click **Add Bookmark**. You can then quickly return to a site that was too busy to give you access.

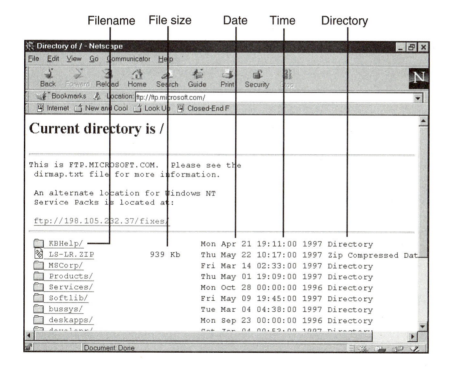

When you connect to an FTP server, you are greeted with a file list.

Downloading (Copying) Files from an FTP Server

You've downloaded plenty of files already by clicking on their links. It's no different on an FTP server. You have two options:

➤ To download a file and play it, click on the file's link. If Navigator or one of your helper apps, plug-ins, or ActiveX controls can play the file, Navigator downloads the file and plays it.

➤ To download a file and save it to your hard drive, right-click on the file and select **Save Link As** or **Save Image As**. Use the Save As dialog box to name the file and specify where to save it.

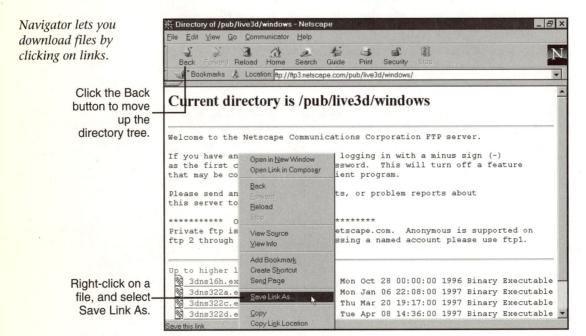

Navigator lets you download files by clicking on links.

Click the Back button to move up the directory tree.

Right-click on a file, and select Save Link As.

ZIP, TAR, and Other Compressed Files

Many files you find at FTP sites are *compressed* in some way, so they take up less storage space and travel more quickly over Internet connections. PC files are commonly compressed into a .ZIP format, requiring you to *uncompress* the files with WinZip or PKZip. Most Mac files are compressed into .SIT or HQX format, for which you will need StuffIt Expander to decompress. Here's a list of other compressed formats you might encounter:

.Z   Compressed with a UNIX compression program.

.z   Compressed with a UNIX pack program.

.shar   Archived with UNIX shell archive.

.tar   Compressed with UNIX tar.

.pit   Compressed with Macintosh Packit.

.zoo   Compressed with Zoo210.

.arc   Packed with PKARC for DOS.

.exe   Self-extracting .ZIP file for a PC.

.hqx   Mac BinHex.

.sea   Self-extracting .SIT file for the Mac.

When downloading files, make sure you get files that can run on your platform: Windows or Macintosh. In other words, if you have a PC running Windows, don't bother downloading a Macintosh .SIT or .SEA file. Most sites also have the shareware utilities you need to decompress the files. Look for a /UTIL directory—that's where you'll usually find them. If you can't find the decompression utilities you need, check Stroud's List at **http://www.stroud.com** or Tucows at **http://www.tucows.com** for links to helpful utilities.

Uploading Files

In addition to grabbing loot off of FTP sites, you can also copy files to some sites (upload files). This allows you to post your favorite shareware, show off graphic images of yourself, and pass along the latest information (assuming you have authorization to upload files to a site).

You can upload files in either of two ways. The easiest way is to go to the FTP site and directory in which you want to place the file, and then drag the file's icon (from Windows Explorer or File Manager) into the Navigator viewing area.

If you don't like that method, you can use the **File/Upload File** command, and use the dialog box that appears to copy the file to the FTP server.

Navigating the Internet with Gopher Menus

There's no trick to getting around in a Gopher server. You simply click on the desired links to follow a trail of menus. Use the Back and Forward buttons to display the previous or next screens, just as you would with Web documents.

The topmost choice in most gopher menus is **About this Gopher**. Click on this link to find out information about the current Gopher, including general descriptions of what's stored on the Gopher and the types of services it offers. Some Gophers may also have restrictions you should read about before using them. To read this document, click on its link. Navigator loads and displays its text.

Many Gopher servers will present links to text files, audio and video clips, and other multimedia files. To play one of these files, simply click on its link. To download the file, right-click on it, and select **Save Link As**. If you want to play around with Gopher and various file types, visit the Minnesota Gopher Server at **gopher://gopher.state.mn.us/**. Click on the **University of Minnesota** link, and click on **Fun & Games**. Enjoy!

Playing Files

Playing a multimedia file from a Gopher server is the same as playing a file from a Web page. Navigator must be equipped with a player designed for the file type you want to play. The player can be a helper app, plug-in, or ActiveX control. See Part 3, "Playing Video, Sound, and Interactive Worlds," for details.

Searching Gopherspace with Veronica

Browsing the Internet with Gopher can be fun, but when you need specific information in a hurry, browsing just won't do. You need a way to search out only those Gopher sites that have the information you want. You need Veronica.

With Veronica, you type search strings that tell Veronica what to look for and how many items to find. Veronica searches its huge index of Internet resources and then assembles a menu of servers that match your search string. For example, you can enter a search string to have Veronica find all sites that contain information about IBM and Apple.

The first, and possibly most time-consuming, step in searching with Veronica is to access a Veronica server. What makes this step so difficult is that Veronica servers are in high demand; you may not be able to gain access when you need it most. The easiest way to access Veronica is to connect to a Gopher server that has a Veronica link, and then click on that link. If you have trouble finding a Gopher that offers Veronica, use your favorite Internet search tool (**http://www.yahoo.com**, **http://www.webcrawler.com**, and so on) to search for **veronica**.

Sometimes, the list of Veronica sites are divided into two groups: one allows you to search all gopherspace, and one searches only for directories. For a quick search that turns up fewer finds, select one of the **Directory Only** options. For a more thorough search, select a **Gopherspace** option. Regardless of which choice you make, Veronica displays a form that allows you to enter your search string. (If you receive an error message when you select one of the Veronica links, just click **OK**, and Navigator should connect you.)

> **Check This Out...**
>
> **Archie, Veronica, and Jughead** The fact that the names **Archie** and **Veronica** stir up images of comic-book characters is no coincidence. Archie (short for "archive") started it all. Veronica, Archie's comic-book girlfriend, followed. There's even a search program called Jughead, which

Click inside the text box, type the words you want to search for, and press **Enter**. For example, type **spanish literature**, and press **Enter**. Veronica looks for all entries that have "spanish" and "literature" in the title, but not necessarily in the order in which you typed the words—Veronica also turns up any occurrences of "literature" and "spanish." Make your search string as specific as possible.

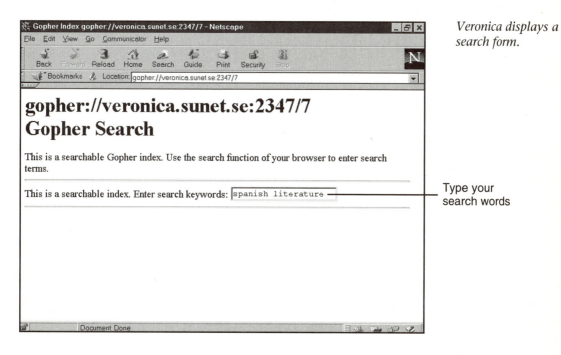

Veronica displays a search form.

Type your search words

The Least You Need to Know

To make this section a bit more interesting, I'm presenting the review material as a list of riddles and questions. The answer for each riddle or question follows it immediately, so don't peek.

➤ At an anonymous FTP site, who's anonymous, you or the FTP site?

   Answer: You are! If the site were anonymous, you'd never find it.

➤ Besides getting a really confused look on your face, what do you do at an FTP site?

   Answer: Copy files.

➤ What do you get when you cross a Web document, an FTP site, and a menu?

   Answer: Gopher.

➤ If Gopher and FTP had a fight, who would win?

   Answer: Gopher, because it contains links to other Internet services, including FTP sites.

➤ What does the URL for every FTP site start with?

   Answer: ftp://

➤ What's the difference between Archie and Veronica?

   Answer: Archie is a boy, and Veronica is a girl, duh!

Chapter 10

Customizing Navigator to Make It Your Own

In This Chapter

- Turn toolbars on or off
- Get rid of that dingy gray document background
- Spruce up your documents with fancy typestyles
- Increase the speed at which Navigator loads pages you have previously visited
- List five preferences you can safely ignore

Navigator has just moved in with you, toting its old look and all its old habits and forcing you to conform. But now you're going to get your chance to mold Navigator into the Web browser of your dreams. Do you want more window room for displaying Web pages? Try turning off the toolbars. Is the text too small? Make it bigger! Is Navigator using too much of your hard drive to store previously viewed pages? Make it stop! Consider this chapter your guide to Navigator empowerment. In the coming sections, you'll learn how to revamp Navigator to look and behave the way you want it to.

Part Deux ➤ *Mastering Netscape Navigator*

As you work through this chapter, keep in mind that some customization settings are not covered in this chapter. You will find instructions on how to enter security settings in Chapter 11, "Digital Certificates, Cookies, and Other Security Issues." To learn how to enter helper application settings, see Chapter 13, "Beefing Up Navigator with Helper Applications." And to enter settings for Netscape Messenger and Collabra, see Chapter 15, "Corresponding with Electronic Mail," and Chapter 18, "Reading and Posting Newsgroup Messages."

Turning Toolbars On and Off

Let's go into this customizing thing as slowly as possible, starting with some simple customization options. The easiest way to customize Navigator is to play with the toolbars. You can turn the toolbars off to provide more room for displaying Web pages, or you can turn them on to provide you with additional navigational tools.

To get the floating Component bar out of the way, simply click its Close (X) button or by opening the **Communicator** menu and selecting **Dock Component Bar**. The toolbar retreats to the status bar, where you can still use it. To bring it back, click the little ridged area on the left of the toolbar, or open the **Communicator** menu and select **Show Component Bar**. (You can move the Component bar when it is displayed full-size by dragging its title bar.) When the toolbar is enlarged, you can right-click in the title bar and select from the following options to control the toolbar's behavior:

➤ **Always on Top** ensures that the toolbar will remain in front of any open window. If you turn this option off, you may have a difficult time finding the toolbar when you need it.

➤ **Horizontal** displays the toolbar horizontally (the default orientation).

➤ **Vertical** displays the toolbar vertically, so you can drag it to the left or right side of the window to get it out of the way.

➤ **Hide Text** removes the text description that appears below each button, making the bar smaller. You can still view the name of a button by resting the mouse pointer on the button.

As for the other toolbars, you already know how to manipulate them individually. If you have forgotten, skip back to "Toolbar Basics" in Chapter 3, "Weaving Through the World Wide Web." One thing Chapter 3 did not mention, however, is that you can turn any of the toolbars on or off. If the toolbars are cluttering the screen, simply open the **View** menu, and click the **Hide** command for the toolbar you want to turn off (for instance **Hide Navigation Toolbar**). To turn the toolbar back on, open the **View** menu, and select the **Show** command for the toolbar you want to see (for instance **Show Navigation Toolbar**).

You can also control the way Navigator displays the buttons. You can display the buttons with pictures only (no text), text only (no pictures), or pictures and text (the default setting). Open the **Edit** menu, select **Preferences**, and select the **Appearance** category. Under **Show toolbar as**, select the desired setting. (The selected setting controls the Navigation toolbar and the Component bar.)

Hot-Key Alternatives

If you turn off the Navigation toolbar, you essentially immobilize your mouse, so you'll need to use your keyboard to navigate:

Ctrl+O	To enter an address (URL)
Ctrl+N	To open a Web page in a new window
Alt+Left Arrow	To display the previous Web page
Alt+Right Arrow	To display the next Web page
Esc	To stop loading a page
Ctrl+R	To reload
Crtl+D	To add a bookmark
Ctrl+B	To edit bookmarks

If you exit Navigator now, and then restart it, any toolbars you turned off stay off. If you used an older version of Navigator (pre-version 3.0), you might remember having to save your changes.

Speeding Up Page Loading

When you hit a graphical Web page, you might notice Navigator shift into low gear. The reason for this is that graphics files are much larger than text files. If you have a slow modem connection, it can take several minutes for Navigator to load all the graphics on a page. To prevent this slowdown, you can tell Navigator not to load the graphics. Open the **Edit** menu, select **Preferences**, and click on the **Advanced** category. Click on **Automatically Load Images** to remove the check from its box.

Now, you can skip around the Web much more quickly. The only trouble is that you won't see any of the pretty pictures. When you reach a page that has pictures you think you might want to view, simply click on the **Images** button in the toolbar. Navigator then reloads the page, along with the pictures. You can turn Automatically Load Images back on at any time by selecting **Edit**, **Preferences**, **Advanced**, **Automatically Load Images**.

Giving Navigator a Makeover

Turning toolbars off is pretty drastic. It's sort of like knocking out a wall in your house or demolishing an entire wing. But what if you just want to add a fresh coat of paint? You can do that in Navigator by changing the font used to display Web document text or changing the background colors. To change the appearance of Navigator, open the **Edit** menu and select **Preferences**.

As you can see from the picture, this dialog box has a bunch of categories, a few of which you have already encountered. We'll skip the Navigator/Applications category, since you'll spend plenty of time there in Chapter 13. We'll also ignore the Navigator/Language category, the Composer category, and most of the options under Advanced. And, we will skip the Mail & Groups category, which you will get to play with in Chapter 15 and Chapter 18. Now that we've whittled down the list to four categories, let's see what's on them.

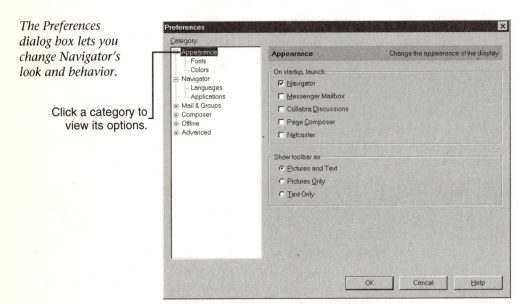

The Preferences dialog box lets you change Navigator's look and behavior.

Click a category to view its options.

A Peek at the Appearance Options

As soon as you open the Preferences dialog box, you see the Appearance category at the top of the list. Click on this category for access to the following options:

On Startup Launch Gives you the option of starting the e-mail program (Messenger Mailbox), the newsreader (Collabra Discussions), the Web page editor (Page Composer), and Netcaster (for Web site subscriptions) automatically when you start Netscape Navigator.

Show Toolbar as Allows you to control the appearance of the buttons in the toolbars. You can choose **Pictures and Text** (for buttons that show both icons and button names) or **Pictures Only** (for buttons without names), or **Text Only** (for buttons with names but not pictures). If you choose Pictures Only, you can still see the name of a button by resting the mouse pointer on it.

Dressing Your Text in the Right Font

If you took a peek at the source document in Chapter 8, "Saving and Printing Your Finds," you know that Web pages consist of a bunch of text and codes. Usually, the codes actually outnumber the text. These codes tell Navigator (or whatever Web browser you might use) how to display a document. They specify the colors to use, the background, and the style of the text. However, codes typically give general orders like "make this text bigger," and "emphasize this text." The browser (Navigator for instance) *interprets* the codes… and there's a lot of room for interpretation.

Because Navigator is in charge of assigning fonts, you can pick the fonts you want to use to style the text. With the Preferences dialog box displayed, click the **Fonts** category (below Appearance). If there is a plus sign next to Appearance, click on it to display the Fonts category.

If you're in the United States or some other country that uses the Latin alphabet for its Web codes, you can probably leave the **For the Encoding** option alone. If you plan on visiting a site in China, Greece, Turkey, or some other country that does not use the Latin alphabet for its codes, select the appropriate setting, so Navigator will be able to translate the codes.

The other two options, Variable Width Font and Fixed Width Font, allow you to change the way Web page text is displayed. A *fixed width font* gives each character the same amount of room. A slender "i" gets the same space as a wide-body "w." Variable width fonts are more communistic—"to each, according to his needs, from each, according to his abilities." In other words, each character gets only the room it needs. Fixed width fonts are usually used to display file names at FTP sites. Variable width fonts are used for most of the text you see on Web pages.

To change a font, open the drop-down list to the right of the font type you want to change, and click on the desired font. To change the font size, open the Size drop-down list, and click the desired size.

Under **Sometimes a document will provide its own fonts**, select the desired option to tell Navigator which fonts to use when a page specifies its own fonts. You can tell Navigator to always use your fonts, to use the document fonts when available, or to use the document fonts only when they don't increase the time it takes the page to transfer. Click **OK** to save your settings.

You can control the look of the text on-screen.

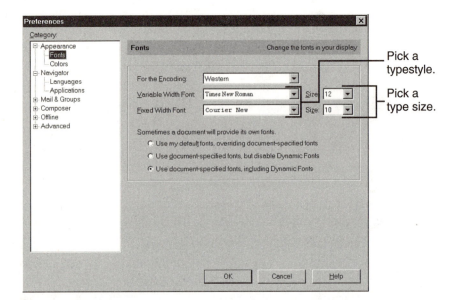

Taking Your Crayolas to the Screen

You've taken it for granted, that dingy gray background that sits behind each Web page you look at is intentional, placed there by one of Navigator's many color settings. How would you like to turn that background white or display a background picture of your favorite actor? You can take control of the Navigator background and the colors that Navigator uses to display text and links. Simply click the **Colors** category, and change any of the following options:

Colors You have three options under colors: Background, Text, and Use Windows Colors. The Use Windows Colors option allows you to use the current color settings in Windows for displaying Web pages. The Background and Text options let you select specific colors for the page background and the Web page text. To select a specific color, click on the **Background** or **Text** button, select the desired color, and click **OK**.

Links You can use the Links options to control the color of links that point to pages you have visited and pages you have not visited. Click on the Visited Links or

Unvisited Links button, select the desired color, and click **OK**. By default, Navigator displays all links as underlined. You can turn underlining off by clicking on **Underline Links** (to remove the check mark).

Always Use My Colors, Overriding Document   Tells Navigator to use your colors and background setting even if the Web page you load is set to display a different color or background. This decreases the time it takes some pages to load, but it can cause problems if the page uses custom colors to make text readable. For example, if you choose to use a white background, and you load a page that uses a dark background with white text, you may not be able to see the text.

Changing the Navigator Settings

Next in the list of preference categories are the Browser preferences. These are the settings that tell Navigator what to do when it starts up and how to keep track of the pages you've visited. To enter browser preferences, open the **Edit** menu, select **Preferences**, and click on the **Navigator** category. You can then enter the following preferences:

Navigator Starts With   This option lets you specify which page you want Navigator to load when you start it. You can select **Blank Page** (if you don't want Navigator to load a page), **Home Page** (to specify a starting page, as explained next), or **Last Page Visited** (to start with the page Navigator had open when you last exited).

Home Page   This option lets you specify the URL of the Web page you want to use as a starting page, if you selected **Home Page** under **Browser Starts With**. This can be the URL for a file on your hard disk, as explained in Chapter 3. You can click **Use Current Page** to insert the URL of the page that is currently displayed.

History   This option lets you specify the number of days you want Navigator to keep track of pages you have visited. You can click the **Clear History** button to delete the history from your hard disk and reclaim some disk space.

Working Offline to Save Time and Money

Navigator lets you work offline to view pages you have already opened. This allows you to download pages during the evening and morning hours when the Internet is less busy, and then view the pages at your convenience. To set the Offline preferences, open the Preferences dialog box, and click **Offline**. You can then choose **Online Work Mode** (to always open pages when you are online), **Offline Work Mode** (to always open pages from your hard disk), or **Ask Me** (to have Navigator display a dialog box when you first start it, asking if you want to work online or offline).

The Download option (directly below Offline) allows you to set options for reading discussion groups (newsgroup messages) offline. For details, see Chapter 18.

To view Web pages offline, it is best to set up channels for your favorite Web pages using Netcaster, as explained in Chapter 7, "Tuning into the Web with Netcaster." You can then have updated pages delivered to you, and view them offline simply by clicking channel buttons.

Tinkering with Some Additional Settings

You've played with the look of Navigator, but what about how it behaves? How much RAM should it use for those Web pages? How much disk space should it use? And do you need to use proxies? These settings can seriously affect Navigator's performance, so let's take a look at them. Open the **Edit** menu, select **Preferences**, and click the **Cache** category, below Advanced. (If the Cache category is not displayed, click the plus sign next to Advanced.)

Establishing a Strong Cache Flow

A *cache* is memory or disk space that Navigator (or any other program) uses to temporarily store data. In Navigator's case, the cache is used to store Web pages you've already loaded, so if you go back or forward to a page, Navigator doesn't have to reload the page from the Web site. The minimum numbers for the disk and memory cache are already entered for you; don't go any lower. If you have scads of disk space or memory, you can increase the numbers so Navigator will "remember" more pages.

Another reason you might want to increase the cache is if you're playing huge files with plug-ins or helper apps. For example, if you're downloading large Shockwave files, you may want to increase the cache, so Navigator will have room to store them.

Clear That Cache!

The buttons next to the disk and memory cache settings (**Clear Memory Cache** and **Clear Disk Cache**) are useful if you have trouble running your other Windows programs, because your system is low on memory. These buttons clear the cache, freeing that storage space for other use.

Chapter 10 ➤ *Customizing Navigator to Make It Your Own*

The last set of options, **Document in Cache Is Compared to Document on Network**, lets you specify how often you want Navigator to check a Web document you've loaded against the original. The less often Navigator has to verify documents, the faster Navigator will run. **Once per Session** is a good, safe setting. **Every Time** is excessive and will slow down an already slow process. **Never** is good if you want to speed up Navigator; you can always reload the page if it doesn't transfer right the first time (just press **Ctrl+R**).

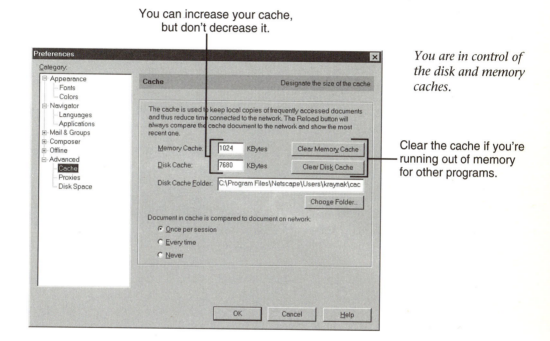

You can increase your cache, but don't decrease it.

You are in control of the disk and memory caches.

Clear the cache if you're running out of memory for other programs.

A Word About the Proxies Category

I know, you're curious about that Proxies category. Go ahead and click on it. You see that the no proxies option (Direct Connection to the Internet) is selected. In case you're wondering, a *proxy* is a server that acts as a sort of middleman. If you're connected to the Internet through a network connection (instead of a modem), your network may have something called a *firewall* that protects the network from unauthorized access. The problem with these firewalls is that they may limit your access to some Internet features. Proxies act as bridges over the firewalls, allowing information to pass freely between the Internet and your network.

If you're connected to the Internet with a modem, leave Direct Connection to the Internet on. If you have a Network connection, ask your network administrator if you need to use proxies. If you do need proxies, the network administrator can tell you which options you need to select, and how to enter information about the proxies.

111

The Least You Need to Know

You don't need to know a whole lot about customizing Navigator. Just remember that the Edit, Preferences command displays a dialog box that presents the lion's share of the customization options. Here's a list to help you remember the rest of the important stuff:

- To hide or display a toolbar, click on its tab. To turn off a toolbar, open the **View** menu, and click on the **Hide** option for the toolbar you want to turn off.

- For quick navigation, turn off Auto Load Images: **Edit, Preferences, Advanced, Automatically Load Images**.

- You can turn an individual toolbar on or off by clicking on its tab, but you learned that in Chapter 3.

- You can change the way Navigator displays Web pages by entering appearance preferences: **Edit, Preferences, Appearance**.

- The Navigator category contains settings that control the way Navigator starts; for example, you can have Messenger and Collabra start automatically when you start Navigator.

- Enter cache preferences (**Edit, Preferences, Cache**) to control the way that Navigator stores the pages you have previously visited.

Chapter 11

Digital Certificates, Cookies, and Other Security Issues

In This Chapter

➤ Confidently send credit card numbers and other sensitive information across the Web

➤ Understand the risks of running Java applets and ActiveX components

➤ Define cookies and prevent Web sites from sending them to you

➤ Censor sites that offer sex, violence, and foul language (assuming you want to)

If you listen to the news, or if you saw Sandra Bullock in *The Net*, you're probably at least a little concerned that while you're fooling around at the *Nando Times* sports server, someone might hack into your computer, grab all your personal information and credit card numbers, and run up an enormous Visa bill at the Mall of America.

I'm not implying that the scenario isn't possible. It's just not all that common. People who steal credit card numbers and personal information usually have more clever ways to get that information, like digging through your trash, paying off an underpaid employee at the Visa office, or breaking into your house and stealing your whole computer.

The point here is that you shouldn't do on the Internet anything you wouldn't do in real life, including handing out your credit card number (or phone number, for that matter) to anyone you don't trust.

This chapter explains some additional security measures you can take in Navigator, and explains some of the security features over which you have no control (so why worry about them?).

Transferring Information Securely on the Net

The biggest security worry on the Internet is the result of one of the biggest improvements on the Web: forms. Forms, such as search forms used in Yahoo! or other search programs, let you enter information and receive feedback. They also allow you to order products by entering your credit card number, register your software, join clubs, and even play interactive games.

The problem with entering any personal information (including credit card numbers) on a form is that the information is not sent directly to the server where that information will be used. Instead, the information bounces around from one server to another until it finds its destination. At any point in this little adventure, someone with the proper know-how can read the information.

How often this happens, no one really knows, but it *can* happen, and that's the concern.

Complete Protection

To *completely* protect yourself, never enter any sensitive information on a form. If you want to order something from a mail-order company, get its phone number from the Web page, and call in your order. Because phone orders travel over private lines (owned by phone companies), there is less chance that someone can grab your credit card number in transit.

Setting Navigator's Security Options

Although the Internet is not completely safe, Navigator does have some built-in security options to help protect you. For one, Navigator displays a warning whenever you enter two or more pieces of information on any form. If you never enter sensitive information, these warnings can become more annoying than useful. However, if you don't trust yourself, keep the warnings on.

Chapter 11 ➤ *Digital Certificates, Cookies, and Other Security Issues*

The following sections explain how to turn Navigator's security warnings on and off, tell whether you are at a secure site (even if the warnings are off), and use other Navigator security features.

Turning Security Warnings On and Off

Navigator's security options provide a gentle reminder that you're entering information that could be read by the wrong person. When the dialog box pops up, all you have to do is confirm that you want to send the information, and Navigator sends it. If the dialog boxes don't bother you, there's no reason to turn them off.

However, most people don't need to be reminded that they're sending information. You typed the information. You clicked on the button to send it. Heck, yes, you want to send it! Once you've gained a little experience on the Web, the warnings become intrusive. When you begin to feel that the dialog boxes are more trouble than they're worth, it's a good sign that you should turn them off.

The easiest time to turn off warnings is when you receive one. At the bottom of the warning dialog box is **Show This Alert Next Time**. If you click on this option, and remove the check from the box, this warning will never disturb you again.

Another way to turn security warnings on or off is via the Security Preferences dialog box. Click the **Security** button in the Navigation toolbar. The Netscape security dialog box appears. Click **Navigator**. You can then select any of the following options to turn them on or off:

Entering an Encrypted Site: Displays a warning whenever you view a Web page that complies with the latest security standards. Why would you turn this on, I wonder?

Leaving an Encrypted Site: This is another warning you can turn off. If you're leaving, why do you care if it's secure?

Viewing a Page with an Encrypted/Unencrypted Mix: If it's mixed, why do you care? Either you can send information securely or you can't. Leave this one off, too.

Sending Unencrypted Information to a Site: This is the option that makes the security warning pop up on your screen all the time. If you don't trust yourself, leave it on.

Enable SSL v2: Turns on data encryption for Web pages protected with the Secure Sockets Layer (version 2) standard. Keep this on, so that when you do enter information on secure Web pages, that information will be encoded.

Enable SSL v3: Turns on data encryption for Web pages protected with the Secure Sockets Layer (version 3) standard. Keep this option on, too. This is the latest security standard from Netscape.

You can turn the security warnings on or off.

Security warning options

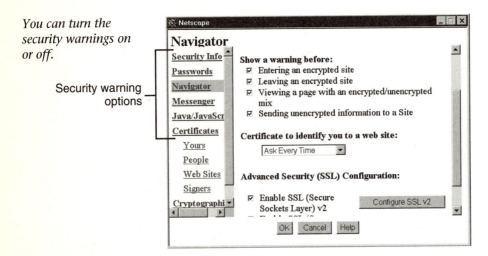

When you're done entering your settings, click on the **OK** button. Even if you turn the warnings off, Navigator has ways of showing you whether you're on a secure Web page. The following section explains.

Is This Site Secure?

If you turn the security warnings off, there are four main ways you can tell that a site is secure:

➤ The URL (in the Location text box) starts with **https** instead of **http**. The "s" indicates that the document is protected by Netscape's SSL (Secure Sockets Layer) protocol.

➤ The **Security** button in the main toolbar shows a locked lock icon. If the icon is unlocked (which it usually is), the site is not secure. Click on this button to view security information about the page.

➤ The lock icon in the lower left corner of the Navigator window is locked. If the lock is open, the document is *insecure*.

Chapter 11 ➤ Digital Certificates, Cookies, and Other Security Issues

➤ The Document Info window shows that the document is secure. To display the Document Info window for the current page, open the **View** menu and select **Page Info**. Look at **Security** (near the bottom of the window) to find out if the document is secure or not.

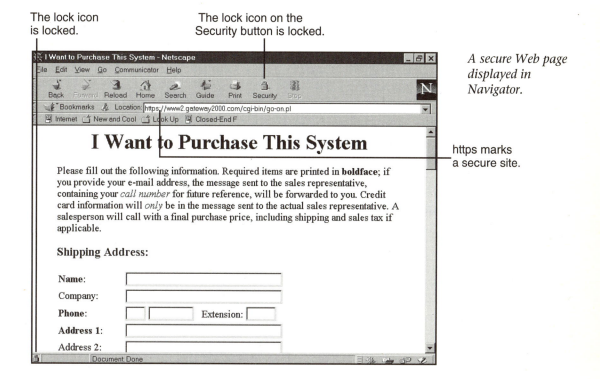

A secure Web page displayed in Navigator.

The lock icon is locked.

The lock icon on the Security button is locked.

https marks a secure site.

Grabbing Some Cookies

Cookies are sort of like tokens that a Web page hands you when you connect to the page or enter information. These cookies stay with Navigator, so that the next time you visit the site, or visit another area at the site, the Web server can identify you. For example, whenever you visit a page, it might give you a cookie to mark how many times you visited. Each time you connect, the Web page will show you how many times you've been to the page.

Cookies are commonly used to collect information about you, such as the number of times you have visited the site. The site creator can then gather general demographics about who is using the site, and where they go when they reach the site. Cookies are also

117

used at shopping pages on the Web. As you add items to your "cart," the page gives you a cookie for each item. When you go to check out, the page knows (from the cookies) which items you have in your cart.

Because cookies allow Web servers to write information to your program (Navigator), there are some possible security risks. If you are concerned about this, you can have Navigator warn you whenever a server attempts to send you a cookie.

To turn on the warning, open the **Edit** menu, select **Preferences**, click the **Advanced** category. Under **Cookies**, select **Warn me before accepting a cookie**, or to reject any cookies, click **Disable Cookies**. Click **OK**.

Using Digital Certificates

If you've wandered the Web much, you've encountered sites that request information from you and then give you a username and password, so you can access additional information at the site. Maybe you had to pay a one-time fee for the additional access, or you had to subscribe to the service.

Of course, you never want to enter the same username and password at each site. If anyone were to steal your password and username at one site, he or she could use it at all the other sites, and really foul up your life. However, keeping track of all your usernames and personal ID numbers can become difficult. To solve this problem, Internet developers came up with the concept of *digital certificates* or *digital passports*.

With a digital certificate, you enter information about yourself one time. The Web server sends you a certificate, which stays with Navigator. Whenever you connect to the site, Navigator identifies you to the site by sending your digital certificate, so you don't have to remember your username or password.

For a fee, you can also apply for a generic digital certificate that you can theoretically use to identify yourself at any site. The following sections explain how to obtain, use, and protect your digital certificates.

Non-Transferable

Each digital certificate works for only one application and on only one computer. If you set up a certificate on your computer at work, it won't work for your computer at home. You need to create a separate certificate for each copy of Navigator you run.

Obtaining and Using Digital Certificates

This digital certificate concept is fairly new, so you may not find many companies (Certifying Authorities) where you can pick up a certificate. One company that offers digital certificates is VeriSign, which you can visit at **http://digitalid.verisign.com/**.

To obtain a certificate from VeriSign (or some other Certifying Authority), click the **Security** button. Under **Certificates**, click on **Yours**, and then scroll down and click the **Get A Certificate** button. This takes you to a Netscape page, which contains links to Certifying Authorities. Click the **VeriSign** link.

Once at VeriSign, you must specify the application for which you want a digital certificate (Navigator), and then enter personal and billing information. VeriSign then sends you a temporary digital certificate. (You will receive your permanent digital certificate, along with instructions on how to install it via e-mail.)

Navigator displays a dialog box, asking if you want to protect your certificate with a password. If you are on a network, you should choose **Yes**, and then enter a unique password. If you're using a computer that no one else has access to, you can choose not to use a password. Navigator then asks you to enter a nickname for the certificate, which will be used in Navigator to identify this certificate.

When you're done, check to see if your certificate has been properly set up in Navigator. Click the **Security** button, and then select **Yours** under **Certificates**. You should see the nickname you entered for the new certificate.

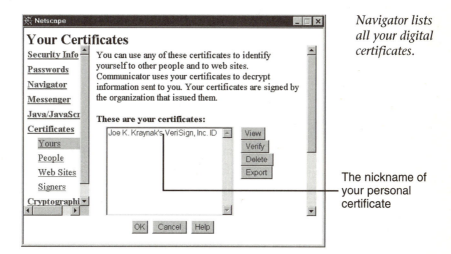

Navigator lists all your digital certificates.

The nickname of your personal certificate

Protecting Your Certificates

If you're using a computer that others may have access to, or you're on a network, you should protect your certificates with a password. When you first obtain a certificate, Navigator asks if you want to give it a password. If you enter a password, Navigator will prompt you to enter it the first time you try to use the certificate during the current session.

You can change your password and password settings through the Netscape security dialog box. Click the **Security** button, and click on **Passwords**. To change your password (or remove password protection), click the **Set Password** button. In the dialog box that appears, enter your old password, and click **Next**. You can then choose to use no password or change the password. Click **Next** again. If you chose to change your password, type the new password into the **Password** and **Type It Again to Confirm** text boxes, and click on **OK**.

You can also change the frequency with which Navigator asks for the password. By default, Navigator prompts you for the password only once each time you use Navigator. You can choose to be prompted each time you use a certificate or at a specified interval (such as 30 minutes).

Using Site Certificates

Each secure Web site is certified by a licensed authority. If you open the security Preferences dialog box, and click Signers, you can view a list of these authorities.

In most cases, you can ignore this list. However, if you hear that the sites certified by a particular authority have had security problems, you can prevent access to sites that this particular authority certified. Or, if you enter information at a site that has been certified by one of the authorities, and the site did something stupid like giving your name and e-mail address to other companies, you can prevent access to sites certified by that authority.

To delete a site certificate entirely (so any sites by that authority will appear as insecure), click on the name of the authority, and click on **Delete Certificate**. To display a warning whenever you attempt to send data to a site that has been certified by an authority, click on the name of the authority, and click the **Edit** button. You can then block access to the site, or have a warning displayed.

Chapter 11 ➤ *Digital Certificates, Cookies, and Other Security Issues*

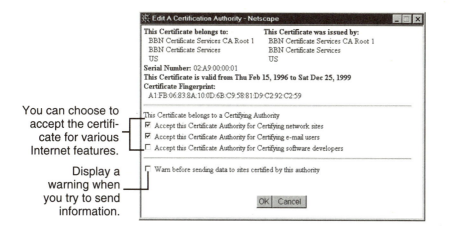

You can control how site certificates are handled.

You can choose to accept the certificate for various Internet features.

Display a warning when you try to send information.

Preventing Viruses from Entering Your System

Picking up a virus on the Internet is sort of like coming home from vacation only to find that someone has broken into your house and stolen all your valuables. You were having so much fun, how could this happen? And, how can you prevent it from happening again? First, follow a few simple rules:

➤ Download programs only from reputable and known sites. If you know the company that created the program, go to its Web page or FTP server, and download the file from there.

➤ Don't accept copies of a program from another person (for example, by e-mail). Although the program may not have contained a virus when the other person downloaded it, the other person's computer may have a virus that infected the program. Ask the person where he or she got the file, and then download the file from its original location yourself.

➤ Run an antivirus program on a regular basis. By identifying and eliminating a virus early, you prevent it from causing additional damage. One of the best antivirus programs on the market is McAfee VirusScan; you can download a trial version at **http://www.mcafee.com/**.

Running an infected program is the most common way you can introduce a virus to your system. However, the Internet poses some additional threats through programmed objects, such as Java applets and ActiveX controls (which you will meet in Part 3, "Playing Video, Sound, and Interactive Worlds").

By default, Navigator is set up to play all types of programmed objects. However, if you hear that viruses have been found in Java applets or ActiveX controls, you may want to prevent Navigator from playing them.

To prevent some types of programmed objects or active content (multimedia files) from playing, open the **Edit** menu, select **Preferences**, and click on the **Advanced** category. Remove the checks from any of the following boxes:

- **Enable Java** allows Navigator to download and play Java applets. If you turn this option off, Navigator will not download Java applets that it finds on Web pages.

- **Enable JavaScript** allows Navigator to play JavaScript (Java codes that are embedded in HTML documents). Turning this off prevents JavaScripts from running on your system.

- **Enable Style Sheets** allows Navigator to use HTML style sheets to display pages that use style sheets. You can safely leave this option on.

- **Enable AutoInstall** lets certain programs, such as ActiveX controls, automatically install themselves on your computer. If you turn this option off, you must manually install these programs if you plan on using them.

Check This Out...

Java and ActiveX Security Issues

Java is a fairly secure programming language, which prevents people from developing programs that could delete files on your system, format your hard drive, or perform other destructive acts. However, programming vandals have created Java applets that can cause Navigator to crash your system, so there is some concern that Java applets may not be completely safe. ActiveX is a less secure Internet programming language. Because ActiveX allows developers to create applets that have access to system commands (such as those used for deleting files and formatting drives), ActiveX applets provide a greater security risk.

Censoring Naughty Net Sites

If you are a parent or teacher, and you want to introduce your kids to the Internet, you need some way to prevent them from accessing sites that broadcast sex, violence, strong language, and other objectionable material. And there are plenty of these sites on the Internet.

Netscape Communicator does not have any built-in features that you can use to censor the Internet. However, there are several specialized programs that can work along with Communicator to block access to objectionable Web pages and Internet newsgroups. Following is a list of some of the better censoring programs along with addresses for the Web pages where you can find out more about these programs and download shareware versions of the products:

- *Cyber Patrol* (at **http://www.cyberpatrol.com**) is the most popular censoring program. It allows you to set security levels, prevent Internet access during certain hours, and prevent access to specific sites. Passwords allow you to set access levels for different users.

- *CYBERsitter* (at **http://www.solidoak.com**) is another fine censoring program. Although a little less strict than Cyber Patrol, CYBERsitter is easier to use and configure. CYBERsitter has a unique filtering system that judges words in context, so that it won't block access to inoffensive sites, such as the John Sexton home page.

- *Net Nanny* (at **http://www.netnanny.com/netnanny**) is unique in that it can punish the user for typing URLs of offensive sites or for typing any word on the no-no list. If a user types a prohibited word or URL, Net Nanny can shut down the application and record the offense, forcing your student or child to come up with an excuse. However, to make the most of Net Nanny, you're going to have to spend a bit of time configuring it.

- *Surf Watch* (at **http://www.surfwatch.com**) is one of the easiest censoring programs to install and use. Surf Watch comes with a list of prohibited sites deemed offensive by its panel of parents and teachers. It also blocks access to pages that contain offensive language.

Although these censoring programs are typically used to prevent children from accessing offensive material, they can also be used in businesses to prevent employees from spending their entire workday at their favorite porno sites.

The Least You Need to Know

The Internet is no place for the paranoid. Wherever you go, whether in real or virtual life, there are some risks involved. To protect yourself or your kids on the Web, here's what you have to do (and not do):

- Don't give your credit card number, phone number, passwords, address, or any other sensitive information to an unknown or untrusted person or company.

- ➤ If your kids are sending e-mail or talking in chat rooms, make sure they know not to give strangers any sensitive information.
- ➤ If you're just starting out, keep Navigator's security warnings on.
- ➤ To change the security settings, click the **Security** button in the Navigation toolbar.
- ➤ Any program you download from the Internet may carry a computer virus; download programs only from reputable sites.
- ➤ If you are introducing your children or students to the Web, supervise them. If you can't always be there, get a censoring program, such as Cyber Patrol.
- ➤ We all worry, but don't forget to have some fun, too.

Part 3
Playing Video, Sound, and Interactive Worlds

Navigator is no slouch when it comes to displaying pictures and playing sound clips. You can surf the Web for hours without encountering a single media file that Navigator cannot play.

However, there are some file types that Navigator cannot play. For these file types, Navigator needs the help of additional applications: helper apps, plug-ins, and ActiveX controls. In this part, you'll learn about all these gadgets, where you can get them on the Internet, how to install them, and how to set up Navigator to use them.

Chapter 12

Going Multimedia with Plug-Ins and ActiveX Controls

In This Chapter

➤ Play video and sound clips that Navigator itself cannot play

➤ Tell the difference between a plug-in and an ActiveX control

➤ Shop for plug-ins from Stroud's List

➤ Grab a plug-in that enables Navigator to play ActiveX components

Navigator can take you around the world, connecting to computers in any of the contiguous and noncontiguous states, and with computers in foreign lands. It can play most audio files, a good selection of video clips, and ninety percent of the graphic files you'll encounter. But if you click a link, and you get this...

...then Navigator needs help in the form of special programs called *plug-ins, helper applications, or ActiveX controls*. In this chapter, you'll learn how to get plug-ins and ActiveX controls off the Internet install them, and start using them to play various media files.

Helper Applications, Plug-Ins, and ActiveX Controls

Back in the old days (about two years ago), Web browsers relied solely on helper applications to play file types that the Web browsers could not handle. Helper applications (*helper apps* or *viewers* for short) are small programs that typically take up little memory and run very fast. Whenever you try to play a file on the Internet that the Web browser cannot handle, the browser downloads the file and runs the helper app assigned to that file type, which then opens and "plays" the file.

Relatively recently, Web browser creators have come up with alternatives to helper apps. Netscape was the first with its *plug-in* idea. Plug-ins are additional computer code that increase the built-in capabilities of the Web browser. Unlike helper apps, which are separate applications, the plug-in becomes part of the Web browser, making it much more efficient for playing media files.

Acknowledging the benefit of the plug-in idea, Microsoft created its own version of plug-ins, calling them ActiveX controls. Like plug-ins, ActiveX controls become part of the Web browser, enabling the Web browser to play file types that it could not otherwise handle.

Although Navigator is designed for using plug-ins, Navigator 4.0 can also use helper applications and ActiveX controls. But which is best? Here's a quick rundown:

- Because there are so many plug-ins designed specifically for use with Netscape Navigator, plug-ins are the best option for adding capability to Navigator. In most cases, you can run the plug-in installation program, and start using the plug-in immediately, without having to mess with any additional configuration settings.

- Helper apps are good if you want to download a media file and play it later. You won't need to fire up your Web browser to play the file. You'll learn how to use helper apps in Chapter 13, "Beefing Up Navigator with Helper Applications."

- ActiveX is an excellent file- and program-sharing technology that was designed to work primarily with Microsoft's Web browser, Internet Explorer. Fortunately, Navigator 4.0 supports ActiveX technology (through the use of a special plug-in), allowing you to download and use ActiveX controls. You may need these controls to play ActiveX components that may be embedded in some Web pages.

File Types that Navigator Can Play

Navigator can play several types of media files without any outside help. It can display images in JPG and GIF formats, Java applets, and other common file types. If you purchased Netscape Communicator, or downloaded the complete package, including plug-ins, Navigator and its plug-ins can handle most of the media files you will encounter on the Web. The following table lists the file types that Navigator and its bundled plug-ins can play.

File Types that Navigator and Its Bundled Plug-Ins Can Play

Program or Plug-In	Description	File Types
Netscape Navigator	Web browser	.html (Web page), .gif (graphic), .jpg, jpeg, jpe (graphic), .txt (text only), Java applets, JavaScript
Cosmo Player	VRML (virtual worlds)	.wrl, .wrz
Netscape Media Player	Streaming Audio Player	.lam
QuickTime	Video player	.mov
NPAVI32 DLL	Video player	.avi
LiveAudio	Audio player	.au, .aif, .aiff, .wav, .mid, .midi, .la, .lma

To play file types that are not listed in the table (for example, PCX images and VDO movie clips), you'll have to download and install either a plug-in or a helper app.

Grabbing Plug-Ins the Easy Way

The easiest way to get the plug-in you need is to try to play a file type that Navigator can't play. Navigator 4.0 is set up to notify you when you need a particular plug-in. If you click on a link that Navigator cannot play, and Navigator "knows" that there is a plug-in available for that file type, Navigator displays the dialog box shown in the following figure, prompting you to download the appropriate plug-in. Click on the **Get the Plugin** button. If the Unknown File Type dialog box appears, click the **More Info** button to display Netscape's Plug-In Finder page.

Now, you're probably wondering just what I did to get this dialog box. In the example, I went to **www.vdo.net**, and clicked on the VDO Guide link. This brought up a list of sites that feature VDO video clips. I followed the trail of links to one of the pages in the VDO Guide, and as soon as I arrived at the page, Navigator displayed the message telling me that I needed another plug-in. If you go to a different page, you may have to click on a link for a VDO clip before Navigator will display the dialog box.

When Navigator knows it needs a plug-in, it prompts you to download and install it.

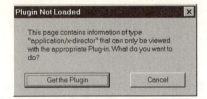

After you click the Get the Plugin button (or click the More Info button in the Unknown File Type dialog box), Navigator opens a new browser window and displays its Plug-in Finder page. Follow the trail of links to the page that contains the link for downloading the plug-in you want. (This trail may be very long and meandering.) When you finally see a link that points to the plug-in, click on the link. The Save As dialog box appears; use this dialog box to save the file to a folder on your hard drive (or to the Windows desktop).

In most cases, after downloading the file, you can simply double-click on it to start the installation process. If the procedure is more complicated, the site from which you downloaded the file should have installation instructions. If you have problems installing the plug-in, return to its home page for instructions.

Visiting the Plug-In Warehouse

You can find links to most of the plug-ins you need, along with information and ratings by pulling up Stroud's List, a helpful Web document kindly constructed by Forrest H. Stroud. To connect to this list, run Navigator and enter the following URL: **http://www.stroud.com**. If you can't pull up this page, go to Yahoo at **http://www.yahoo.com**, and search for **Stroud's**. This displays a list of links for various servers that mirror Stroud's List. Pick the server nearest you.

When you get there, click on the big Stroud graphic at the top of the page. Then, scroll down the page until you see the Main Menu, as shown in the following figure. (Another good place to grab plug-ins is Tucows at **http://www.tucows.com**.)

Check the Date

Stroud's List resides on several Web sites which update the list at varying intervals. At the bottom of the Main Menu is a Mirror Sites link; click on it to view a list of the other sites. When you go to a mirror site, check the date at the top of the page to see when it was last updated. Try to find the site that was updated most recently.

Chapter 12 ➤ *Going Multimedia with Plug-Ins and ActiveX Controls*

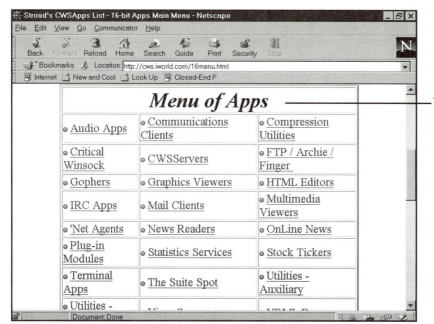

Stroud's Consummate Winsock Applications list has links to all the plug-ins you need.

— The Main Menu

From the Main Menu, click on the **Plug-in Modules** link. This takes you to a page that lists common plug-in modules.

Although the Plug-in page offers links to many of the most popular Navigator plug-ins, the list is not very comprehensive. For example, the list does not include the plug-in version of FigLeaf, a graphics viewer that comes both as a helper app and plug-in. If you can't find the plug-in you need, go back to Stroud's Main Menu, and click on a link for an application category. For example, you might click on **Audio Apps** for a sound player, **Graphics Viewers** for an image viewer, or **Multimedia Viewers** for video players. You might have to go to the app's information page to find out whether it is offered as a plug-in.

Stroud's list also rates the plug-ins, indicates whether the plug-in has been tested, and shows the size of the file you're about to download. Be sure to check out this information before downloading. You don't want to download a 4-megabyte file only to find out that it's not what you expected. To read a brief review of the product and compare it to other products in its category, click on the **Full Review** link.

131

Part 3 ➤ Playing Video, Sound, and Interactive Worlds

Stroud's has an entire page full of useful plug-in modules.

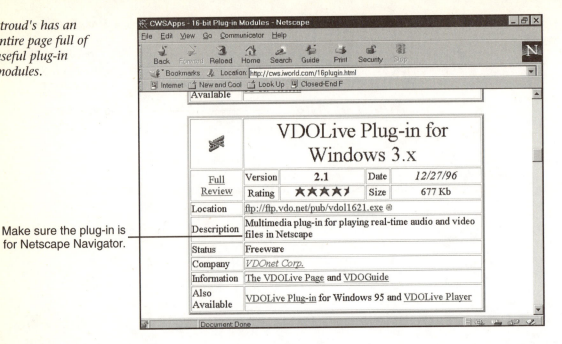

Make sure the plug-in is for Netscape Navigator.

You should also make sure you are getting the latest version of the plug-in. Many plug-ins are for older versions of Navigator. Some of these plug-ins will work with Navigator 4.0, but some will not. The best way to find out if the plug-in will work with Navigator 4.0 is to go to the home page of the company that developed the plug-in. If the current plug-in does not work with Navigator 4.0, the page will usually indicate when the new version of the plug-in will be available for downloading.

Netscape's Plug-In Page

Another good place to find out about the latest Navigator plug-ins is at Netscape. Open Navigator's **Help** menu, and select **About Plug-ins**. At the top of the page is a link called **click here** that takes you to a page that has links to plug-ins.

Downloading from Stroud's

When you're ready to download the file, click on the link next to Location, and then follow the trail of links and on-screen instructions to download the file. Make sure you get the right version of the helper app (Windows 3.1, Windows 95, or Macintosh).

Although Stroud's list may not distinguish between these operating systems when listing the helper apps, the download site typically displays a form that lets you specify your operating system, or displays links for the various versions.

	VDOLive Plug-in for Windows 3.x			
Full Review	Version	2.1	Date	12/27/96
	Rating	★★★★✓	Size	677 Kb
Location	ftp://ftp.vdo.net/pub/vdo1621.exe			
Description	Multimedia plug-in for playing real-time audio and video files in Netscape			
Status	Freeware			
Company	VDOnet Corp.			
Information	The VDOLive Page and VDOGuide			
Also Available	VDOLive Plug-in for Windows 95 and VDOLive Player			

From Stroud's List, you can download most applications.

Click on this link to go to the download site.

Before You Download

Before you start downloading files and sticking them all over your hard drive, you should create a separate temporary directory or folder for your files. You might want to call it something like Plugins. You can then place all the original downloaded files in this folder. When you are done installing these plug-ins, you can delete the Plugin folder and all the files it contains. Otherwise, you'll clutter your hard drive.

Downloading Files with Navigator

You learned all about using Navigator to copy files from the Internet in Chapter 9, "Driving Off-Road to FTP and Gopher Sites."

I'm not going to assume that everything proceeded as planned. If you couldn't connect to the computer that holds those precious plug-ins, you have two options. You can try later (during the Letterman show, and at the crack of dawn are good times), or you can try downloading the files from somewhere else.

If you've tried several FTP sites, and you keep receiving error messages telling you that access has been denied, Navigator may not be sending your e-mail address as a password. Open the **Edit** menu, select **Preferences**, and click the **Advanced** category. Make sure there is a check in the box next to **Send Email Address as Anonymous FTP Password**.

Installing and Uninstalling Plug-Ins

The best part about plug-ins is that you don't have to mess with setting up the application to play files of a particular type. You install the plug-in, and Navigator takes care of the rest. (Yes, that's right—you plug it in, and it works).

The only trouble is that plug-ins do supplant any other plug-in or helper application designed to handle the same file type. So, if you install the plug-in and you decide you'd rather use a helper app instead, you have to uninstall the plug-in (fairly easy), and then reassociate the file type with your helper app (a pain).

Into Which Folder Should I Install My Plug-Ins? Whenever you install a plug-in, the installation program prompts you to specify the directory or folder in which Navigator is installed. If you pick the wrong folder, the plug-in won't work. Before you begin the installation, use Windows Explorer or File Manager to find the netscape.exe file; when you find it, write down the complete path to it. If you're using Windows 95, check the C:/Program Files/Netscape/Communicator/Program directory.

Installing a Plug-In

Installing a plug-in is easy. When you download the plug-in, you end up with a self-extracting, usually self-installing file on your hard drive. Before running the file, shut down Navigator. While you're at it, close your other programs, too, just in case anything bombs during the installation. The easiest way to install the plug-in is to display the file you downloaded (in Windows Explorer or File Manager), and double-click on it. Then, follow the instructions.

In a few cases, the self-extracting file might not be self-installing. After decompressing the file, you may have to go into the directory where the extracted files are stored and run **Setup.exe** or **Install.exe**. If you extract a file, and it places DISK directories on your drive (disk1, disk2, disk3, and so on), the DISK1 directory usually contains the Setup or Install file. Double-click on the **Install** or **Setup** file to run it.

Uninstalling Plug-Ins

Plug-ins typically come with their own uninstall utility. To remove a plug-in in Windows 95, open the **Control Panel**, and double-click on the **Add/Remove Programs** icon. Click on the name of the plug-in you want to uninstall, as shown in the following figure, and then click on the **Add/Remove** button.

Chapter 12 ➤ *Going Multimedia with Plug-Ins and ActiveX Controls*

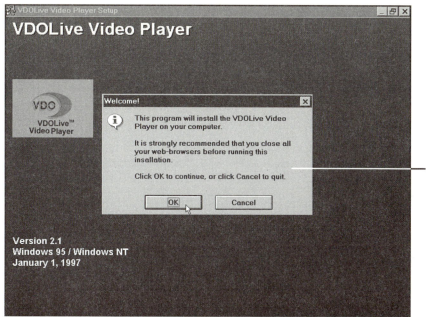

Most plug-ins can install themselves.

Follow the on-screen installation instructions.

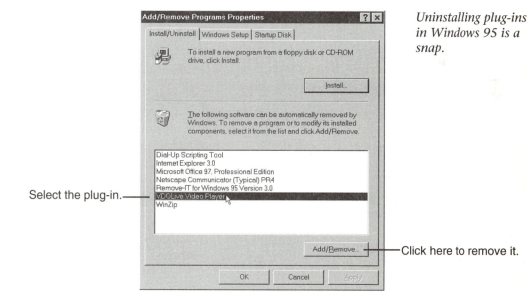

Uninstalling plug-ins in Windows 95 is a snap.

Select the plug-in.

Click here to remove it.

Windows 3.1 does not have an Add/Remove Programs feature, so you'll have to rely on the plug-in's uninstall utility. Change to the directory that contains the plug-in's program files, and double-click on its uninstall icon. Follow the on-screen instructions to complete the operation.

Can I Find Out Which Plug-Ins Are Installed?

To find out which plug-ins are installed, open Navigator's **Help** menu and click on About Plug-ins. A page appears, listing all the plug-ins you've installed, including Information about which file extensions they're linked to.

Playing ActiveX Controls

ActiveX is a technology that lets Web page developers stick all sorts of cool animations, programs, and other objects on a page, and lets you play them. ActiveX consists of the following three components:

- ➤ **ActiveX Controls** are sort of like plug-ins. They reside on your computer and enable your browser (Navigator) to play ActiveX components.

- ➤ **ActiveX Documents** are documents that you can open and edit in any application that supports ActiveX. For example, you can open a Word document or an Excel spreadsheet right in the Web browser.

- ➤ **ActiveX Scripting** is a programming language that allows Web developers to write and insert small applications on their Web pages and coordinate other ActiveX components. JavaScript and VBScript are two ActiveX scripting languages.

To play ActiveX components, Navigator needs a special plug-in. As with most plug-ins, you can get the ActiveX plug-in by going to a Web page that has ActiveX components, clicking on a component to play it, and then following the instructions. Try it:

1. Go to Microsoft's ActiveX Gallery at **http://www.microsoft.com/activex/gallery**. This displays a page that has links to several companies which have created ActiveX controls.

2. Click on the link for an ActiveX control you want. This displays a page that describes the control and presents you with a link for downloading and installing it.

3. Click on the link for downloading and installing the control. The Plugin Not Loaded dialog box appears, indicating that Navigator does not have the plug-in it needs.

4. Click on the **Get the Plugin** button. (If you receive the Unknown File Type dialog box, click on the **More Info** button.) Navigator displays Netscape's Plug-in Finder page. Follow the instructions to get the ActiveX plug-in (ScriptActive from NCompass) and install it on your computer.

You can also get the ScriptActive directly from NCompass, before you start trying to play ActiveX components. Visit NCompass at **http://www.ncompasslabs.com**. ScriptActive also includes the capabilities of DocActive, a plug-in that enables Navigator to open ActiveX documents (created in Microsoft Word, Excel, PowerPoint, and other applications that support ActiveX documents).

> **Check This Out...**
>
> **ActiveX Controls at Stroud's** You can check out a collection of popular ActiveX controls at Stroud's Consummate Winsock Applications site: **http://www.stroud.com**.

Once you have the plug-in you need, you can start playing ActiveX objects. The process is fairly simple. When you encounter a page that has an ActiveX component for which you have no ActiveX control, Navigator downloads the control, installs it, and uses the control to play the ActiveX component.

The Least You Need to Know

If you have lots of free hard disk space and a couple of days off work, you can have fun with plug-ins. Here's all you have to do:

➤ Don't worry about plug-ins. Just click links until Navigator tells you that it needs a specific plug-in, and then follow instructions.

➤ If you try to play a file, and Navigator displays the Unknown File Type dialog box, click the **More Info** button to see if Navigator knows which plug-in you need.

➤ You can get most of the plug-ins you need from **http://www.stroud.com** or one of its mirror sites.

➤ After you download a plug-in file, run it; this decompresses the file and usually installs the plug-in.

➤ In most cases, after downloading the plug-in, you can return to the site from which you downloaded it to play some demos specially designed for that plug-in.

Chapter 13

Beefing Up Navigator with Helper Applications

In This Chapter

- ➤ Find and download a sound player, movie player, and picture viewer
- ➤ Associate a particular file type with a helper application that can play it
- ➤ Name a couple Web sites that act as helper application warehouses
- ➤ "Play" any multimedia link simply by clicking on it

Assuming you didn't skip the previous chapter, you know that plug-ins are the best tools around for playing the various media files you will inevitably encounter on the Web. However, there may not be a plug-in for every file type, and a particular plug-in may not be the best tool for playing files of a specific type. In such cases, you may be better off downloading and installing a *helper application*—a stand-alone application that Navigator can automatically call to action when needed.

In this chapter, you'll learn how to get helper applications off the Internet, install them, and set them up so that Navigator can use them.

How Do Helper Applications Help?

Check This Out...

Helper Applications
Also known as *ex-ternal viewers* (or *helper apps*), helper applications are programs that play the Web's multimedia files, including photos, sounds, and video clips. Typically, these programs run quickly and use little memory.

Helper applications are programs that perform the specialized jobs that Navigator by itself is unfit to manage. Whenever you click a link that Navigator can't play, Navigator loads the file to disk, and then summons (spawns) the helper application associated with that file. The helper application loads the file and plays it.

Sound simple? It's absolutely brainless, assuming you have everything set up correctly. However, setting up everything to run correctly takes some effort. You have to get and install the helper applications, and then tell Navigator which application goes with each type of file you might want to play.

Decompressing and Installing the Software

Some files you download come as self-extracting compressed files. These files end in EXE for PCs or SEA for Macs. To decompress the file, double-click on its name. The file decompresses itself and then usually runs an installation program that installs the application.

If the file ends in ZIP or HQX, you must use a decompression utility to unzip the file. In Windows, use WinZip; you can get it at **www.winzip.com**. To install WinZip, first download the file and run it. WinZip comes as a self-extracting file that basically installs itself. To use WinZip to decompress your other files, take the following steps:

1. In Windows Explorer or File Manager, double-click on the zipped file you want to decompress. This runs WinZip. The WinZip window displays the names of all the files that are packed in the zipped file.

2. Click on the **Extract** button. The Extract dialog box appears, asking you to pick a folder or directory for the unzipped files.

3. Make sure **All Files** is selected, and then pick the drive and folder or directory into which you want the unzipped files placed.

4. Click the **Extract** button. WinZip decompresses the files and places them in the specified folder.

To decompress an HQX file using StuffIt Expander (for the Mac), drag the compressed file over the StuffIt Expander button, and release the mouse button. StuffIt Expander does the rest.

Once you've unzipped the helper application files you downloaded, read the installation instructions that came with each application for any quirky installation steps. (The instructions are usually in a file called README.TXT or INSTALL.TXT, which you can open in Windows Notepad or WordPad.) With some applications, you can simply unzip the application, create an icon for it, and start using it. Others may require that you run a separate Setup program (in File Manager or My Computer, look for a file called SETUP.EXE or INSTALL.EXE, and then double-click on it). When you're done, you should have an icon you can double-click to run the application.

Mapping Files to Their Helper Applications

I hate to break it to you, but installing the helper applications is only half the story. Now, you must tell Navigator which applications to run for each type of multimedia file you encounter on the Web. For example, if you click a movie link, Navigator must know whether it should run the audio player, the graphic viewer, or the movie player. You need to *associate* each file type you might encounter with a helper application that can load and play that file type.

You can associate program types to helper applications on-the-fly. If you click a link for a file that's not associated with a helper application, Navigator displays the Unknown File Type dialog box essentially saying, "What do you want me to do?" You can then click **Save File** and worry about the file later, or click **Pick App** to associate this file type to a helper application. If you click **Pick App**, you're presented with the Configure External Viewer dialog box. Click the **Browse** button, and use the dialog box that appears to select the program file for the viewer (helper application) you want to use.

If you don't like that idea, you can set up your helper applications ahead of time, and completely avoid the Unknown File Type dialog box. Navigator will automatically run the helper application when you try to load a file it cannot handle. To associate files, here's what you do:

1. Run Navigator (you don't have to be connected to the Web).

2. Open the **Edit** menu, and select **Preferences**. The Preferences dialog box appears.

3. Click the plus sign next to Navigator, and click **Applications**. You now see the page of options you can select to specify how you want Navigator to handle various file types.

4. In the Description list, click the type of file you want to associate with a helper application, and click the **Edit** button. For example, you might click **MPEG Video** to associate MPEG video files with an MPEG Player. Here's a list of common file types and the helper applications that play them:

141

Extension	Helper Application
JPG	LView
GIF	LView
AVI	AviPro
MPG	MPEG
MP2	MPEG
WAV	Windows Sound Recorder

(If the desired file type is not in the list, you can click the **New Type** button to create a new file type.)

5. Click inside the **MIME Type** text box, and type the MIME type for any of the files you want this helper application to play. (If you are unsure of the MIME type, create a new file type as explained following these steps, and associate the helper application to a file name extension rather than to a MIME type.) Following is a list of common MIME types:

MIME Type	File Types
application/msword	DOC, DOT, WIZ
application/pdf	PDF
application/x-compress	ZIP
application/x-conference	NSC
audio/basic	AU
audio/x-aiff	AIF, AIFF
audio/x-mpeg	MP2, MPA, ABS, MPEGA
audio/x-pn-realaudio	RA, RAM
audio/x-wav	WAV
image/gif	GIF
image/jpeg	JPEG, JPG, JPE, JFIF, PJPEG, PJP
image/x-ms-bmp	BMP
image/x-xbitmap	XBM
midi/mid	MID

Chapter 13 ▶ Beefing Up Navigator with Helper Applications

MIME Type	File Types
midi/rmi	RMI
text/html	HTML, HTM, HTT
text/plain	TXT, TEXT
video/mpeg	MPEG, MPG, MPE, MPV, VBS, MPEGV
video/quicktime	MOV
video/x-ms-asf	ASF, ASX
video/x-msvideo	AVI
x-world/x-vrml	WRL, WRZ

6. Click the **Application** option. This tells Navigator that whenever you choose to load a file of this type, it should run the associated helper application.

7. Click the **Browse** button. The Open dialog box appears, prompting you to select the file that runs the helper application.

8. Change to the drive and folder (or directory) in which you installed the helper application.

9. In the file name list, click the executable program file (the file that launches the helper application), and then click the **Open** button.

10. To have Navigator prompt you before downloading and opening files of this type, make sure there is a check in the **Ask me before opening downloaded files of this type** box. Click **OK**.

11. Repeat Steps 4–10 to associate additional file types with their helper applications.

12. Click **OK** when you're done.

While editing a file type, you may have noticed the **Navigator** option (above Application). This option tells Navigator to play the file itself. Navigator can play graphic files in the GIF or JPG format, but they won't look as clear as graphics displayed in a dedicated graphics program, such as LView Pro or Paint Shop Pro. This option is available only for certain file types.

Although the file type list includes most of the file types you'll commonly encounter on the Web—and then some—you may come across a file type that's not on the list and that requires a special helper application. In such a case, you can click the **New Type** button and create your own association. You'll get a dialog box asking for a Mime and Sub Mime type, which has nothing to do with Marcel Marceau.

You can quickly associate files with helper applications.

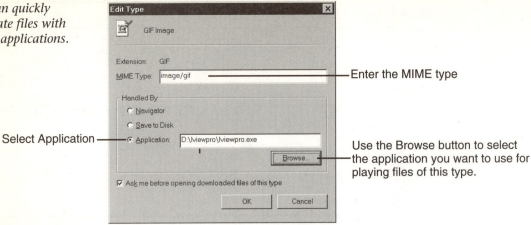

— Enter the MIME type

Select Application —

— Use the Browse button to select the application you want to use for playing files of this type.

MIME Short for *Multi-purpose Internet Mail Extensions*, MIME is a protocol that controls all file transfers on the Web. Navigator uses MIME to recognize different file types.

Type a description of the file type in the Description text box. Tab to the File Extension text box, and type the file name extension(s) for the file type(s) you want to associate to a helper application. For example, you might type **pcx bmp** to associate PCX and bitmapped graphics to a graphics viewer. If you know the MIME type, tab to the MIME text box, and type the MIME type. If you are unsure of the MIME type, leave the box blank; if Navigator can't recognize the MIME type of an incoming file, Navigator uses the file name extensions you enter to determine which helper application to run.

Click inside the **Application** text box, and click the **Browse** button. Use the Open dialog box to select the file that runs the desired helper application, and click the **Open** button. Click **OK** when you're done. You now have a new entry in the Description list. You can edit this entry at any time.

One Helper App Per File Type

Be careful to assign only one helper application to a particular file type. If you assign two helper applications to a file type, Navigator may choose to run the wrong helper application. If another helper application or plug-in is assigned to the file type you want to use, first remove that file name extension from the list of extensions assigned to that plug-in or helper application.

Playing Multimedia Links

Playing a multimedia link is as easy as clicking on the link. Navigator downloads the file and then runs the helper application, which loads and plays the file. All you have to do is sit back and watch.

Keep in mind that multimedia files can take loads of time to transfer, even if you have a direct (network) connection. The total time it takes depends on the speed of your connection, the size of the file, the amount of traffic on the server, the distance of the server from your computer, and the speed of your computer. Photos, graphics, video clips, and sound clips can be hefty. These files take a long time to transfer and consume a great deal of memory and disk space.

> **My Plug-In Insists on Playing the File!** Whenever you install a plug-in, it takes over the job of playing files of a particular type. If you want to use your helper application to play that file type, you must uninstall the plug-in.

Do It! Cinema, Sounds, and Photos

In your wanderings, you're sure to stumble across some Web sites that offer video and sound clips, photos, and on-screen art. Although I hate to spoil the thrill of discovery, I feel compelled to mention a few sites that are sure to impress you:

> **Internet Underground Music Archive:** Stores sound clips of little-known bands. You can download short clips or entire songs.
>
> http://www.iuma.com/
>
> **Kid's Corner:** A site for kids and by kids, Kid's Corner offers plenty of graphics for the younger set.
>
> http://wwwsmart.com/~shui/PV/Kids.html
>
> **Hollywood Online:** Contains pictures of your favorite Hollywood stars along with video clips and soundtracks.
>
> http://www.hollywood.com
>
> **Perry-Castaneda Library Map Collection:** Offers maps of Africa, the United States, the Middle East, Europe, and maps of several major cities around the world.
>
> http://www.lib.utexas.edu/Libs/PCL/Map_collection/Map_collection.html
>
> **Yahoo! (a guide to the World Wide Web):** Yahoo! provides an index of cool Web sites, so you'll have to click a couple of links to get what you want. Click the **Entertainment** link, and then click **Comics**, **Multimedia**, or something else that catches your eye. You're sure to find some neat clips.
>
> http://www.yahoo.com

You can download music clips of lesser-known artists.

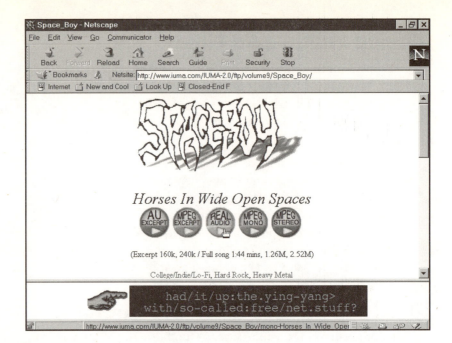

A Word About Sound and Video Quality

Eight-bit sound cards and standard VGA monitors just can't keep up with the sounds and clips stored on the Web. If you're still stuck with the old technology, maybe the Web will provide the incentive for you to upgrade.

If you have a Super VGA monitor and a 16-bit or better sound card, make sure they're set up to play at the highest quality. If you have your Super VGA monitor set to display only 16 colors, your pictures and video clips will look like snowstorms. Make sure you set your monitor to display at least 256 colors. Also, check your sound card setup to make sure it's in 16-bit, stereo mode.

The Least You Need to Know

Now that you can watch movies and listen to sound clips, you probably already know everything you want to know. However, if you get bored with all that sensory stimulation, read the following review items:

➤ A helper application is a small, streamlined program that can play files which Navigator is incapable of playing.

➤ You might prefer using plug-ins instead. See Chapter 12, "Going Multimedia with Plug-Ins and ActiveX Controls."

➤ To use a helper application, you have to get it, install it, and associate it with a specific file type.

➤ Assuming your helper applications are set up correctly, you can play a multimedia link simply by clicking on it.

➤ Sometimes, you're better off saving a file and then playing it later... especially if you get a juicy clip off one of the movie galleries.

Chapter 14

Exploring Java, Shockwave, and Virtual Worlds

In This Chapter

➤ Understand why there are so many coffee metaphors on the Web

➤ Play interactive Java applets

➤ Interact with multimedia Shockwave presentations

➤ Explore virtual, three-dimensional worlds with Cosmo Player

In Chapters 12, "Going Multimedia with Plug-Ins and ActiveX Controls," and 13, "Beefing Up Navigator with Helper Applications," you were busy downloading and playing video clips, audio recordings, pictures, and other types of multimedia files, as if you were channel surfing on your TV. You acted as some passive voyeur, hungry for more sensory stimulation than the Web could serve up. Aren't you ashamed of yourself? I didn't think so.

If your hard drive isn't full yet, you'll get a chance to interact with your downloads. Sounds warm and fuzzy, eh?

The Web is exploding with interactive programs, games, tutorials, and presentations that you should experience firsthand. In this chapter, you'll get your chance by playing Java applets, visiting Shocked sites, and exploring three-dimensional, interactive worlds. I'll even tell you where to find the best interactive games.

What Is Java?

Java is the first and most popular programming language for the Web. Developed by Sun Microsystems, Java is a tool that allows programmers to create small applications (called *applets*) that you can download and run. These applets are similar to old DOS shareware programs. For example, with a loan calculator applet, you can type in the amount you borrowed, the interest rate, and the term, and the calculator will determine your monthly payment. Another applet might allow you to shoot missiles out of the sky. Although the current crop of applets is not very powerful, that is about to change, as programmers become more experienced with Java and as the Java programming language develops.

To run a Java applet, you need a Java-enabled Web browser. Fortunately, Navigator is the most Java-enabled browser around. Navigator is optimized to support all the advanced features of JavaScript 1.1 and is working to implement more features from JavaScript 1.2.

When you encounter a link to a Java applet, all you have to do is click the link. Netscape Navigator downloads the Java code, interprets it, and starts the applet. Once the applet is downloaded, it's on your computer, and you can use it just like any of your other applications (although you have to run these applets through Navigator).

Don't Wait for Me

In the next section, I'll tell you where to look for Java applets. But you can look for yourself. Connect to your favorite search page on the Web, and search for **Java applet**. You'll find scads of them.

Can These Applets Hurt Me?

Sun Microsystems, creator of Java, claims that Java has built-in safeguards that prevent programmers from inserting any viruses or destructive code into their applets. But saying that to a hacker is like poking Mike Tyson in the eye. As soon as you claim that your code is secure, every hacker who was busy chugging a Mountain Dew drops his drink and starts trying to figure out ways to crack it.

It's no different with Java. Although Java is relatively safe, there are ways to insert destructive code into Java applets. You can visit the Hostile Applets page at **http://www.math.gatech.edu/~mladue/HostileApplets.html**, to check out some of these codified vandals.

Chapter 14 ➤ *Exploring Java, Shockwave, and Virtual Worlds*

Does that mean you shouldn't play Java applets? Of course not! You just need to be a little careful, play Java applets that look legitimate, and if you hear of a destructive applet, avoid it.

However, if you're worried, you can disable Navigator's Java feature. Open the **Edit** menu, select **Preferences**, and click **Advanced**. Click on **Enable Java** and **Enable JavaScript** to remove the checks from the boxes. While you're at it, you can click on **Enable stylesheets** and **Enable AutoInstall** to turn off those options. Now, Navigator won't download or play Java Applets, automatically load stylesheets, or allow Web pages to update Navigator by adding features automatically. Happy?

HotJava Required?

If you connect to a Java site, and you see a message saying that HotJava is required, you probably won't be able to play the applets at that site. HotJava is the other Java-enabled Web browser created by Sun Microsystems (yes, the creators of Java). HotJava is on the cutting edge of Java code, so it may be able to play Java applets that Navigator can't handle. However, because Netscape and Sun are currently collaborating on developing Java, Netscape Navigator should be able to handle most of the Java components you will encounter.

Playing Java Applets

There's no trick to playing Java applets. You don't have to install a plug-in or set up a helper application. So, let the fun begin.

To play a cool simulation of how airplanes land at a typical airport, go to **http://www.db.erau.edu/java/pattern/**. When the applet window appears on your screen, click the **Start Sim** button in the upper right corner of the window. The planes start circling the airport, landing, and pulling into the hangar.

Turn Off the Toolbars

Java applets commonly use more screen than Navigator has to offer. When playing applets, consider turning off the toolbars at the top of the screen.

151

Java landing simulation.

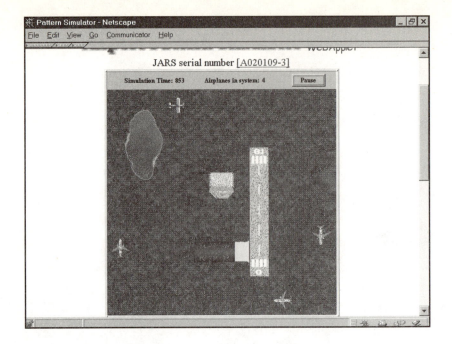

You've been cooped up in your office too long. You probably haven't seen the news, and you have no idea what the weather's doing. Do you care? If so, you can check out Blue Skies for an interactive Java weather report at **http://cirrus.sprl.umich.edu/javaweather/#Java**. Once you get there, click on the link for the type of weather information you want (for example, Precipitation or Surface Temperature). This displays a weather map with hot spots (no pun intended) that you can click on to get weather data for a specific city or area of the country.

Okay, I won't bore you anymore with this tour of Java applets. You get the idea. The applet runs, you stare at the controls on the screen, and figure out what you need to click on to use it. Easy stuff. However, I will give you the URLs of a couple Java repositories on the Web, so you have some idea where to look for these little Java gems.

The first place is JARS (the Java Applet Rating Service). This place not only contains links to thousands of Java applets, but it also rates the applets, so you can screen out the losers. Connect to JARS at **http://www.jars.com/**.

When you've exhausted the JARS Java applets, check out Café del Sol, where employees of Sun Microsystems display their Java creations: **http://www.xm.com/cafe/**. This is also a good place to find more information about Java, including information on how to start creating your own applets (or check out *The Complete Idiot's Guide to JavaScript, Second Edition* by Aaron Weiss).

Chapter 14   Exploring Java, Shockwave, and Virtual Worlds

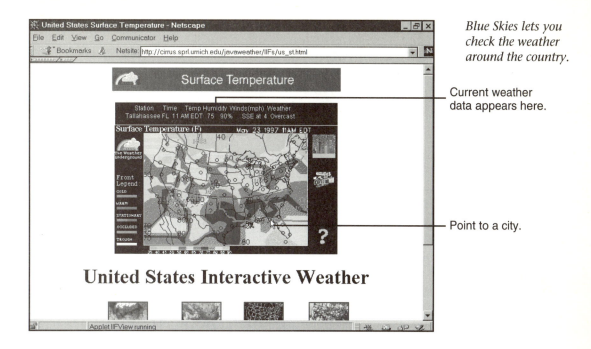

Blue Skies lets you check the weather around the country.

Current weather data appears here.

Point to a city.

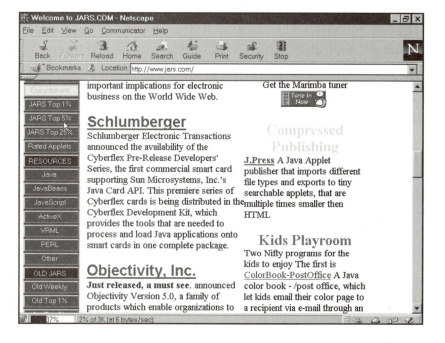

At JARS, you'll find links to thousands of applets.

153

Getting Shocked!

Multimedia presentations have become the latest time-wasting device in corporate America. Media specialists, middle management, and ambitious hourlies are all trying to impress each other with their fancy presentations and multimedia training programs, while the Japanese figure out better ways to build cars.

Okay, okay, I'll get off the soapbox.

At any rate, multimedia presentations have finally hit the Web. A company called Macromedia, maker of programs such as Macromedia Director and FreeHand, has made it possible for multimedia developers to quickly and easily publish their presentations electronically on the Web. Along with its superior file-compression technology, Macromedia presentations are becoming more popular and more accessible.

Downloading and Installing Shockwave

To view Macromedia presentations on the Web, you need a special program called Shockwave, which Macromedia offers for free. You can find the beginning of the download link trail on Macromedia's home page at **http://www.macromedia.com/Shockwave/**. Once you've found a link for downloading the file, click on it, specify the directory in which you want the file stored, and then wait patiently while Navigator downloads it.

This gives you a self-extracting, self-installing file. Change to the folder in which you saved the file, and double-click on it. Then, follow the on-screen installation instructions. When the installation is complete,
a dialog box appears, asking if you want to go to Macromedia to test Shockwave. Make sure **Yes, go to www.macromedia.com** has a check mark next to it, and then click the **Finish** button.

Which Directory Is Navigator in?
The Shockwave installation prompts you to specify the directory in which you installed Navigator. If you pick the wrong directory, Shockwave won't run when you click on a link for a Shocked page. You may have to use Windows Explorer to find the netscapt.exe file; when you find it, write down the complete path to it. If you're using Windows 95, check the C:/ProgramFiles/Netscape/Communicator/Program directory.

Chapter 14 ➤ *Exploring Java, Shockwave, and Virtual Worlds*

Playing with Shockwave

Once you've installed Shockwave, fire up Navigator and return to Macromedia's home page at **http://www.macromedia.com/**. Here, you'll find a link for a list of sites that have Shockwave demos. The following figure shows Steve's Tequila Race, where you can slam down virtual shots of tequila and see the effects on your senses.

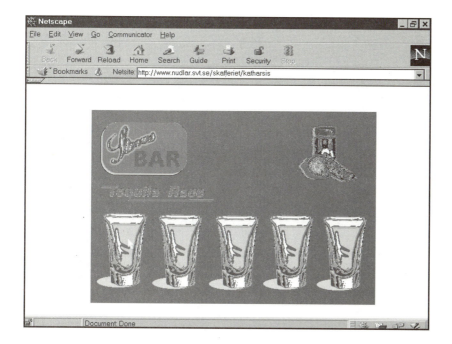

Click on a glass to slam a shot.

No Macromedia sites will look the same. The presentation (or "movie"), not Shockwave, determines the controls displayed. When you visit shocked sites, be prepared to be... er... shocked.

What Is VRML?

VRML (sounds like "vermal"; stands for Virtual Reality Modeling Language) is another programming language that allows developers to create applications they can place on the Web. However, VRML lets these developers create interactive, three-dimensional worlds that you can walk through, fly over, and explore. For example, at the Ziff Davis Terminal Reality site, you can take a virtual elevator to various levels of its bookstore, board the ZD cruise liner to sail to Nubble's Treehouse, or fly the blimp to Paragraph International.

155

Part 3 ➤ *Playing Video, Sound, and Interactive Worlds*

In the following sections, you'll learn how to use Netscape's Cosmo Player VRML player and other VRML browsers to explore these virtual worlds and see for yourself what they have to offer.

With VRML, you can explore three-dimensional worlds.

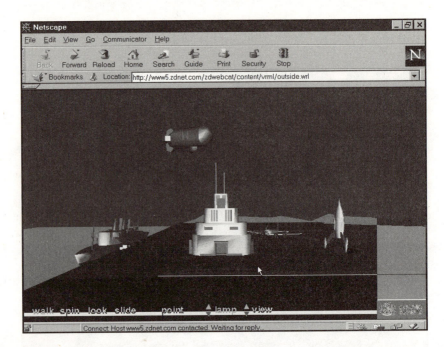

VRML Hazards

Don't go too crazy downloading and installing a bunch of VRML browsers. Most browsers are four or more megabytes as compressed files, and can consume as much as ten megabytes when installed. VRML files are no lightweights either. Make sure you have enough disk space before proceeding.

Using Netscape's Cosmo Player

One of the best VRML browsers out there is Netscape's own Cosmo Player. If you downloaded and installed the version of Communicator with plug-ins, you already have Cosmo Player, and Navigator is set up to use it.

Chapter 14 ➤ *Exploring Java, Shockwave, and Virtual Worlds*

Cosmo Player is a plug-in for Navigator, so you don't have to set it up as a helper application. As soon as you click on a link for a VRML file (most end in .gz or .wrl), Navigator downloads the file and starts playing it.

Navigating with Cosmo Player

To see how this VRML thing works, connect to ZD3D Terminal Reality, the world you saw earlier in the chapter at **http://www5.zdnet.com/zdwebcat/content/vrml/outside.wrl**. When you first connect, the world will look dark. Click on **lamp** at the bottom of the window to light the world.

Unlike most virtual worlds or 3-D objects you'll encounter on the Web, Terminal Reality has hotlinks. If you move the mouse pointer over the cruise liner, building, plane, blimp, or rocket, a brief description of the link appears, telling you where the link will take you if you click on it.

> **Techno Talk**
>
> **GZ Files**
> GZ stands for GZip, a compression utility used to squish VRML files so they take up less hard disk space and travel faster through the phone lines. Most VRML browsers have a built-in decompression utility that automatically decompresses GZipped files, so you don't have to worry about it.

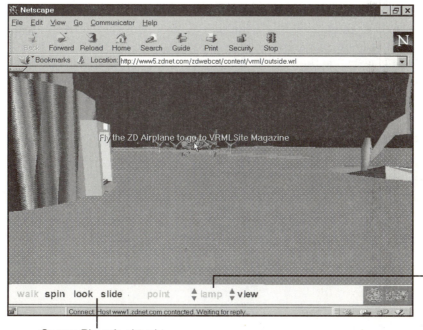

Cosmo Player supplies the controls you need to explore.

Click on lamp to light the world.

Cosmo Player's virtual world controls

157

At the bottom of the window are Cosmo Player's controls. You've already used the lamp button to light the world. Most of the other buttons control your movement through the world. For example, if you click on the walk button, you can drag the mouse in the viewing area to saunter through the streets and approach objects. Here's a list of all the buttons and what they do:

walk lets you walk through the scene. Drag the mouse pointer or use the arrow keys to walk.

spin pivots the world on an imaginary center point. Click on this option and then drag the mouse to spin the world or object in three-dimensional space. If this option is off, you can right-drag to spin.

look lets you move your point of view. You're standing still, moving your head to focus in on different areas of the world or on different objects, but you can't approach these objects, as you can with the walk option.

slide shifts the world up, down, left, or right when you drag the mouse. If this option is off, you can Alt+drag to slide.

point takes you closer to an object. Point and click on an object, and you'll walk right up to it. If this option is off, you can Ctrl+click to point.

lamp illuminates the scene. Click on it again to turn off the lights.

view returns you to the original view of the world.

For additional controls, try right-clicking inside the viewing area. This displays a shortcut menu with gobs of options. Some sites offer a bunch of rooms or viewpoints where you can go in a hurry. Right-click inside the viewing area, point to **View Points**, and click on the desired viewpoint.

VRML Control Panel

Unlike Java applets, each of which comes with its own set of controls, VRML worlds have no built-in controls. The VRML browser supplies the controls, so you'll be working with the same controls no matter which world you explore.

Chapter 14 ➤ *Exploring Java, Shockwave, and Virtual Worlds*

Exploring Some Worlds

Terminal Reality is one of the best worlds you'll find on the Web. Other places might just provide VRML objects, such as trees, spheres, and cones that you can spin around in three-dimensional space (oh boy!). So as you hunt for other worlds, don't get your hopes up.

I'll take you to a couple other worlds on the Web that offer some neat features that you won't find in other worlds. When you're done here, assuming you want to explore some more worlds on your own, pull up a Web search page and search for **VRML world**. The resulting list should give you plenty of links to explore.

First, let's drop by the VRML Mall at…. I have to warn you before you enter this URL. This Mall is huge. And when I say huge, I mean it's going to take you a good part of your adult life to download it. (Don't try downloading it with a 28.8 Kbps or slower modem.) I wrote most of this chapter while waiting for the Mall to open. The VRML mall is a virtual world that acts as sort of a mega-mall where you can shop for other VRML worlds. To shop at the mall go to **http://www.ocnus.com/models/mall.wrl**. When the world finally arrives, you can enter the mall and click on links to load other worlds.

Okay, now you've mastered all the controls, right? Right-click on a spot in the viewing area. A pop-up menu appears giving you about a hundred more navigational options. Point to **View Points**, and you'll get a list of rooms that group the worlds in categories, such as Animals or People. Click on the desired group.

For some fun, visit Grafman's VR World at **http://www.graphcomp.com/vrml/**. This site has a few offbeat characters from the world of animation that you can take control of and have a little fun. Don't leave without visiting the virtual-reality, randomly generated bunny or the virtual snowman. Grafman's virtual gallery is also a visual treat, although it takes a while to download.

As you wander and explore, you might also want to check out some of the worlds at Planet 9. When Planet 9 first started, the worlds were no match for ZD3D, but they have since made ZD3D look amateurish. You'll feel as though you're moving through some advanced gaming world as you explore. You can go to Planet 9 at page **http://www.planet9.com**. When you get there, use links to find the various virtual worlds and cities.

At Planet 9, you can visit several virtual cities, including Las Vegas.

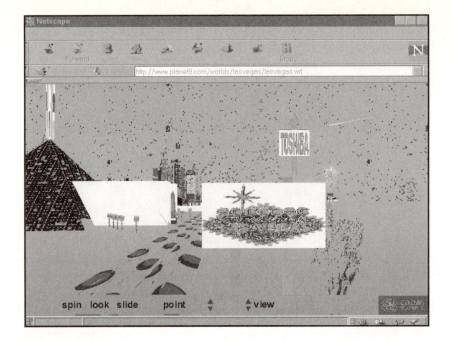

Other VRML Browsers

Cosmo Player is no slouch in the VRML department. Its simple controls and the point option are enough to get my vote for top VRML browser of the year. I've used about ten other browsers, and Cosmo Player stacks up with the best of them. WIRL and Pioneer are the other two VRML browsers I would recommend. Here's where you can get them if you're interested in taking them for a test drive:

> WIRL: **http://www.vream.com/3wirl.html**
>
> Pioneer: **http://www.caligari.com/**

Another browser that has received positive reviews is *VRealm*, although I find its controls infuriatingly frustrating. *VR Scout* isn't bad. It offers simple controls, like those used in Cosmo Player, but when you drag the mouse pointer to move an object, it's likely to fly off your screen. *WebSpace* is another popular browser with lousy controls. And last, but not least, is *WorldView*, which has the best-looking opening screen of all VRML browsers. When you start it, WorldView displays a spinning globe. WorldView looks more like a Web browser than a VRML browser, but it's positioning itself in the market for when the Web goes entirely 3D... sometime in the next century.

Chapter 14 ➤ *Exploring Java, Shockwave, and Virtual Worlds*

The Least You Need to Know

With all the new interactive files and programs on the Web, it's tough to stay abreast of all the changes, or even speculate on where the Web is going. However, Java, VRML, and Shockwave have established themselves as the prime tools for creating and playing interactive Web pages. As you play, keep the following in mind:

➤ Java applets are small applications that are typically embedded in Web pages.

➤ Navigator is a Java-enabled Web browser, so it can play Java applets without the help of a plug-in or helper application.

➤ Shockwave allows you to play interactive games and presentations created with Macromedia's AuthorWare, Director, and other authoring tools.

➤ Navigator comes with its own VRML browser, called Cosmo Player, but you can install and use other VRML browsers in its place.

Part 4
Talking to Other People

Futurists predicted that the '90s would be the Information Age. They were wrong. With people toting around cellular phones, jabbering in Internet chat rooms, penning millions of e-mail messages each day, and posting personal pages on the Web, the '90s have become the Golden Age of Communication.

In this part, you'll learn how to use Netscape Communicator's communicator tools, which can help you join the age of communication. You'll learn how to quickly send e-mail messages, read and post messages in newsgroups, place long-distance voice calls over the Internet, and even have virtual conference meetings (assuming you can get someone else to show up).

Chapter 15

Corresponding with Electronic Mail

In This Chapter

➤ Send a letter without licking a postage stamp

➤ Put your e-mail address on your business card

➤ Grab mail from your mailbox

➤ Use Composer's fancy formatting options to make your e-mail missives look like Web pages

The U.S. Postal Service has made all sorts of improvements in an attempt to make their service more attractive. You want me to name one? Okay, they released the Marilyn Monroe stamp. Oh yeah, and they came out with those self-adhesive stamps, so you can still taste your coffee after applying the stamp.

But the mail is still slow. A letter you send today usually takes several days to reach its destination. Fortunately, the Internet has provided an alternative: *electronic mail* (*e-mail* for short). This postage-free alternative sends e-mail across the country, or around the world, in a matter of minutes or hours instead of days. In this chapter, you'll learn how to send and receive e-mail using Netscape Messenger.

How E-Mail Works

Everyone who uses the Internet has a personal e-mail address, which usually consists of the person's username and the domain of the service provider (for example, jsmith@aol.com). Each user also has an e-mail "box," in which incoming messages are stored. Whenever you send an e-mail message, it is placed in the person's e-mail box, where it stays until the person uses her e-mail program to read it. E-mail programs, such as Netscape Messenger, allow you to compose and send e-mail messages to other Internet users and read messages that arrive in your inbox. If you're not sure what your e-mail address is, check with your service provider.

Running Netscape Messenger

Because Netscape Messenger is a component of Netscape Communicator, there are all sorts of ways to run Messenger. To run Messenger by itself, open the Windows **Start** menu, point to **Programs**, point to **Netscape Communicator**, and click on **Netscape Messenger**. You can also run Messenger from the other Communicator components:

➤ In Navigator, Collabra, or Composer, open the **Communicator** menu and click on **Messenger Mailbox**.

➤ In the Component bar, click on the **Mailbox** button. (Remember, the Component Bar appears in the lower right corner of the window or as a floating toolbar.)

➤ To display a window for creating a message to send, open the **File** menu, point to **New**, and click on **Message**.

➤ To have Messenger start automatically when you double-click on the Netscape Communicator icon, open the **Edit** menu, select **Preferences**, and click on **Appearance**. Under **On Startup Launch**, click on **Messenger Mailbox**.

You Have to Set It Up First

As with anything on the Internet, e-mail requires some setup before you can use it. You have to enter your return address, specify an e-mail server (sort of like a P.O. Box number), and enter your name. Although this takes a little longer than it takes to lick a postage stamp, it's almost as easy and you only have to do it once!

Chapter 15 ➤ *Corresponding with Electronic Mail*

The most important Messenger settings you need to enter concern the address of the server that's in charge of handling incoming and outgoing e-mail messages. To enter the required information, you must edit the Mail & Groups preferences. Here's what you do:

1. Open the **Edit** menu and select **Preferences**. (You can do this in Navigator, Messenger, or any of the other Communicator components.)

2. Click on the plus sign next to **Mail & Groups** to display a list of categories.

3. Click **Identity**, and enter the following information in the Identity panel:

    Your name: This is your legal name (for example, John Smith).

    Email address: This is the address people will use to write to you or respond to your messages. E-mail addresses typically start with your username or number, followed by the at sign (@) followed by the domain name of your Internet service provider. For example, an America Online member might have an e-mail address that looks like **studlyfox@aol.com**.

    Reply-to address: If you want people to reply to an e-mail address other than the e-mail address you entered above (for instance, if you have two e-mail accounts), enter the preferred e-mail address here.

    Organization: If you work for a company or run your own business, you can enter its name here.

    Signature File: A signature is a file you create (typically in a text editor) that includes additional information about you, or a clever quote. (For instructions on how to set up a signature file, see "Identify Yourself," near the end of this chapter.)

4. Click **Mail Server**, and enter the following information in the Mail Server panel:

    Mail server user name: This is the username you use to log in to your Internet account (for example, jsmith).

    Outgoing mail (SMTP) server: This is the address of the server in charge of handling outgoing mail. It usually starts with "mail" or "pop" followed by your service provider's domain name. For example, if your e-mail address were **jsmith@internet.com**, your outgoing server's address would be **mail.internet.com**.

> **Incoming mail server:** This is the address of the server that handles incoming e-mail messages. This entry typically starts with "pop," followed by your service provider's domain name. For example, if your e-mail address were **jsmith@internet.com**, your incoming server's address would be **pop.internet.com**.
>
> **Mail Server type:** Choose the type of server used for incoming mail: POP or IMAP. Obtain this information from your service provider.

5. Click the **OK** button to save your settings and close the dialog box. If you have trouble connecting to your mail server later, perform these same steps to change settings or correct any typos you might have made.

You can enter other customization options by opening the **Edit** menu, selecting **Preferences**, and clicking on the other options under Mail & Groups. For details, see "Configuring Netscape Messenger," later in this chapter. However, before you start messing with customization options, move on to the next sections to learn the basics of sending and reading e-mail.

Writing (and Sending) an E-Mail Message

Once you've entered your e-mail settings, you can start churning out e-mail messages. Click the **New Msg** button in the toolbar. The Message Composition window appears. You can also open this window by performing any of the following steps:

➤ Open the **File** menu, point to **New**, and click **Message**. (Perform the same steps in Messenger, Composer, Navigator, or Collabra.)

➤ Press **Ctrl+M**. This works in Messenger, Navigator, or Collabra.

➤ To send a Web page via e-mail, first display the page you want to send in Navigator or Composer, and then open the **File** menu and select **Send Page**.

➤ Some Web pages have a link that you can click on to send a person an e-mail message. If you click on the link, Navigator runs Messenger and displays the Composition window.

Click inside the **To** text box, and type the e-mail address of the person to whom you're sending the message. For example, you might type **cmiller@aol.com**. Click inside the **Subject** text box, and type a brief description of the message. Now, click inside the big message area at the bottom of the dialog box, and type your message. Assuming you want to send only the message you typed, click the **Send** button to send it. If you want to format the text, attach a file, send a copy of the message to someone else, or enter some other fancy options, read on.

Chapter 15 ➤ Corresponding with Electronic Mail

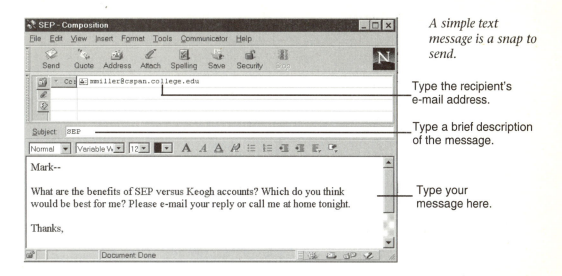

A simple text message is a snap to send.

Type the recipient's e-mail address.

Type a brief description of the message.

Type your message here.

Pronouncing an E-Mail Address

If you want to be cool, you have to be able to pronounce your e-mail address properly. If your address is jsmith@weidner.cyber.edu, you would say, "jsmith at weidner dot cyber dot edu." Just remember that @ = "at" and . = "dot." E-mail addresses are usually in lowercase, so you don't have to specify case unless one or more characters is uppercase.

Attaching Files to E-Mail Messages

To send a file along with your e-mail message, click the **Attach** button and select one of the following options:

File Sends a file that's on your hard disk (such as a graphic or sound file or a document you created). Use the dialog box that appears to select the drive, folder, and name of the file you want to send, and then click on the **Open** button. (You can send more than one file by selecting **Attach, File** again.)

Web Page Sends the Web document that's currently displayed in Navigator. Just click on the **OK** button. You can then select **As Is** to send it as an HTML document (a Web page) or select **Convert to Plain Text** to send the Web document as a text file.

My address book card Ignore this option for now. You will learn how to use an address book card in Chapter 17, "Creating and Using an Address Book."

169

After selecting the file(s) or Web page you want to send, click the **OK** or **Open** button. You're returned to the Composition window, and the file's name(s) is inserted in the **Attachment** text box.

Another way to attach files is to click on the **Attach Files & Documents** tab (just below the To tab), and then click on the blank area to the right of the tab. This opens the Enter file to attach dialog box, which prompts you to select a file from your hard drive. Select the desired file, and click **Open**. You can repeat the step to attach additional files.

When you're ready to send your message (along with any attached file), click the **Send** button. Or, open the **File** menu and select **Send Now** or **Send Later** (Send Later is useful if you are composing messages offline to reduce connect charges). Messenger sends the message. Because the message may take any of several paths on the Internet, it may arrive in seconds, minutes, or hours. Mail typically bounces around several Internet sites before reaching its destination (especially if there's a lot of traffic).

Getting Fancy with Formatting Tools and Graphics

In and of itself, Netscape Messenger is an excellent e-mail program. What makes Messenger really excel, however, is its integration with Netscape Composer. You can use Composer's formatting tools in Messenger to change the size, color, or style of your text; to insert graphics and lines; to add lists; and to insert tables.

Before you go through the trouble of using these fancy formatting options, make sure the recipient's e-mail program can display the message in all its glory. If the recipient is using the current version of Netscape Messenger or Microsoft's Internet Mail, you're safe, but most older e-mail programs cannot display graphics or formatted text. In such cases, the recipient will be able to read the text part of the message, but all the fancy formatting will appear only as a bunch of ugly Web codes that make the text difficult to read.

As with most text formatting options, you can format your text before or after you type it. If you are formatting existing text, drag over the text before selecting the desired format. You can apply most text formatting via the Composer toolbar, as shown in the following table.

The Composer Toolbar's Formatting Controls

This Control		Does This
Normal ▼	Paragraph Style	Lets you format the text in an entire paragraph. Open the drop-down list, and select the desired style.
Variable W ▼	Font	Lets you pick a different type style for selected text.

This Control		Does This
`12 ▼`	Font Size	Provides a list of seven text sizes from -2 (smallest) to +4 (largest).
	Font Color	Sets the color of selected text.
A	Bold	Makes text bold.
A	Italic	Makes text italic.
A	Underline	Underlines text.
	Remove All Styles	Removes all fancy formatting.
	Bullet List	Transforms selected paragraphs into a bulleted list.
	Numbered List	Transforms selected paragraphs into a numbered list.
	Decrease Indent	Decreases the distance that text is indented from the left margin.
	Increase Indent	Increases the distance that text is indented from the left margin.
	Alignment	Lets you select from a list of alignment options: Left, Right, or Centered.
	Insert Object	Displays a list of objects you can insert: Link (to a page or resource on the Internet), Target (to point to a specific place on a linked page), Image (to insert a picture), Horizontal Line (for dividing sections of text), and Table (to arrange text in rows and columns).

Although the Composer toolbar offers the most common formatting options, you can access these same options and additional options via the Format menu and the Insert menu. For example, to format text, open the **Format** menu, and select **Font**. This displays the Font dialog box, shown in the following figure, which gives you much more control over the appearance of your text. These formatting options are explained in greater detail in Chapter 23, "Formatting and Publishing Your Page," in relation to using the formatting tools to spruce up Web pages.

The Font dialog box gives you more text formatting options.

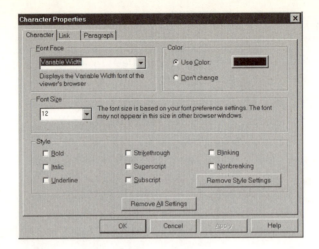

If you have a graphic file on disk, you can insert it in your e-mail message (although images slow the message transfer). Position the insertion point where you want the image inserted. Click on the **Insert Object** button, and click on **Insert Image**. The Image Properties dialog box appears, prompting you to pick a graphic. Click on the **Choose File** button, use the Choose Image File dialog box to pick the graphic file you want to insert, and then click **Open**.

You can enter additional settings to control the way text wraps around the image and to change the size and dimensions of the image. These settings are discussed in Chapter 20, "Making a Simple Web Page." For now, simply click on the **OK** button. Composer inserts the selected image into your e-mail message. You can drag the image to move it or drag one of its edges to resize it.

Sending a Copy of the Message to Another Person

Sometimes, you must send the same message to several people. For example, say you're having a party and you want to invite all your online pals. You can send one message and have it go to all the people you want to invite. To address a message to more than one person, simply address the message to the first person, and then click on the box below the **To** button (or simply press **Enter**). This inserts another To button and places the insertion point in the text box next to it. Keep clicking and typing until you have entered an e-mail address for each recipient.

If you select the To option to send a copy to another person, the copy is sent just as if you had e-mailed the message separately to that person. There are a couple other ways to send the message to another person. Click the **To** button, and select any of the following options:

- **Cc** (carbon copy) sends a duplicate message to a second person, and notifies the main recipient that you sent a copy of the message to someone else.

- **Bcc** (blind carbon copy) sends a duplicate message to a second person, but does not notify the main recipient that you sent a copy of the message to someone else. (Pretty sneaky, eh?)

- **Group** posts the message in a newsgroup, rather than sending the message to a specific person. See Chapter 18, "Reading and Posting Newsgroup Messages," for details.

- **Reply-To** does not send a copy of the e-mail message to another address. It tells the main recipient to send any reply to the e-mail address you type as the Reply-To address. When the recipient receives your e-mail and enters the Reply command, the e-mail program will automatically address the reply to the Reply-To address, not to your address.

- **Followup-To** is similar to the Reply-To option. It tells the main recipient to send any follow-up messages to an e-mail address other than yours.

Entering Other Message Options

To the left of the area that you use to address your message are three tabs: Address Message, Attach Files & Documents, and Message Sending Options. The Address Message tab displays the text boxes into which you type the recipients' addresses. The Attach Files & Documents tab displays a list of the files you are sending as attachments. The Message Sending Options tab lets you enter the following settings:

Encrypted codes the message to prevent people from peeking at it in transit. The message is decoded by the recipient's e-mail program.

Signed inserts a signature at the end of the message. A signature is a file you create (typically in a text editor) that includes additional information about you, or a clever quip.

Uuencode instead of MIME for Attachments allows you to use Uuencode to encode attached documents and files. Select this option only if you know that the recipient's e-mail program is set up to use Uudecode to receive attachments.

Return Receipt tells the recipient's mail server to automatically send you a confirmation message when the recipient retrieves the message. This lets you know that the person received your message.

Priority lets you specify how important the message is. Some e-mail programs, including Messenger, can display the importance of a message next to the message's description.

Format is initally set to Ask Me, so Messenger displays a dialog box whenever you send a message, asking if you want to send it with fancy formatting or as a plain text message. You can choose to send this message as plain text, with HTML codes (fancy formatting), or as a mix of text and HTML.

Composing Mail Offline

If you have a bunch of messages to write and send, consider composing the messages offline (when you are not connected to the Internet), so you don't tie up your service provider's computer and rack up additional connect-time charges. Simply run Netscape Messenger without connecting to the Internet. After composing a message, open the **File** menu, and select **Send Later** to place the message in the Outbox (on your hard drive). To send the messages later, connect to the Internet, run Messenger, open the **File** menu, and select **Send Now**.

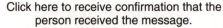

Click here to receive confirmation that the person received the message.

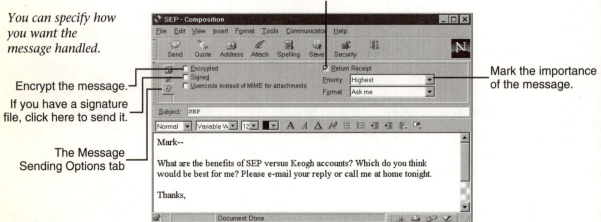

You can specify how you want the message handled.

Encrypt the message.

If you have a signature file, click here to send it.

The Message Sending Options tab

Mark the importance of the message.

Reading and Responding to Incoming Mail

As with paper mail, once you start sending e-mail and telling people your e-mail address, e-mail messages will start to arrive in your inbox. You need some way to connect to the e-mail server (where incoming messages are stored), retrieve your messages, and read them. The following sections explain how to use Messenger to retrieve and read incoming messages and respond to them.

Retrieving and Reading Your Mail

To read incoming e-mail messages, start Messenger using any of the techniques explained earlier in this chapter. Click on the **Get Msg** button, or press **Ctrl+T**. A dialog box appears, prompting you to type your e-mail password (this is usually the same as the login password supplied by your service provider). Type your password and click **OK**. Messenger checks your electronic mailbox. If you haven't received any mail, a dialog box appears, telling you that your box is empty (I hate when that happens). Click **OK**.

If you do have mail, Messenger retrieves it and displays a list of message descriptions. Double-click on a message description to display the contents of the message in its own window. Another way to read a message is to click on its description. If you have a window that's split into two panes, the contents of the message appear in the lower pane. If your window has only one pane, click on the blue triangle in the lower left corner of the window. This splits the window into two panes; the top pane displays a list of message descriptions, and the bottom pane displays the contents of the currently selected message. You can drag the divider between the panes to change their relative sizes.

In Chapter 16, "Managing Your E-Mail Messages," you will learn how to use this window to delete messages, move them to other folders, view messages you have sent, and much more.

Whether you display a message in its own window or use the main message window, you can move from one message to the next by clicking on the **Next** button. You can also use the commands on the **Go** menu to scroll through the messages: **Next Message**, **Next Unread Message**, **Previous Message**, or **Previous Unread Message**, and so on.

Part 4 ➤ *Talking to Other People*

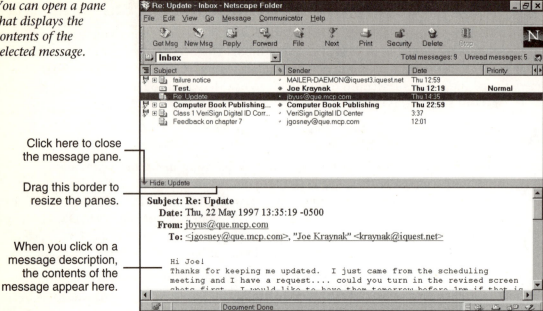

You can open a pane that displays the contents of the selected message.

Click here to close the message pane.

Drag this border to resize the panes.

When you click on a message description, the contents of the message appear here.

Viewing and Saving Attachments

If the incoming e-mail message contains an attachment, Messenger automatically downloads the attachment and places it in a temporary storage area on your hard drive. The message itself will contain a link that points to the file. You can open the file as if you were working in Navigator; simply click on the link. Messenger then runs the program associated with the attachment's file type and opens the attachment in that program (or in Navigator, if Navigator can display the file).

You can also save the attachment to a specific folder on your hard drive. Right-click on the link, and click on **Save Link As**. Use the Save As dialog box to pick the folder in which you want the attached file placed, and click **Save**.

Responding to Messages

As you read your mail, you will undoubtedly want to respond to a message, especially if you're caught up in a flame war with your ex.

To respond to an e-mail message, first click the message to which you want to respond. Now, you have a couple options—you can reply to the sender, or (if the person sent the message to other people) you can reply to everyone. Take one of the following steps:

- ▶ To reply only to the sender, press **Ctrl+R**. To reply to the sender and to all the people that the original message was sent to, press **Ctrl+Shift_R**.

- ▶ Click on the **Reply** button, and click on **Reply to Sender** or **Reply to Sender and All Recipients**. (These options are also available on the Message Reply menu.)

- ▶ To forward the message to someone else, without responding to it yourself, click on the **Forward** button or press **Ctrl+L**. (If you forward a message, you can still type your own message. It will be attached to the message you forward.)

The dialog box that appears looks a lot like the dialog box you saw earlier in this chapter (when you sent your first e-mail message). The only difference is that the Send To and Subject text boxes are already filled in for you. Type your message inside the message area, add any attachments, and click the **Send** button.

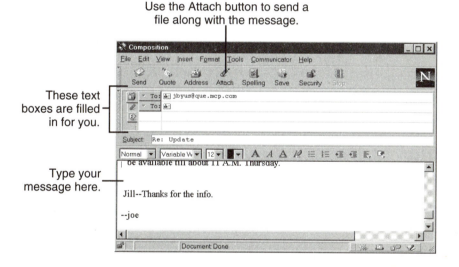

Use the Attach button to send a file along with the message.

These text boxes are filled in for you.

Type your message here.

You can quickly reply to any e-mail message you receive.

Quoting the Previous Message in Your Reply

When you respond to a message, sometimes it's a good idea to quote a portion of the message to which you are replying. This quote provides a context for your reply and helps the other person recall what he or she said. By default, Messenger inserts quotes in the original message in your reply. To turn off this option, open the **Edit** menu, select **Preferences**, click the plus sign next to **Mail & Groups**, click **Messages**, and click **Automatically quote original message when replying**.

If you turn off the automatic quote option, you can quickly quote a message by clicking on the **Quote** button. The quoted text is inserted after the insertion point, and a right angle bracket (>) is inserted at the beginning of each quoted line.

Now, don't get carried away with quotes. Every day I receive e-mail messages that include quotes from entire conversations. These messages clog the arteries of the Internet and consume unnecessary space on the e-mail server (not to mention the space on my hard drive). If you must use the Quote button, go back into the message area and delete all but the most essential lines of the quote.

Right-Click Menus

You can save a lot of time in the Mail window by using your right mouse button. To reply to a message, right-click on its description, and click **Reply to Sender**. To delete a message, right-click and select **Delete**. Try right-clicking on various items in the Mail window to see which options are available for each item.

Configuring Netscape Messenger

Now that you have mastered the basics of composing and reading messages, you may want to configure Messenger to save yourself some time and to make it conform to the way you work.

To customize Messenger, open Messenger's **Edit** menu, select **Preferences**, and click on the plus sign next to **Mail & Groups**. This displays the preferences for Netscape Messenger, as shown in the following figure.

You can change Messenger's appearance and make it work the way you want it to.

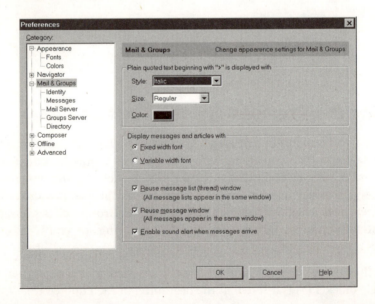

The following sections explain many of the customization options. However, some of the customization options are for creating an address book and for managing your messages; those options are explained in detail in Chapters 16 and 17.

Changing the Way Messages Are Displayed

With **Mail & Groups** selected, you can change any of the settings to control the way messages appear:

- ➤ The first couple options let you control the appearance of quoted text. By default, when you reply to a message, Messenger inserts text from the message to which you are responding in order to help the recipient keep track of the conversation. You can use the Style, Size, and Color buttons to change the way this quoted text is displayed.

- ➤ The options under **Display messages and articles with** allow you to pick a font for the text that makes up messages you receive. A fixed-width font gives each character the same amount of space, an anorexic "i" gets the same space as a corpulent "m." A variable width font gives each character the room it needs.

- ➤ The **Reuse message list (thread) window** option tells Messenger to display all the message lists in a single window. If you turn this option off, Messenger opens a new message list window whenever you choose a different message folder (such as Outbox or Sent).

- ➤ The **Reuse message window** option tells Messenger to use the same window to display the contents of any message you double-click on. If you turn this option off, Messenger displays the contents of each message you double-click on in its own separate window, which can quickly clutter your desktop.

- ➤ **Enable sound alert when messages arrive** simply tells Messenger to sound a beep when you receive messages.

Changing Options for Outgoing Mail

To change the options for outgoing messages, click Messages (below Mail & Group). The Messages panel has a bunch of options you can safely ignore. The options you want to focus on are right at the top of the panel. To have Messenger automatically quote messages when you reply to them, make sure there is a check mark next to **Automatically quote original message when replying.** If you don't use any fancy formatting in your e-mail messages, remove the check from the **By default send HTML messages** box. That gets rid of Composer's toolbar and prevents you from inadvertently adding formatting codes that a recipient's e-mail program can't handle.

As for the other options on the Messages panel, here's a quick rundown, so you'll know why you don't need to mess with them:

Wrap long lines at ___ characters tells Messenger to automatically wrap long lines of text, so the recipient does not have to experience funky line breaks. Enter a number no larger than 72.

Automatically email a copy of outgoing messages to lets you specify an e-mail address of someone to whom you want to send a copy of all the e-mail messages you send. I guess this option is designed for those who have to justify their worth as human beings. You can choose **Self**, if you need to justify your worth as a human being to yourself.

Automatically copy outgoing messages to a folder allows you to specify a folder in which to save the mail you send and the messages you post to newsgroups. You'll learn more about this option in Chapter 16. For now, just ponder the question of why you might want to e-mail a copy of outgoing messages to yourself when Messenger automatically saves a copy of all outgoing messages in a separate folder anyway.

The Least You Need to Know

If you really want to get into this e-mail thing, check out any of the many e-mail books at your friendly neighborhood bookstore. However, if you just want to send and receive e-mail messages through Netscape Messenger, you have to know only four things:

1. To send an e-mail message, run **Messenger**, and click on the **New Msg** button.
2. To check for incoming messages, run **Messenger**, and click on the **Get Msg** button.
3. To read an e-mail message, double-click on the description of the message in the list of messages.
4. To reply to a message that's currently displayed, click on the **Reply** button.

Chapter 16

Managing Your E-Mail Messages

In This Chapter

➤ Manage all your e-mail and news postings from the Netscape Message Center

➤ Dump old e-mail in the trash

➤ Create your own inbox folders

➤ Compact folders to conserve drive space

As the mail starts pouring in, you'll soon become a prolific writer, even if you never had any intentions of becoming a prolific writer. Soon, your landfill... er, inbox, will be heaped with messages and ongoing dialogs with friends, relatives, and colleagues. You need some way to organize this opus, and clean it up.

Fortunately, Netscape Messenger contains all the management tools you need to group, delete, copy, and move messages. It even comes with the equivalent of a trash compactor, which you can use to remove the free space left behind when you delete messages from your Inbox.

Using the Message Window and Message Center

To organize your mail, you can use either of two windows: the Message (Inbox) window or the Message Center. You saw the Message window in the previous chapter. It displays a list of messages you received. You read a message by double-clicking on its description. The Message Center is a better tool for creating and managing the various folders in which Messenger stores messages: the Inbox, Outbox, Drafts, Sent, and Trash folders. Before we get into the specifics of using these windows to manage your messages and folders, let's take a look at some of the basic controls that these windows offer.

Taking Control of the Message Window

You know how to use the Message window to read the messages you received. In Chapter 15, "Corresponding with Electronic Mail," you even learned how to display the message content pane, to display the content of the selected message at the bottom of the window. Following are additional ways you can change how the Message window displays your messages (see the following figure):

Change Folders: This drop-down list (just above the message pane) lets you select the folder that contains the messages you want to work with: Inbox (messages you received), Outbox (messages you chose to Send Later), Trash (messages you deleted), Drafts (messages you saved as drafts), Sent (messages you have sent), and Unsent Messages (messages you chose to send later).

Resize Column Headings: Above each column in the list of messages is a column heading (Subject, Sender, Date, and so on). You can drag the line that separates these headings to resize the columns. For example, you may want to give your message descriptions more room.

Move Column Headings: You can drag a column heading to the left or right to move a column. For example, you might want to place the Sender names first.

Sort Messages: You can click on a column heading to sort the messages according to the entries in that column. For example, to sort the messages by date, click on Date at the top of the date column. Click the column heading again to flip the sort order; for instance, if you sort by date, you can click the Date again to switch from earliest messages first to earliest messages last. The column heading all the way on the left expands the list to show all related messages.

Display More Columns: The Message window does not initially display all the available columns. On the far right end of the column heading bar are two buttons that let you display or hide columns. Click the left arrow button to display more columns or the right arrow button to hide columns.

Chapter 16 ➤ *Managing Your E-Mail Messages*

Go To Message Center: All the way on the right, just above the column headings is the Message Center button. You can click this button to display the Message Center window, described in the following section.

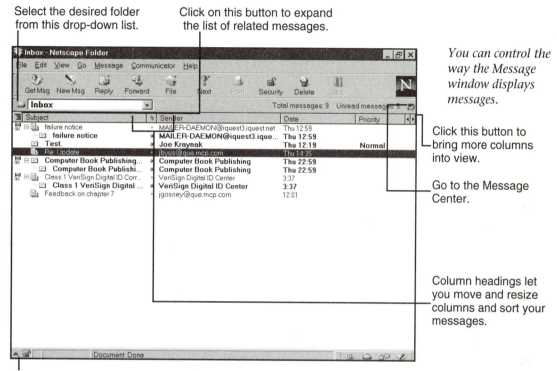

Select the desired folder from this drop-down list.

Click on this button to expand the list of related messages.

You can control the way the Message window displays messages.

Click this button to bring more columns into view.

Go to the Message Center.

Column headings let you move and resize columns and sort your messages.

This button displays the message contents pane.

Nickel Tour of the Message Center

The Message center provides a communications hub from which you can access both e-mail messages and newsgroups. It doesn't display a list of messages, but it does display all the Messenger folders and the names of any newsgroups you have subscribed to (or will subscribe to in Chapter 18, "Reading and Posting Newsgroup Messages"). You can go to the Message Center by clicking on the Message Center button, as explained in the previous section, or by selecting **Communicator, Message Center** from any of the other Communicator programs (or press **Ctrl+Shift+1**). As you can see in the following figure, the Message Center is ideal for working with folders, but lacks features for working with individual messages.

183

The Message Center displays a list of folders for storing messages.

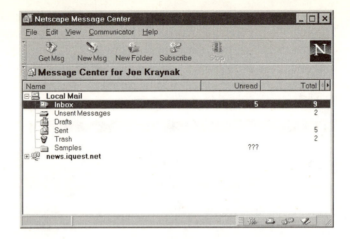

Organizing Messages with Folders

The first step in reorganizing your messages is to create a folder. For example, you might create a folder for each person you frequently correspond with or one for business and one for personal messages. To create a folder, take the following steps:

1. Go to the Message Center.

2. Click on the folder below which you want the new folder to be created. To place the folder on the same level as the Inbox folder, click on **Local Mail** at the top of the folder list.

3. Open the **File** menu and select **New Folder**. The New Folder dialog box appears, prompting you to type a name for the folder.

4. Type a name for the folder, and click **OK**. The new folder appears. You can now copy and move messages to this new folder, as explained in the next section.

Selecting, Moving, Copying, and Deleting Messages

Whenever you receive a message, the message is added to the Inbox folder. When you send messages, they're added to the Sent folder. These folders quickly become overcrowded, making it nearly impossible to find a specific message later. To help, you can create folders, as explained in the previous section, and then move messages to the folders you created.

Chapter 16 ▶ *Managing Your E-Mail Messages*

Before you can move messages, you must select them. You can select a single message by clicking on its name. To select additional messages, hold down the **Ctrl** key while clicking on their names. You can select a range of neighboring messages by clicking on the top message in the range, and then holding down the **Shift** key while clicking on the bottom message in the range. The Edit, Select Message menu offers some fancy commands to select messages:

Thread   Selects all messages that have the same title.

Flagged   Selects all messages that you've flagged. To flag a message (mark it as important or as a message you want to respond to later), select the message, open the **Message** menu, and click on **Flag**.

All Messages   Selects all messages in the currently open folder.

After selecting the messages, you can quickly move them to a different folder. Right-click on any one of the selected messages, point to **File Message**, and click on the folder in which you want them moved. Another way to move messages is to click on the **File** button in the toolbar, and then select the folder from the file list, as shown in the following figure.

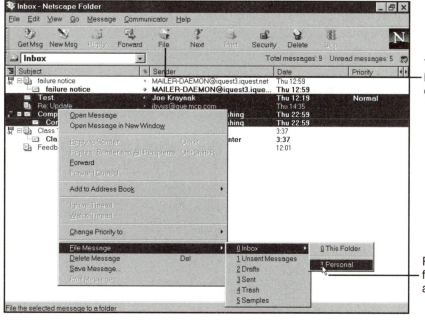

You can easily move selected messages to another folder.

You can click on the File button and select the destination folder.

Right-click on a selected file, point to File Message, and select the folder.

185

Taking Out the Trash You can quickly nuke all the messages in the Trash folder. Open the **File** menu and select **Empty Trash Folder**.

To delete messages, first select them, and then click the **Delete** button in the toolbar, or press the **Del** key. The deleted messages are sent to the Trash folder. If you delete a message by mistake, you can move it from the Trash folder to one of your other folders, as explained in the previous paragraph. If you delete a message from the Trash folder, it's gone for good.

As you delete messages from folders, Messenger removes the message but leaves a gap where the message used to be. This gap consumes disk space. To remove these gaps, you should *compress* your folders whenever you do any major clean-up. To compress your folders, open the **File** menu and select **Compress Folders**.

Telling Messenger Where to Place Incoming Messages

Once you have created specific folders, you can create *mail filters*, which tell Messenger where to store specific incoming messages. For example, say you create a folder for all your correspondence with Sharon Stone; you name the folder Sharon. Now, you want all incoming messages from Sharon Stone placed in this folder, so you don't have to move them later. Say Sharon's e-mail address is **sstone@hollywood.com**. You can create a mail filter that tells Messenger to place all messages from sstone@hollywood.com directly into the Sharon folder. Cool, huh? Let's do it:

1. Create the folder in which you want a group of specific messages stored.

2. Open the **Edit** menu and select **Mail Filters**. The Mail Filters dialog box appears.

3. Click on the **New** button. The Filter Rules dialog box appears, as shown in the following figure.

4. Type a name to help identify the filter (for example, Sharon's Letters).

5. Use the three controls below the filter name to enter instructions Messenger can use to identify these messages. In the figure, the instructions tell Messenger to look in the *Sender* field to see if it *contains* the text sstone@hollywood.com. (You can click the More button to add another filter and make your instructions even more specific.)

6. In the next line down, pick the desired action you want Messenger to perform on these messages. In the figure, the instructions tell Messenger to *Move to folder* specifically to the folder named *Sharon*.

7. Make sure the **Filter Is On** option button is selected at the bottom of the dialog box, and click **OK**. This returns you to the Mail Filters dialog box, where you can create another filter.

8. Repeat the steps to create additional mail filters, if desired. When you are done, click **OK**.

Is There Any Way to Filter Out Junk Mail?

Yes. If you're getting a lot of junk mail from a specific company, you can choose to automatically delete those messages. Create a mail filter to filter out messages from the address that's sending you the junk mail. Select **Delete** from the list of actions you want Messenger to perform. For a more permanent solution, write to the junk mail source and ask to have your name removed from its mailing list. USE ALL CAPS to get its attention.

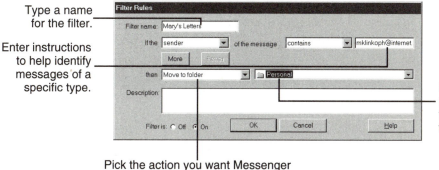

Type a name for the filter.

Enter instructions to help identify messages of a specific type.

Pick the action you want Messenger to take on these messages.

You can pick the folder in which you want specific incoming messages stored.

If you choose to move messages, pick the folder in which you want them placed.

Sorting Your Messages

Long lists of messages can become somewhat unwieldy. To help, Messenger can sort the messages for you by date, subject, and even by sender. To sort your messages, you can click on a column heading in the Message window, as explained earlier in this chapter.

187

Another way to sort messages is to double-click the folder whose messages you want to sort, open the **View** menu, point to **Sort**, and choose one of the following options:

by Date   Sorts messages by date. If you turn Ascending off, recent messages appear first in the list.

by Flag   Places flagged messages at the top or bottom of the list depending on the selected sort order (Ascending or Descending).

by Priority   Sorts messages according to importance, assuming that the sender specified a priority level.

by Sender   Sorts messages alphabetically by the sender's name.

by Size   Sorts by message size.

by Status   Places unread messages at the top of the list when Ascending is on or at the bottom of the list if Descending is on.

by Subject   Sorts messages alphabetically by their descriptions. With Ascending off, messages that start with Z would be listed before messages that start with A.

by Thread   Keeps all messages with the same description together, regardless of the date.

by Unread   Sorts the same way as if you selected by Status (go figure).

Ascending   Sorts messages in ascending order. For example, if you sort by date, earlier messages will be listed first. If you sort by subject, messages are sorted alphabetically, starting with A.

Descending   Sorts messages in descending order. For example, if you sort by date, more recent messages are placed at the bottom of the list.

Tracking Down Misplaced Messages

Although sorting can help you arrange messages in some logical order, you might still have trouble finding a specific message. Fortunately, Messenger can help. Open the **Edit** menu and select **Search Messages**. This displays a dialog box that prompts you to pick the folder(s) you want to search and enter unique text that the misplaced message contains.

Chapter 16 ➤ *Managing Your E-Mail Messages*

Making Messenger Check for Mail Automatically

If you stay connected to the Internet all day, you might want to set up Netscape's Mail Notification feature to have Messenger automatically check for incoming mail at a specified interval (say every 15 to 30 minutes). At the specified interval, Messenger logs in to your e-mail server, and notifies you (by beeping or displaying a special icon in the taskbar). To use Netscape Mail Notification, take the following steps:

1. Establish your Internet connection.

2. Select **Netscape Mail Notification** (from the Netscape Communicator Program group). In Windows 95, you would select **Start**, **Programs**, **Netscape Communicator**, **Utilities**, **Netscape Mail Notification**. A pinwheel icon appears on the right end of the Windows taskbar. The pinwheel spins whenever Mail Notification is checking for mail. If you have mail, the icon changes into a picture of an envelope with a waving red flag.

3. Rest the mouse pointer on the Mail Notification icon. A tool tip message pops up, indicating the number of new messages.

4. If you have new messages, right-click on the icon, and select **Run Mail**. The Messenger window appears. You can then click the **Get Msg** button to retrieve the messages.

5. To enter preferences for Netscape Mail Notification, right-click on its icon in the Windows taskbar, and click on **Options**. The Netscape Mail Properties dialog box appears, as shown in the following figure.

6. Enter the desired settings, and click **OK**. (The most important setting is the one that tells Mail Notification how often to check for new messages.)

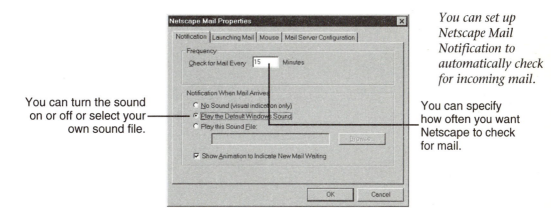

You can set up Netscape Mail Notification to automatically check for incoming mail.

You can turn the sound on or off or select your own sound file.

You can specify how often you want Netscape to check for mail.

189

The Least You Need to Know

You don't really need to know anything in this chapter to use e-mail, but once you know the following, you can run a clean, well-organized post office:

➤ Use the Message Center to create additional folders for storing your messages.

➤ To create a new folder, select the folder below which you want the new folder placed. Open the **File** menu and select **New Folder**.

➤ To move messages from one folder to another, select the messages, click on the **File** button, and click on the folder to which you want the messages moved.

➤ You can tell Messenger how to treat specific messages by creating a mail filter. Open the **Edit** menu and select **Mail Filters**.

➤ To find a misplaced message, open the **Edit** menu and select **Search Messages**.

➤ When you delete messages, they are placed in the Trash folder. To empty the trash, open the **File** menu and select **Empty Trash Folder**.

Chapter 17

Creating and Using an Address Book

In This Chapter

➤ Store the names and e-mail addresses of all your pen pals in an electronic address book

➤ *Insert* e-mail addresses instead of typing them

➤ Perform mass mailings to groups of selected recipients

➤ Make a business card and attach it to outgoing messages

Internet e-mail addresses are about as easy to remember as international phone numbers. They can be a combination of long usernames, disjointed numbers, and domain names that snake across the screen like the mighty Mississippi. Nobody expects you to remember these addresses, but if you don't enter them precisely as they appear, your mail will never reach its destination.

The solution to this problem is to create an e-mail address book. With an address book, you can address your e-mail messages simply by selecting a name from the book, rather than by typing the address. You can even create a group of recipients to automatically send them all the same message. In this chapter, you will learn how to use Messenger's address book.

Adding E-Mail Addresses to Messenger's Address Book

Messenger has a default address book, in which you can immediately start to insert e-mail addresses. To display this address book, open the **Communicator** menu (in Messenger, Navigator, or Collabra), and click **Address Book** (or press **Ctrl+Shift+2**). The Address Book window appears.

To add an e-mail address to your book, click the **New Card** button in the Address Book toolbar. The New Card dialog box appears with the Name tab up front, as shown below. Enter the person's first name, last name, and e-mail address in the appropriate text boxes. (You can move to a text box by tabbing or by clicking in it with the mouse.) You can also enter the person's username in the Nickname text box, and type any additional information in the Notes text box, although these entries are optional. (If you open your address book in Navigator as a Web page, any text in the Notes text box will be displayed.) To start a new line in this text box, press **Ctrl+Enter**. If the person prefers to receive text only messages, make sure there is no check in the **Prefers to receive rich text (HTML) mail** check box.

You can enter additional information about the person, including the person's mailing address and phone number. To enter this information, click on the **Contact** tab, and type entries in the appropriate text boxes. When you're done, click **OK**.

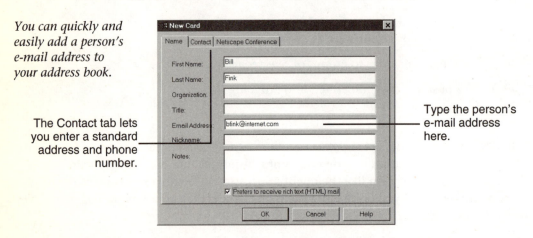

You can quickly and easily add a person's e-mail address to your address book.

The Contact tab lets you enter a standard address and phone number.

Type the person's e-mail address here.

To delete a person from your address book (sorry it didn't work out), click the person's name, and press the **Del** key (or click the **Delete** button).

Lifting E-Mail Addresses from Messages

In the previous section, you learned the standard way to add e-mail addresses to the Address Book. There's a much easier way, assuming that the person has sent you a message. Click on the message to select it (or double-click on it to display the message in its own window). Open the **Message** menu, point to **Add to Address Book**, and click on **Sender** (to add the e-mail address of the sender) or **All** (to add the e-mail addresses of all the recipients, assuming that this message was sent to additional recipients).

> **Save Your Address Book**
> Use the **File, Save As** command to save the address book. To use the addresses in the address book, use the **File, Import** command. This appends the addresses from the selected file to Messenger's default Address Book.

> **Editing an Address Book Entry**
> If your friend or relative moves or picks a new e-mail address, you'll have to change it. Open the Address Book window, and then double-click on the name of the person whose information you want to change (or right-click on the name, and select **Card Properties**). This opens the same dialog box you used to add the person to your address book.

Adding Addresses from Online E-Mail Directories

One of the coolest new features of Netscape Messenger is that it allows you to search e-mail directories on the Web and add any e-mail addresses you find to your address book. For example, say you're searching for long lost relatives to write to. You can search an online directory by last name and then add any e-mail addresses that the search discovers to your address book.

To search a directory, click on the **Directory** button in the Address Book window's toolbar. This opens the Search window. Open the **Search for Items** drop-down list, and click on the directory you want to search (for example, Four11 Directory). Use the three controls below the directory name to enter your search instructions. The following figure shows a search by name for records that contain the name Stucky. You can click on the **More** button and enter additional instructions to limit the search (for instance, you can specify a city or state). Click the **Search** button.

Assuming the search turned up some e-mail addresses, the addresses are listed at the bottom of the window. To add an address to the Address Book, click on the address, and then click on **Add to Address Book**.

Online directories can help you find e-mail addresses when you know the person's name.

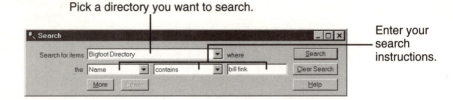

Pick a directory you want to search.

Enter your search instructions.

Importing an Address Book

Making the switch from one e-mail program to another is a drag. You spend hours creating an address book, and then you find that there's no way to use that address book in your new e-mail program. You have to create your new address book from scratch.

Messenger can't help you solve this problem. However, you may be able to import the names and addresses into Messenger's address book. First, check your e-mail program, to determine if there is any way to export the address book in a format compatible with Netscape Messenger (good luck!). If you get lucky and successfully export the addresses, you can then take the following steps to import them in Messenger's address book:

1. In the Address Book window, open the **File** menu and select **Import**. The Import Address Book File dialog box appears.

2. Select the file that contains the addresses you want to import, and click on the **Open** button. Messenger opens the file and adds its addresses to the Address Book.

Inserting Addresses from the Address Book

Now that you have some e-mail addresses in the address book, how do you use them? Here's what you do:

1. Display the Message Composition window for sending an e-mail message, and click inside the **To** text box.

2. Click the **Address** button in the toolbar. This displays your list of e-mail addresses.

Chapter 17 ➤ *Creating and Using an Address Book*

3. Click the address to which you want to send this message, and then click **To**. This adds the selected e-mail address to the This message will be sent to the list at the bottom of the window. You can repeat this step to send the message to additional recipients.

4. (Optional) You can send a carbon copy or blind carbon copy of the message to additional recipients. Click on the person's name, and then click the **Cc** (carbon copy) or **Bcc** (blind carbon copy) button.

5. Click on the **OK** button when you're done. Then, take any additional steps to send the message.

There's another way to send a message to somebody in the Address Book. Open the Address Book, click the person's name, and click the **New Msg** button. Messenger opens the Message Composition dialog box, and addresses the message to the person you selected.

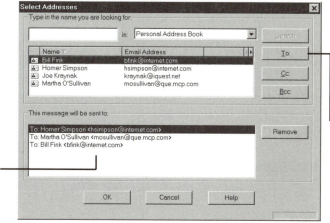

You can insert e-mail addresses from the Address Book.

Click on the recipient's name, and then click To.

The e-mail message will be sent to all the people listed here.

Searching for E-Mail Addresses

The Address Book window displays the names in your Address Book. You can use this window to search an online directory for e-mail addresses. At the top of the window, type the name of the person to whom you want to send the message, and then open the drop-down list, and select the directory you want to search. Click the **Search** button.

195

Part 4 ▶ *Talking to Other People*

Doing Mass Mailings with Mailing Lists

Occasionally, you may find yourself sending the same message to the same group of people. For example, maybe you work in a small company or you work on a team (Go team!) that requires you to distribute memos to everyone. Whatever the case, you can create mailing lists that contain the names and e-mail addresses for all the members in your group. Then, instead of entering each person's e-mail address separately, you can simply select the mailing list.

To create a mailing list, display the Address Book window, and click the **New List** button in the toolbar. The Mailing List dialog box appears, as shown on the following page. Type a name for the mailing list; for example, you might type **Department Memo**. You can add a nickname and description for the mailing list, but these entries are not required.

Click next to the card icon in the bottom section of the dialog box, and start typing the name of one of the recipients you want to add to the list. When you start typing, Messenger completes the entry for you (from the address book). When the person's name is displayed, press **Enter**. You can then start typing the next person's name. After entering the name of the last recipient, click **OK**.

When you compose a message, you can quickly address the message to everyone on the mailing list. Simply click inside the **To** text box in the Message Composition window, and click the **Address** button. From the list of addresses, select the name of the mailing list you created. Messenger inserts the mailing list name into the To text box. When you send the message, it will be sent to everyone on the mailing list.

You can create a mailing list to send the same message to several people.

Type a name for the mailing list.

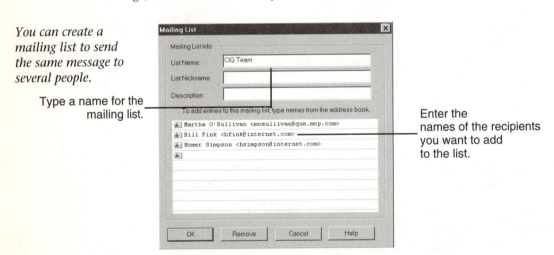

Enter the names of the recipients you want to add to the list.

196

Making and Using Your Own Electronic Business Card

In Chapter 15, "Corresponding with Electronic Mail," you learned how to attach a signature file to your outgoing e-mail messages. Messenger also allows you to create an electronic business card (called a "personal card"), containing information such as your full name, mailing address, home phone number, and so on. You can then send this card along with your messages.

To create a personal card in the Address Book, open the **Edit** menu, and select **Preferences**. Click the plus sign next to Mail & Groups, click **Identity**, and click the **Edit Card** button. The Card for ____ dialog box appears, with the Name tab in front. Enter your first name, last name, and e-mail address in the appropriate text boxes. You can add a nickname and notes about yourself, but these entries are optional. Click on the **Contact** tab and type any additional entries, such as your mailing address and phone number. The Netscape Conference tab includes information about how to contact you via Netscape Conference (see Chapter 19, "Free Long Distance with Conference").

Click **OK** to save your card. This returns you to the Preference dialog box. To attach your card to all outgoing messages, click **Always attach Address Book Card to messages**. (If you leave this off, you can attach the card to only selected messages, as explained next.) Click **OK**.

To attach your card to a selected outgoing message, first create the message you want to send. Then, open the **File** menu in the Message Composition window, point to **Attach**, and select **My Address Book Card**.

The Least You Need to Know

Although adding names and e-mail addresses to the Address Book takes a little time and effort, it pays off in the long run. As you use the Address Book, keep the following points in mind:

➤ You can display the Address Book from any of Communicator's component programs; open the **Communicator** menu and select **Address Book**.

➤ The easiest way to add an e-mail address to the Address Book is to lift it from a message that contains the address. Display the message, open the **Message** menu, point to **Add to Address Book**, and click on **Sender** or **All**.

➤ For a real thrill, click on the **Directory** button in the Address Book's toolbar, and use the resulting dialog box to search an online e-mail address directory.

➤ If you frequently send the same e-mail message to the same group of people, create a mailing list that includes everyone's e-mail address.

➤ You can create a personal address card and attach it to all of your outgoing messages, assuming of course that you want everyone to know your mailing address and phone number.

Chapter 18

Reading and Posting Newsgroup Messages

In This Chapter

➤ Tell the difference between a newsgroup and newspaper

➤ Have a general idea of what's in a particular newsgroup just by looking at its URL

➤ Navigate a newsgroup by clicking on links

➤ Connect to and read messages in at least five newsgroups

If you've never encountered newsgroups, you might have a somewhat distorted image of what they are. Maybe you think that newsgroups provide up-to-the-minute online news... news on demand. You click a link to get the latest sports scores, click another link to see a national weather map, and click still another link to view CNN Headline News.

That's not quite what Internet newsgroups are all about. A *newsgroup* is more of a discussion group, an electronic bulletin board on which users exchange messages. For example, you might post a message in a body art newsgroup asking for instructions on how to pierce your belly button. Other people will read your messages, and some of those people will post responses, telling you just what to do. They might even offer to do it for you!

Part 4 ▶ Talking to Other People

If It's News You Want...

If you're looking for genuine news, you can find plenty of it on the Web. **http://www.yahoo.com/headlines/** alone will give you enough news about current events, sports, business, and weather to keep you busy for hours. You can also find stock and news ticker plug-ins to keep you posted about late-breaking news. Look at Stroud's (**http://www.stroud.com**) for WinStock, Personal Stock Monitor, and other ticker-tape plug-ins. The Yahoo! News Ticker is a great tool for supplying all types of news information. If that's not enough news, use your favorite Web search tool to search for "news ticker."

There are thousands of newsgroups on the Internet, dealing with just about any topic you can think of... everything from Christianity to body art to dog training. Netscape Collabra is the key that unlocks the door to these newsgroups. In addition, if your company has an intranet, you can use Collabra to create your own discussion groups, where you and colleagues can exchange information and ideas.

USENET

Most newsgroups are part of a larger organization called USENET, which is short for *user's network*. USENET sets the standards by which the various newsgroups swap information.

Starting Netscape Collabra

Because Netscape Collabra is a component of Netscape Communicator, there are all sorts of ways to run Collabra. To run it by itself, open the **Start** menu, point to **Programs**, point to **Netscape Communicator**, and click on **Netscape Collabra**. You can also run Collabra from the other Communicator components:

➤ In Navigator, Messenger, or Composer, open the **Communicator** menu and click on **Collabra Discussion Groups**.

➤ In the Component bar, click on the **Discussion Groups** button.

➤ To display a window for creating a message to post, open the **File** menu (in any of the Netscape Communicator components), point to **New**, and click on **Message**.

➤ To have Collabra start automatically when you double-click on the Netscape Communicator icon, open the **Edit** menu, and select **Preferences**. Click on **Appearance**, and then, under **On startup, launch**, click on **Collabra Discussions**.

Before You Can Read Newsgroups...

To read messages posted in a newsgroup, you have to tell Collabra which newsgroup server you want to use. Hopefully, your service provider already supplied you with the domain name of its newsgroup server. If you don't have this information, get on the phone to your service provider (yes, again), and find out.

When in Doubt, Guess

If it's 2 a.m., and you can't contact your service provider, guess the domain name of your service provider's news service. You can usually just add "news." to the beginning of your service provider's domain name entry. For example, if the general domain name is internet.com, the news server address should be news.internet.com. (Many service providers post this information at their Web sites.)

Once you have the information you need, open the **Edit** menu, and select **Preferences**. Click the plus sign next to Mail & Groups, and click on **Groups Server**. Now, click inside the **Discussion Groups (news) server** text box, and type the domain name of your service provider's newsgroup server. Don't change the entry in the News Directory text box, unless you have some good reason for changing it. This entry tells Collabra where to store information about the newsgroups you decide to read.

While you're looking at the Groups Server options, make sure **Ask me before downloading more than 500 messages** has a check mark next to it. This prevents Collabra from cluttering your disk with more message descriptions than your hard drive can handle. Click **OK** to save your changes.

Specifying a newsgroup server in Collabra.

Type the domain name of your newsgroup server here.

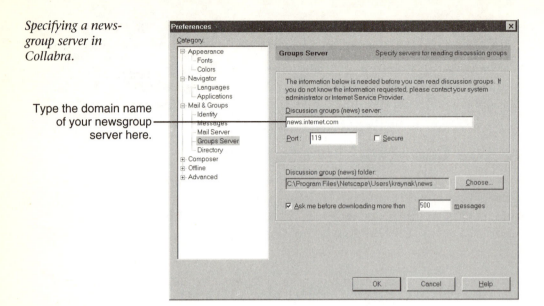

Doing Newsgroups from Navigator and Collabra

Communicator offers a couple ways to open a newsgroup and read its postings. If you're in Navigator and you pull up a page that has a link for a newsgroup, simply click on the link. Navigator automatically runs Collabra, which then connects to the newsgroup and displays a list of messages in that group. Double-click on the message description to display the contents of the message.

Another way to connect to a newsgroup from Navigator is to enter the URL of a newsgroup. Of course, you have to know a newsgroup's URL before you can enter it. The URL for a newsgroup must start with **news:**. Here are some URLs to try:

>news:alt.comedy.british

>news:humanities.lit.authors.shakespeare

>news:hawaii.sports

>news:alt.startrek.borg

>news:sci.anthropology

The more standard way of connecting to newsgroups is to have Collabra download a list of available newsgroups from your news server. You can then pick a newsgroup from the list. The following sections show you just what to do.

Chapter 18 ➤ *Reading and Posting Newsgroup Messages*

Dissecting Newsgroup Addresses

A newsgroup address can tell you a great deal about the newsgroup, if you know how to read it. The first part of the address indicates the newsgroup's overall subject area; for example, **comp** stands for computer, **rec** is for recreation (hobbies, sports), **sci** stands for science, **soc** is for social topics, and **alt** is for alternative topics. The second part of the address indicates, more specifically, what the newsgroup offers. For example, **comp.ai** is about computers, specifically covering artificial intelligence. If the address has a third part (most do), it focuses even further; for instance, **comp.ai.philosophy** discusses how artificial intelligence can be applied to philosophical questions.

Grabbing a (Long) List of Newsgroups

Although Navigator makes it convenient to access newsgroups via links, you can't rely on these chance encounters to find the newsgroups you want. Instead, you should use Collabra to display a list of all the available newsgroups, so you can see what's out there.

To display a list of available newsgroups, click the **Subscribe** button in Collabra's toolbar. The Subscribe to Discussion Groups dialog box appears, and Collabra starts to download newsgroup names from your news server. This process may take several minutes. If Collabra displays a warning, indicating that it cannot connect to the news server, click **OK**, and then open the **Server** drop-down list at the bottom of the dialog box, and select your news server (the server you set up earlier in this chapter). You might have to click the **Get Groups** button to tell Collabra to start downloading the list of newsgroups.

When Collabra has finished downloading the newsgroup names, it displays a list of the newsgroups, as shown on the following page. You might notice that some of the newsgroups have a plus (+) sign next to their names. Click on the plus sign to view additional newsgroups under this newsgroup heading. You can display all of the subgroups by clicking on the **Expand All** button. Note that Collabra displays a number next to each newsgroup indicating the number of messages in the newsgroup. This tells you how active the newsgroup is; if there are no messages, it makes little sense to subscribe to the newsgroup.

Collabra displays a list of newsgroups available on your news server.

Newsgroup names appear here.

Click on a plus sign to see a list of subgroups.

Click these arrows to view more or fewer columns.

You can expand or collapse all subgroups.

Subscribing to a Newsgroup

When you find a newsgroup that catches your eye, you should *subscribe* to it. When you subscribe to a newsgroup, Collabra places the newsgroup name on a list of subscribed newsgroups, so you can quickly access messages in only those newsgroups you care about. To subscribe to a newsgroup, take any of the following steps:

➤ In the Subscribe to Discussion Groups dialog box, click on the newsgroup to which you want to subscribe, and click on the **Subscribe** button.

➤ In the Subscribe to Discussion Groups dialog box, click on the dot in the Subscribe column next to the desired newsgroup. The dot changes into a check mark, indicating that you have subscribed to the newsgroup.

➤ In the Message Center window, open the **File** menu and select **Subscribe to Discussion Groups**. This displays the Subscribe to Discussion Groups dialog box.

If you used the Subscribe to Discussion Groups dialog box to subscribe to newsgroups, click the **OK** button to close it and return to the Message Center window. Click on the plus sign next to your news server. The Message Center displays the names of all the newsgroups you subscribed to, as shown on the following page. You can double-click on a newsgroup's name to display a list of messages posted in that newsgroup.

Chapter 18 ➤ *Reading and Posting Newsgroup Messages*

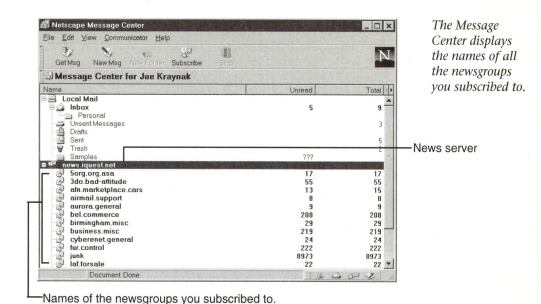

The Message Center displays the names of all the newsgroups you subscribed to.

To unsubscribe to a newsgroup, you can delete it from the Message Center. Just click on the newsgroup's name, and press the Delete key. You can also use the Subscribe to Discussion Groups dialog box. Click on the check mark next to the name of the newsgroup you want to unsubscribe from.

Reading Newsgroup Messages

Okay, now that you know all about connecting and subscribing to newsgroups, you're probably dying to read some messages. Here's what you do:

1. Run Collabra, if it's not already running. This displays the Netscape Message Center window.

2. Click on the plus sign next to your news server's name. A list of subscribed newsgroups appears.

3. Double-click on the name of the newsgroup whose postings you want to view. The Netscape Discussion window appears, displaying a list of messages in the selected newsgroup.

4. Double-click on a message to display its contents. The message appears in its own Netscape Message window.

5. Click the **Next** button to read the next unread message. (You can select options from the **Go** menu to read the next or previous message.)

205

Another way to read messages is to divide the Netscape Discussion window into two panes (it may already be divided into two panes). If the window displays a single pane, click on the blue triangle in the lower left corner of the window to display the message contents pane. Whenever you click on a message description in the upper pane, the contents of the message appear in the lower pane. You can use the drop-down list just above the message list to select a different subscribed newsgroup or to change to your Inbox folder or another folder.

You can display a list of messages and the contents of the selected message in a single window.

You can select a subscribed newsgroup from this list.

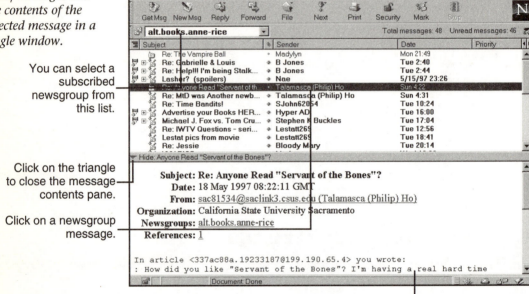

Click on the triangle to close the message contents pane.

Click on a newsgroup message.

The contents of the message appear here.

Check This Out... Article, Newsgroup, Message Center

If you plan on doing newsgroups, you had better hone your window juggling skills. When you double-click on a newsgroup in the Message Center, the Discussion window appears, showing a list of messages in the selected newsgroup. If you then double-click on a message, the Message window appears. Below the Netscape N logo in the Message and Discussion window is a button you can click to quickly switch to the previous window. In the Message window, click on the button to go back to the Discussion window. In the Discussion window, click on the button to return to the Message Center.

Viewing Replies to Posted Messages

As you are reading messages, you might notice that some message descriptions have a plus sign next to them. This indicates that someone else has posted a reply to the original message. Click on the plus sign to view the reply(ies). You can then click on the description of the reply to view its contents. To collapse the list of replies, click on the minus sign to the left of the original message.

A message and its replies are called a *thread*. To skip from one thread to another, open the **Go** menu and select **Next Unread Thread** (or press the **T** key). This allows you to proceed through the list of unread messages without having to view each message.

Sorting and Searching for Messages

If you connect to a newsgroup that contains hundreds of messages, sifting through the list may seem like an exercise in tedium. To help, you can sort the messages. Simply click on the heading above the column whose entries you want to sort. For example, to sort by name, click on the **Sender** column heading. To sort by message description, click on the **Subject** heading. You can change the sort order (for instance, from A-Z to Z-A) by clicking again on the column heading.

If you know of a specific subject or sender that you want to search for in the message list, you can use Collabra's search tool to hunt down messages. Take the following steps:

1. Open the **Edit** menu and select **Search Messages**. This displays the Search Messages dialog box.

2. Open the **Search for items in** drop-down list, and select the specific newsgroup you want to search.

3. Use the next three controls to specify what you want to search for. In the example, shown below, we are about to search the body of messages that contain "stan laurel." (Some servers allow searches on a limited number of fields; for example, you may be able to search only the Subject field, not the Body.)

4. You can click the **More** button and enter additional search instructions to narrow the search.

5. Click the **Search** button. Collabra performs the specified search, and displays a list of newsgroup messages that it found. Double-click on a message description to read the message.

Part 4 ➤ *Talking to Other People*

Collabra can search for messages about a specific topic or from a specific author.

Select the newsgroup you want to search.

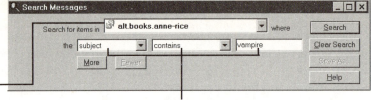

Enter your search instructions.

Other Newsgroup Management Options

The Netscape Message window is very similar to the Mail Message window, and offers many of the same options for sorting and displaying messages. Refer to Chapter 16, "Managing Your E-Mail Messages," for details.

Replying to Newsgroup Messages

Before you post messages to a newsgroup, familiarize yourself with the newsgroup. Hang out, and read existing messages to obtain a clear idea of the focus and tone of the newsgroup. Reading messages without posting your own messages is known as *lurking*. Newsgroups encourage lurking, because it provides you with the knowledge you need to respond intelligently and to avoid repeating what has already been said.

You can reply to a message by posting your reply in the newsgroup, by sending a private reply via e-mail, or by posting and sending an e-mail reply. (Check the original message to determine if the sender requested a reply method.) If you post the reply, it appears in the newsgroup, where anyone can read it. The person to whom you are replying will have to check the newsgroup to read your reply. If you reply via e-mail, your reply goes only to the person who posted the original message. To send or post your reply, take the following steps:

1. Select the message to which you want to respond.
2. Click on the **Reply** button, and select the desired option:

    Reply to Sender e-mails your reply only to the person who wrote the original message.

    Reply to Sender and All Recipients e-mails the reply to the person who wrote the original message and to any individuals that the original message was addressed to.

Reply to Group places your reply only in the newsgroup, where everyone, including the person who posted the original message, can read the reply.

Reply to Sender and Group posts the message in the newsgroup and e-mails a copy of your response to the person who wrote the original message.

3. The Netscape Composition window appears. If desired, you can address the message to additional newsgroups or individuals. See Chapter 15, "Corresponding with Electronic Mail," for details.
4. Type your message in the message area at the bottom of the window.
5. Click the **Send** button. Collabra sends your reply as instructed.

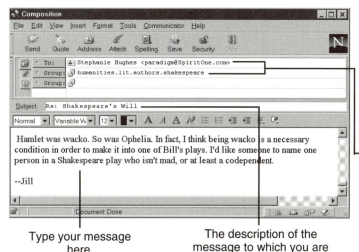

Replying to a newsgroup message is very similar to composing and sending e-mail messages.

This message will be posted to a newsgroup and e-mailed to an individual.

Type your message here.

The description of the message to which you are responding appears here.

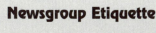

Newsgroup Etiquette

To avoid getting verbally battered in a newsgroup, follow a few simple rules. Don't insult any person or attack any topic of conversation. Post messages that pertain to the newsgroup and topic of conversation (read the entire conversation before adding your own two cents). And don't advertise in a newsgroup unless the newsgroup is especially designed for advertising. Oh yeah, DON'T SHOUT by using all capital letters in your message.

Starting a New Discussion

As you gain experience in a particular newsgroup, you might decide to venture out and start your own conversation. For example, if you're into hot rods, and you need a bumper for your '64 Corvette, you might want to post a message asking if anyone knows where you can find the bumper.

To start a conversation, first activate the newsgroup in which you want to post your message. Then, click the **New Msg** button. The window that appears is very similar to the window you use to reply to messages, except in this dialog box, the Subject text box is blank. Click inside the **Subject** text box, and type a description for your message.

Now, click inside the big text box at the bottom of the window, and type your message. When you're done typing, click the **Send** button. Your message is posted in the active newsgroup. You can now check the newsgroup on a regular basis, to see if anyone has replied to your message. And don't be surprised if you receive replies via e-mail!

Check Your Spelling

Avoiding misspellings and typos in your newsgroup messages is just as important as avoiding them in e-mail. Before you send a message, click the **Spelling** button in the toolbar. For fancy formatting options, see Chapter 20, "Making a Simple Web Page."

Receiving and Sending Files in Newsgroups

In some newsgroups, people like to trade files instead of simple text messages. In gaming newsgroups, for instance, gamers may post shareware versions of their favorite games or add-ons that make the game more challenging and fun. In a photography newsgroup, you might find digitized landscape photos or portraits.

In the past, swapping files in newsgroups was a pain. You usually had to download several parts of a coded message, assemble the parts to create one file, and then decode the monster you just created. With Communicator, the process has become as easy as transferring files on the Web. Collabra is now capable of displaying inline images, such as GIFs and JPEGs (graphics), text files, and HTML coded documents (Web pages).

If Collabra cannot display an attached file, it displays a link for the file, just as you might see on a Web page. You can then click on the link to display the Save As dialog box and save the file to your hard drive.

Chapter 18 ➤ *Reading and Posting Newsgroup Messages*

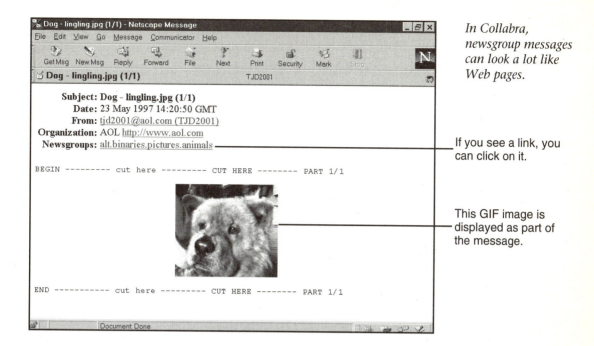

In Collabra, newsgroup messages can look a lot like Web pages.

If you see a link, you can click on it.

This GIF image is displayed as part of the message.

You can change the way Collabra displays attachments. Open the **View** menu, point to **Attachments**, and click on **Inline** to display attachments as part of the newsgroup message, or **As Links** to display them as highlighted text you can click on.

Reading Newsgroups Offline

You can spend a lot of time sifting through heaps of newsgroup messages in search of interesting tidbits. If your service provider or phone company charges you for connect time, lurking can become quite an expensive habit. To help, Collabra allows you to download messages from selected newsgroups and then read those messages offline. Here's what you do:

1. In the Message Center, open the **File** menu and select **Go Offline**. The Download dialog box appears.

2. Click the **Select Items for Download** button. A list of subscribed newsgroups appear.

3. Under Choose, click the dot next to each newsgroup you want to read offline. The dot changes into a check mark. Click **OK**.

4. Make sure **Download Discussion Groups** is selected. You can also choose to download mail and send mail messages before going offline.

211

5. Click the **Go Offline** button. The Downloading Articles dialog box appears, displaying the downloading progress.

6. You can now disconnect from the Internet and read your messages offline. To go back online, open the **File** menu and select **Go Online**.

The Least You Need to Know

Dealing with newsgroups is easy, once you know what you're doing. While you're learning, you should be aware of the following problems that might trip you up:

➤ If you receive an error message indicating that your news server does not exist, make sure you specified the correct news server to use, and that you selected the correct news server in the Message Center.

➤ Collabra uses several windows, and it's tough trying to keep track of them all:

> **Message Center:** This window gives you access to all your e-mail folders and the subscribed newsgroups.
>
> **Netscape Discussion:** This window displays a list of messages in the selected newsgroup.
>
> **Netscape Message:** This window displays the contents of the currently selected message.

➤ To display a list of available newsgroups, click the **Subscribe** button.

➤ To subscribe to a newsgroup, click on the newsgroup's name in the Subscribe to a Newsgroup window, and click the **Subscribe** button.

➤ To reply to a newsgroup message, select the message, click the **Reply** button, and select **Reply to Sender**, **Reply to Sender and All Recipients**, **Reply to Group**, or **Reply to Sender and Group**.

➤ To start your own newsgroup discussion, open the newsgroup, and click on the **New Msg** button.

Chapter 19

Free Long Distance with Conference

In This Chapter

➤ Use one of those Internet telephone programs you've heard so much about

➤ Save 100 percent on long-distance calls *without* switching to MCI or Sprint

➤ Understand why the other person's voice sounds so fuzzy

➤ Pretend you're a high-powered business executive collaborating on a project using Conference's Whiteboard feature

You've no doubt heard all the buzz about Internet Phone, WebPhone, and other programs that let you bypass phone companies (and their sky-rocketing rates) by placing calls over the Internet. Well, here's your chance to take one of these programs for a test drive without sinking 50 bucks in a separate program. Netscape Communicator includes an Internet phone program called Netscape Conference, which offers the following features:

➤ **Toll-free phone calls:** If you have a sound card, speakers, and a microphone, and you have a friend who has a computer that is similarly equipped, you can place voice calls over the Internet without paying the telephone company.

➤ **A shared drawing board:** The Netscape Conference Whiteboard lets you join online conferences and display a picture on the monitors of all the conference participants, so you can doodle together.

- **Chat tool:** If the voice thing doesn't work out, you can type messages back and forth.
- **Collaborative Web browsing:** You can wander the Web with a friend. This makes the Web all warm and fuzzy, giving you a feeling of camaraderie.
- **File exchange tool:** If a friend or colleague needs a file, all she has to do is ask. You can send the file immediately.

In this chapter, you will learn how to set up Netscape Conference and take advantage of all these features.

Can You Really Make Free Long-Distance Calls?

Yep, it's free, but if you have a slow modem connection to the Internet, don't get your hopes up. To carry on live phone conversations, Conference has to record your voice, digitize it, and then send this huge, digitized recording over the Internet, where it bounces off of several nodes en route to its destination. The sound is typically of a very low quality and it suffers huge delays. However, this tool works pretty well over a fast cable connection or on an intranet. Even over a fairly fast modem connection (28.8Kbps), you may be disappointed with the voice features.

What You (and the Person You're Calling) Need to Get Started

You can't just plug your phone into your modem and use Conference to start placing calls. The setup is a little more complicated than that.

First, your computer has to have a few accessories in order to function as a phone. It needs a sound board, speakers, a microphone, and Netscape Conference. Second, you can't just dial up an ordinary telephone. The person on the other end must have a computer with a sound card, speakers, and a microphone, too. And this person must also have Conference (or a compatible Internet phone program).

Now, when you call this person, she has to know you're calling and have her computer all set to answer (otherwise, you'll have to leave a voice mail message). The computer on the other end must be actively connected to the Internet, and it must be running Conference (or a compatible Internet phone program).

Chapter 19 ➤ *Free Long Distance with Conference*

Alright, with all the caveats out of the way, and assuming you have someone to call (or someone to call you), we can embark on this futuristic phone adventure.

No Sound Card?!

If you don't have a sound card, you can still use Conference's Chat Tool, Whiteboard, collaborative Web browser, and file exchange tools, but you won't be able to make voice calls or use the voice mail feature. In short, you really should have a sound card if you're doing the Web.

Setting Up Netscape Conference

To run Conference, select **Netscape Conference** from the Netscape Communicator program group (in Windows 95, select **Start, Programs, Netscape Communicator, Netscape Conference**). You can also run Conference by opening the **Communicator** menu in Navigator, Messenger, Collabra, or Composer, and selecting **Conference** (or press **Ctrl+5**).

This starts Conference and runs the Setup Wizard. (If the Setup Wizard does not run, open the **Help** menu and select **Setup Wizard**.)This Wizard is a series of dialog boxes that lead you through the process of configuring Conference to work with your sound card, speakers, microphone, and modem. This is a one-time deal, so don't fret. Just follow the on-screen instructions, and keep clicking on the **Next>** button.

During the setup, the Wizard displays the dialog box shown below, allowing you to create a business card. This card is used to help the person you're calling identify you. Type as much or as little information as you want the other person to know about you.

Phone Taps?

If you're worried about somebody tapping your phone call, you should worry. The Internet isn't the most secure place to carry on sensitive phone conversations. Your messages bounce off public servers on their way to their destination, making it easy for people with the proper know-how and free time to eavesdrop. Have fun, but watch what you say. If you are still concerned about privacy, check out PGPfone (Pretty Good Privacy) at **http://web.mit.edu/network/pgpfone/**.

The only tricky part is if you want to add a photo of yourself, or a photo of the person you're impersonating. The photo will appear in the upper right corner of your business card. You can insert a photo in either of two ways:

➤ Scan in a picture of yourself, and save it as a JPEG, GIF, BMP, or TIFF file. Click on the little folder icon next to **Photo**, and use the **Open** dialog box to select it.

Part 4 ➤ *Talking to Other People*

➤ In your graphics program, display the image you want to appear on your business card, select it, and use the Copy command to place it on the Windows clipboard. Then, click on the little clipboard icon next to Photo to insert the clipboard contents.

Near the end of the setup, the Wizard prompts you to test your audio levels but provides the option to skip the test. Don't skip the test. The test adjusts the Silence Sensor, which enables Conference to automatically switch between the microphone and the speakers when you are conversing. When the setup is complete, click on the **Finish** button. You're now ready to use Conference.

Your business card will identify you to the people you call.

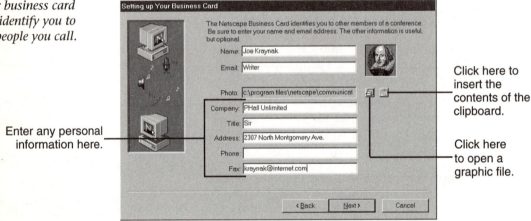

Enter any personal information here.

Click here to insert the contents of the clipboard.

Click here to open a graphic file.

What's This Silence Sensor All About?

If you have a full-duplex audio card, it can record and receive sound at the same time, just as on a telephone. However, if you have a half-duplex sound card, it cannot record when it is playing. In such cases, Conference uses the Silence Sensor to automatically turn off audio play when you are talking, and turn it back on when you stop talking. Without the Silence Sensor, you would have to click the microphone button before talking, and then click the speaker button to hear the other person.

Chapter 19 ➤ *Free Long Distance with Conference*

Placing a Call and Hanging Up

Okay, you've been waiting to try out this Conference program. Here's what you do:

1. Connect to the Internet, and run Conference. The Netscape Conference window appears, as shown in the following figure.

2. In the **E-mail address** text box, type the e-mail address of the person you want to call. For example, you might type **jsmith@internet.com**.

3. Click the **Dial** button. Conference attempts to locate the person online, and checks to determine if the person has a compatible Internet phone program running. If the person is available, Conference displays an invitation on that person's screen.

4. If the person accepts your invitation and starts talking into her microphone, you will be able to hear her voice. (At this point, the main Conference window is displayed on both your screen and the other person's screen.)

5. You can start talking, and the other person will be able to hear your voice.

6. You can have a conference call by inviting other people to join your conversation. As long as these other people are not already engaged in another conference, they'll be able to see your invitation.

7. To view the business card of someone else who's involved in the conference, click the person's picture or the big Netscape Conference logo.

8. At some point, you may wish to hang up. Open the **Call** menu and click on **Hang Up**.

If you have trouble hearing the other person (or if the other person has trouble hearing you), you can crank up the volume. To adjust the microphone volume, drag the slider under Microphone to the right to increase volume or to the left to decrease it. To adjust the volume of the other person's voice, drag the slider under Speaker.

The little sliders to the right of the microphone and speakers buttons allow you to readjust the silence levels. For example, you may need to increase the silence sensitivity for the microphone if the person on the other end is not receiving any audio signals from you.

Part 4 ➤ *Talking to Other People*

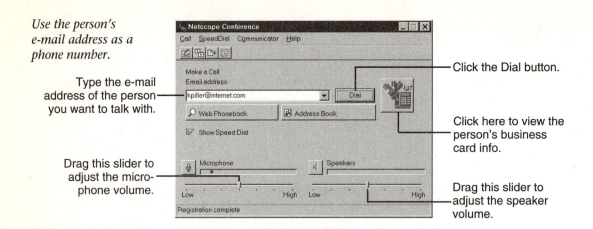

Use the person's e-mail address as a phone number.

Type the e-mail address of the person you want to talk with.

Drag this slider to adjust the microphone volume.

Click the Dial button.

Click here to view the person's business card info.

Drag this slider to adjust the speaker volume.

Finding a Person in the Web Phonebook

If Conference displays an error message indicating that it cannot contact the person using the e-mail address you entered, you may be able to locate the person by selecting his name from the DLS (Dynamic Lookup Service). The DLS is a remote server at Netscape, Four11, or other companies who choose to provide this service. It keeps track of all users who want to be listed. If the person you are looking for has chosen to be listed, you can use the DLS to help Conference find that person.

In the Netscape Conference window, click on the **Web Phonebook** button. This runs Navigator, which opens a page displaying an alphabetical index. Click on the letter for the name you want to look up (your friend's first name or last name may be used as identification). The page displays a list of all the people whose name starts with the letter you selected. If you see your friend's name, click on it. Navigator runs Conference, which then attempts to contact your friend.

To make it easy for your friends and colleagues to find you, you should make sure that you have made your contact information available to the DLS. Open the **Call** menu and select **Preferences**. Click on the **Network** tab. Under Servers, place a check in the **List my name in phonebook** check box. Click **OK**.

Chapter 19 ➤ *Free Long Distance with Conference*

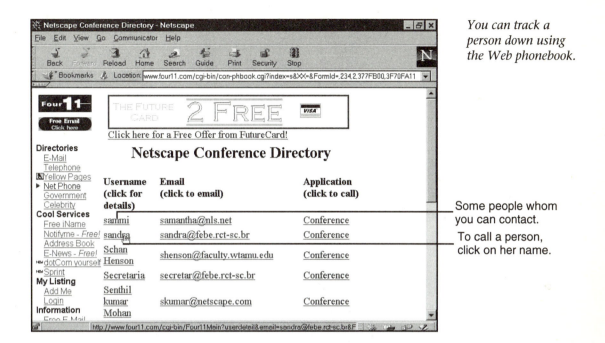

You can track a person down using the Web phonebook.

Some people whom you can contact.

To call a person, click on her name.

Using Your Address Book to Place Calls

Another way to place a call is to use the address book entries you typed in Chapter 17, "Creating and Using an Address Book." In the Netscape Conference window, click the **Address Book** button. This opens the address book you created. Double-click on the name of the person you want to call. The Card for ___ dialog box appears. Click on the **Netscape Conference** tab. Open the **Address** drop-down list, and select one of the following options:

Netscape Conference DLS Server: This option tells Conference to look for the person using the default DLS server. (You can select the default DLS server by opening the **Call** menu, selecting **Preferences**, and selecting the desired server.)

Specific DLS Server: This option lets you enter the address of the DLS server that the person typically uses to connect. If you choose this option, type the address of the server in the text box directly below the Address drop-down list.

Host Name or IP Address: Select this option if you want to track down the person using her e-mail address. If you select this option, type the person's e-mail address in the text box directly below the Address drop-down list; for example, type **smith@internet.com**. (As an alternative, you can type the person's IP address, which is a number such as 170.98.130.78. However, many servers assign each person a different IP address whenever the person signs on, making this number unreliable.)

219

Part 4 ➤ *Talking to Other People*

Once you have entered a person's e-mail address as the Conference address, you can quickly call the person. Run Netscape Conference, and click on the **Address Book** button. In the Address Book dialog box, click on the name of the person you want to call, and then click on the **Call** button. Conference attempts to contact the person. If Conference is successful, and the person accepts your invitation, you can start talking. (If the person is unavailable, Conference prompts you to leave a voicemail message. See "No Answer? Leave a Voicemail Message," later in this chapter.)

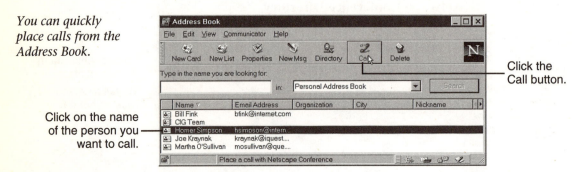

You can quickly place calls from the Address Book.

Click on the name of the person you want to call

Click the Call button.

Creating Speed Dial Buttons

You can create buttons for people you call frequently. In the Netscape Conference window, click on the **Show Speed Dial** option (directly below the Web Phonebook button). Six Speed Dial buttons appear. Click on one of the buttons. The Speed Dial Edit dialog box appears, prompting you to enter settings for this button. Enter the following:

Name   This is the name of the button.

Email   Type the e-mail address of the person whom you wish to use this button to call.

DLS Server   Type the URL of the DLS server that the person uses.

Direct Address   If you prefer to connect directly (without using the DLS server), type the person's direct e-mail address here. A direct e-mail address is a number, such as 206.246.170.92. But as I said before, the person may be given a different IP (direct) address each time she signs on.

Click **OK**. Conference creates the button. You can now quickly call the person by clicking on the appropriate Speed Dial button. You can edit a Speed Dial button by right-clicking on it.

No Answer? Leave a Voicemail Message

If the person you're trying to contact is unavailable or refuses to answer, Conference displays a dialog box asking if you want to leave a voicemail message. To leave a message, click the **Yes** button. Conference then displays the Message Composition window, just as if you had decided to send an e-mail message, and Conference prompts you to record your voice message. Click the **Record** button, speak your message into the microphone, and click **Stop**. Click the **Send** button.

Your voice message is saved as a WAV file and is inserted as an attachment into an e-mail message that's addressed to the person. You can type a text message instead of or in addition to the recorded message. Click the **Send** button.

Record your voice message or simply compose an e-mail message.

If the person can't take your call, leave a message.

No Sound?

If you have trouble hearing someone or she has trouble hearing you, even after you and your partner have adjusted the speaker and microphone volumes, something may have run afoul with Windows or in one of your sound card programs.

Windows 95 has a gazillion ways to set your sound output and microphone input volume. The easiest way is to right-click on the speaker icon in the taskbar, and click on **Volume Controls**. Drag all the sliders to the top. If there is no slider for your microphone, open the **Options** menu, select **Properties**, and make sure all the check boxes at the bottom of the dialog box (except PC Speaker) are selected. This should display the sliders you need to set the volume.

If you have Windows 3.1, and you're using SoundBlaster, or one of the many SoundBlaster clones, look for a program group that contains the SoundBlaster program icons. Double-click on the Creative Mixer icon, and use its control panel to crank up the volume. For some strange reason, the Microphone slider likes to creep to the bottom.

Check This Out...

Priceless Troubleshooting Tip

If you can't figure out what's wrong, try using some other audio program to record sounds. In Windows, you can use the Windows Sound Recorder. If you can record and play back sounds successfully with it, but not with Conference, the problem is with Conference, not Windows. Conference also comes with its own audio troubleshooter. Open the **Help** menu and select **Troubleshooting Audio**.

Answering Incoming Calls

If you know someone is going to call you at a particular time, connect to the Internet and run Conference. When the person calls, an invitation pops up on your screen. Accept the invitation, and start talking. Once you accept the invitation, the main Conference window appears on your screen.

You can have Conference automatically answer incoming calls (or reject all calls). To set your preferences, open the **Call** menu. To have Conference accept all invitations, select **Auto Answer**. To refuse all invitations, select **Do Not Disturb**.

Typing Messages with the Chat Tool

If you don't have a sound card, or you're tired of talking into a microphone and interrupting each other, you can type messages back and forth using Conference's Chat Tool.

In the Conference window, click on the **Chat** button (the one with the two message bubbles on it), and the Chat Tool window opens. Type a message in the area at the bottom of the window, and click on the **Send** button or press **Ctrl+Enter**. Your message pops up on the other person's screen. Any messages that the other person sends you pop up on your screen. (You can send an entire text file by clicking on the **Include** button, the one with the open folder on it.)

You can save a transcript of the conversation (in case you decide to sue the person later). Click on the **Save** button, or open the **File** menu and select **Save**.

When you're done chatting, and you want to return to your voice call, open the **File** menu and select **Close**.

Chapter 19 ➤ *Free Long Distance with Conference*

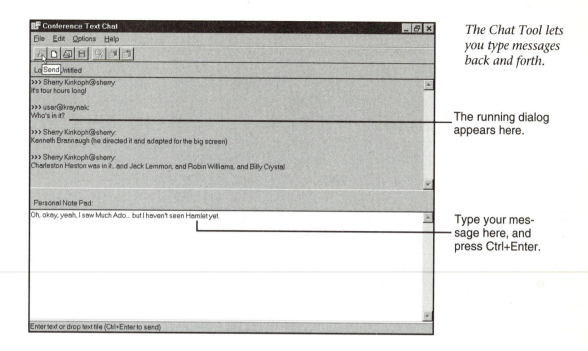

The Chat Tool lets you type messages back and forth.

The running dialog appears here.

Type your message here, and press Ctrl+Enter.

Collaborating with Whiteboard

Conference's Whiteboard is a tool that allows you to send pictures to the other person and annotate them. Such tools have become much more popular now that all the companies in corporate America are giving their employees the opportunity to become self-employed or sending them home as telecommuters. With Whiteboard, you can collaborate on projects and doodle together during virtual corporate meetings.

With Whiteboard, you can send graphics files across the Internet, just as if you were sending a typed message. If you don't have any graphics files, you can display what you want to send (a document, spreadsheet, whatever) and have Conference capture and send the screen. This image then pops up on your colleague's screen, and you can start to mark it up.

Here We Go! Using the Whiteboard

To use Whiteboard, click on the **Whiteboard** button in the Conference toolbar. You can then send an image from disk by opening the **File** menu and selecting **Open** (or by clicking the **Open File** button in Whiteboard's toolbar). Use the dialog box to select the file you want to send, and click on **Open** or **OK**.

223

If you're using Windows 95, you can capture a screen and send it. Display the image you want to send, and then open the **Capture** menu and select **Desktop**. You can capture and send only the open window (instead of the entire desktop), by selecting **Window** from the **Capture** menu. Or, you can send a portion of the screen by selecting **Capture/Region**, and then dragging over the area you want to send. However you do it, the image is immediately sent to all the people in the conference (and it pops up on your screen).

Once the image is there, anyone in the conference can start drawing on the screen by using Whiteboard's drawing tools, as shown below. Click on the button for the tool you want to use, and then drag the mouse to draw. It's just like drawing in Paintbrush.

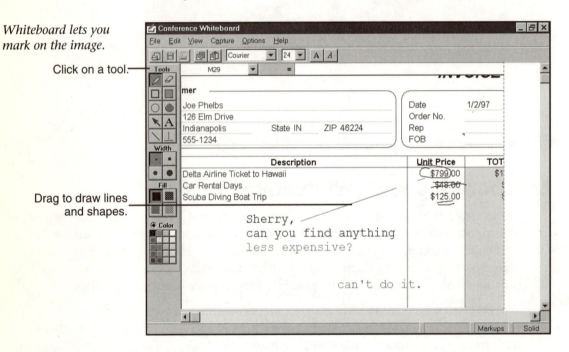

Whiteboard lets you mark on the image.

Click on a tool.

Drag to draw lines and shapes.

The Whiteboard work surface consists of two layers: an image layer and a drawing layer. If someone in the group drags the mouse all over the screen and turns the display into a primordial blob, you can clear the drawing layer and start over. Open the **Edit** menu and select **Clear Markups**. This removes all markings from all conference participants, leaving the original image clean. To scrap the entire work area, including the original image, select **Edit/Clear Whiteboard**.

Team Web Browsing

As you are talking, you might find the need to point to some informative, or at least interesting, pages on the Web. Conference offers a new tool that allows one conference participant to lead the other conference participants on a tour of Web pages. In order for this to work, all conference participants must be using Conference and Navigator. Take the following steps to lead the tour:

1. Click on the **Collaborative Browsing** button. The Conference Collaborative Browsing Tool dialog box appears, prompting you to take the lead.

2. To lead others on a tour, click the **Control the Browsers** check box.

3. Click the **Start Browsing** button. Navigator automatically starts on all the conference participants computers, and loads your starting page.

4. Use Navigator to load the pages that you want the Conference participants to see. Whenever you load a page, that page pops up on everyone's screen.

5. To stop browsing, click the **Stop Browsing** button. This closes all the browsers and returns you to your Conference call.

6. If another participant wants to take the lead, she must click the **Control the Browsers** button, and you must relinquish your role as fearless leader.

Sending Files

People commonly swap files over the Internet via e-mail and newsgroups. Now, you can immediately send files to conference participants. This comes in handy when you are working with others on a project and need to share documents and data.

To send one or more files, click on the **File Exchange** button in Conference. Netscape's File Exchange window appears, as shown in the following figure. Click on the **Open** button, use the **Add File to Send List** dialog box to select a file you want to send, and click **Open**. This adds the file to the File(s) to Send list. You can use the **Open** button to add more files to the list.

If you are sending text-only files, open the **Options** menu and select **Ascii**; to send program files or formatted documents, open the **Options** menu and select **Binary**. (You can also choose the Compress option to increase the speed at which they truck through the phone lines.) When you are ready to send the files, click the **Send** button, or press **Ctrl+Enter**. The files are then sent to all the conference participants. When they receive the files, Netscape's File Exchange window pops up on their screens, displaying a list of the files they received. The conference participants can then click on the **Save** button and save the files to their hard drives.

Part 4 ➤ *Talking to Other People*

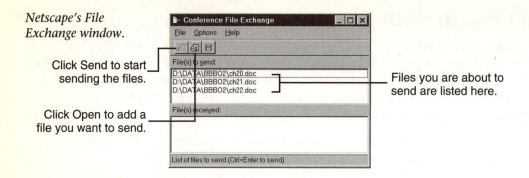

Netscape's File Exchange window.

The Least You Need to Know

Conference is a fairly easy tool to use to place voice calls over the Internet. Here's all you have to remember:

➤ You can run Conference by selecting it from the Netscape Communicator program group or from the Communicator menu in Navigator, Messenger, Collabra, or Composer.

➤ Before calling, make sure you get the person's e-mail address, and let him know when he'll be receiving a call.

➤ To call a person, type the person's e-mail address in the **E-mail address** text box, and click the **Dial** button.

➤ Once you are connected, you can use the Chat tool, Whiteboard, and Collaborative Browsing tool to carry on a virtual meeting.

➤ To disconnect when you are done talking, open the **Call** menu and select **Hang Up**.

Part 5
Publishing Your Own Web Pages

You've mastered the Internet. You can wander the Web, use Internet search tools, send and receive e-mail, poke around in newsgroups, and even make free, long-distance "phone" calls across the Internet. You're probably feeling pretty smug right now.

However, you can't consider yourself an Internet master until you've accomplished one more feat—placing your own page on the Web. In this part, you will learn how to use Composer, along with a few other tools, to create your own Web page and place it on the Web. As an added bonus, this part provides a few sites where you can publish your Web page for free and publicize it, so people can find it.

Chapter 20

Making a Simple Web Page

In This Chapter

➤ Use Composer and Netscape's Page Wizard to whip up a Web page

➤ Steal someone else's Web page and modify it

➤ Transform your bookmarks into a Web page

➤ Name three places where you can create and post a Web page simply by filling out a form

Admit it, the Web is cool. At any time of the day or night, you can hit the Web and pull up pages containing text, pictures, video clips, and a host of other media. You've tapped into the source, you've seen the light, and now you want to express yourself on the Web. Maybe you want to post your resume, introduce the world to your wonderful family, publish your poems that nobody else would print, show off your home, or simply provide a list of links to other pages that you find interesting.

Whatever the case, you want to publish a Web page, but you don't know where to start. Well, you've come to the right place. In this chapter, you'll learn how to create a simple Web page, using Netscape Composer, the Netscape Page Wizard, and some predesigned pages. By the end of this chapter, you will be the proud mother (or father) of your very own Web page!

Webtop Publishing with Composer

When you wander the Web, pulling up pages and clicking on links, it's easy to forget that behind each attractive page is a text file that contains the codes that tell Navigator how to display the page. If you haven't seen these codes yet, run Navigator and open a page that interests you. Open Navigator's **View** menu and select **Page Source**. Navigator displays the coded HTML file that it used to render the current Web page.

What Exactly Is HTML?

HTML (short for Hypertext Markup Language) is a set of standard (and standard wannabe) codes that tell Web browsers how to display Web pages. For example, the <H1> code tells Web browsers that the text following the code is a heading. The Web browser interprets the code and displays the text in a large, usually bold, typeface. HTML includes many codes for formatting lists, paragraphs, and tables, and for inserting graphics, sounds, and other objects. Because the browser is in charge of interpreting these codes, a Web page usually does not look the same in any two browsers.

Behind every Web page is a text file that contains HTML codes.

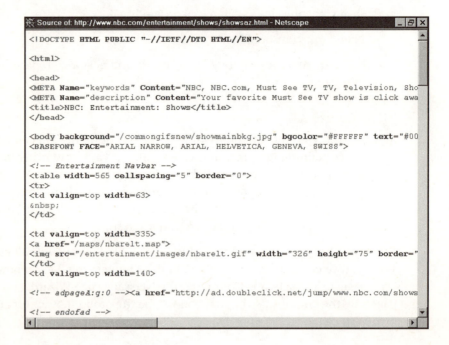

Chapter 20 ➤ *Making a Simple Web Page*

In the old days, Web page developers created Web pages by manually typing all these codes in a text file, and then saving the file with the HTM or HTML extension. Although you can still do that, many software companies have created special Web page editing programs (also called HTML editors), which take care of the coding for you. These programs act as word processing or desktop publishing programs for the Web. You type the text, format it, and add graphics and other objects; the HTML editor inserts the necessary codes for you.

Netscape Composer is Netscape Communicator's HTML editor. Formerly available only in Netscape Gold, Composer now plays a central role in the Communicator package, providing the following enhancements:

➤ **Page Wizards and Templates** give you something to start with, so you never have to create a Web page from scratch. You'll learn how to use Wizards and templates later in this chapter.

➤ **E-mail Support** allows you to enhance your e-mail messages with fancy text, bulleted and numbered lists, tables, graphics, and links.

➤ **Easy Web Publishing** lets you save your Web pages directly to a Web server on the Internet or on your company's intranet with a single click of a button. See Chapter 23, "Formatting and Publishing Your Page," for details.

➤ **Spell Checking** (a new tool) checks your Web pages and e-mail messages for spelling errors and typos.

Running Composer

You can run Composer in Windows 95 by selecting it from the **Start, Programs, Netscape Communicator** menu. In Windows 3.1, change to the Netscape Communicator program group, and double-click on the Netscape Composer icon. Because Composer is an integral part of the Communicator suite, there are other, more convenient methods of running Composer:

➤ Click on the **Composer** button in the Component bar, or press **Ctrl+4**.

> **Check This Out...**
>
> **Composer Plug-Ins?**
> Netscape designed Composer using open standards, so third-party developers can develop plug-ins for Composer, such as grammar checkers and image editors. When you're looking for plug-ins, keep an eye out for Composer plug-ins.

Part 5 ▶ *Publishing Your Own Web Pages*

▶ Open the **Communicator** menu in any of the other Communicator components (for instance Messenger or Collabra), and select the **Page Composer** option.

▶ To edit an existing page, you can open it directly in Composer. In Navigator, select **File, Open Page**. Type the URL of the page you want to open, and make sure **Composer** is selected. Click the **Open** button.

▶ You can start creating a Web page immediately by opening Navigator's **File** menu, pointing to **New**, and selecting **Blank Page**, **Page From Template**, or **Page From Wizard**.

▶ Open the page in Navigator, open the **File** menu, and select **Edit Page**.

However you choose to run Composer, the Composer window eventually appears. The following figure shows Composer displaying a Web page template from Netscape. Note that the Composer window contains tools that you might see in any standard word-processing application, including a formatting toolbar for styling text, and a standard toolbar for cutting, copying, pasting, and performing other common tasks. You will learn how to use several of these tools in this chapter.

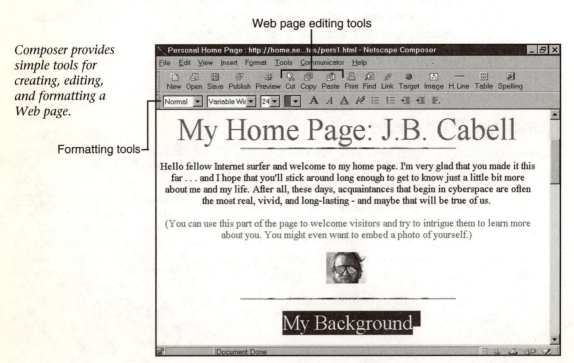

Composer provides simple tools for creating, editing, and formatting a Web page.

Step-by-Step Web Pages with the Wizard

Netscape offers an online Wizard that leads you step-by-step through the process of creating a Web page. You simply click on the items you want to add to your page, follow the instructions, and fill out a few forms. The Wizard slaps together the page. You can then save the page to your hard drive, publish it, or open it in Composer to modify it.

To run the Wizard, first connect to the Internet and run Netscape Composer. Click the **New** button in Composer's toolbar, and click the **From Page Wizard** button. Navigator (not Composer) displays the Wizard page, consisting of three frames. Scroll down to the bottom of the upper right frame and click the **Start** button.

> **Check This Out...**
>
> **The Ever-Changing Wizard** The Wizard is actually stored at Netscape's Web site, where it may be modified, so the steps for using the Wizard may differ when you finally get around to making your page.

The upper left frame contains instructions for using the Wizard, and the upper right frame has a preview of the page you're designing. The underlined links in the left frame are commands for the Wizard. You click on these commands to add elements to your page. Click the **give your page a title** link. A simple form with just one field appears in the bottom frame. Drag over the existing text, type your page title, and click the **Apply** button.

Follow the remaining instructions in the left pane to add items to your Web page. For example, you can type an introduction, add links to other Web pages, add an e-mail link (so visitors can quickly send you an e-mail message), and select a color combination. When you are done, click the **Build** button to see your finished page.

At this point, you might think you're finished, but you still need to save your page. The page is at Netscape's site, not on your computer, so you have to save the page to your hard drive. Don't just use the File, Save As command, because Navigator will drop out any graphics you may have added to the page. Instead, take the following steps:

1. Open the **File** menu and select **Edit Page**. Netscape Composer runs, displaying the page you just created.

2. Click the **Save** button. The Save As dialog box appears.

3. In the Save As dialog box, type a name for the file in the **File name** text box, and select the drive and folder in which you want the page stored. (It's a good idea to use a separate folder for your Web page and all associated files.) Click **Save**.

The Wizard lets you create a Web page online.

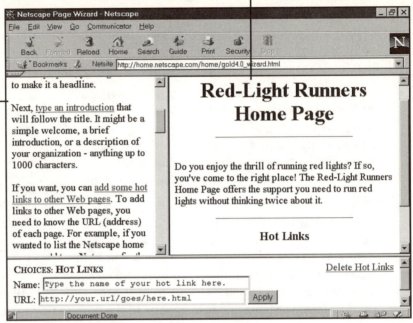

Follow the instructions here to make your page.

This frame lets you preview your page.

Can I Use Any Name for My Web Page? If you are publishing your Web page on your service provider's Web server, ask your service provider if you need to use any special file name. Many service providers demand that you name your file **index.htm** or **index.html**, because Web browsers automatically open the index.html file whenever they connect to a directory that has a file of this name.

4. A Saving Document dialog box appears, listing each text and graphics file as it downloads, and counting off the number of files it has left to download. When the download is complete, the page appears in Composer, ready for you to edit.

The page might look a little funny in Composer. If the page contains a numbered list, for instance, Composer does not display actual numbers next to the paragraphs. Instead, it displays placeholder icons. To see the page as it will appear in a Web browser, click the **Preview** button. This opens the page in Navigator (Composer may prompt you to save the file before opening it in Navigator). You can then switch back to Composer to edit the file.

Chapter 20 ➤ *Making a Simple Web Page*

Click the Preview button to see how the page will look on the Web.

Your page appears in Composer, where you can tweak it.

Creating Your Own Web Page Using a Template

Web page templates are nothing more than existing Web pages that you can modify and use as your own Web pages. Netscape has a collection of templates grouped by category: Personal/Family, Company/Small Business, Department, Product/Service, Special Interest Group, and Interesting and Fun.

You can open any of these templates in Netscape Composer, and use Composer's tools to edit the text, add graphics, add your own links, change the background, and modify the page in any way you wish. To use one of these templates, take the following steps:

1. Run Navigator or Composer. Open the **File** menu, point to **New**, and select **Page From Template**. (In Composer, you can click the **New** button and select **From Template**.) Navigator displays the New Page from Template dialog box.

2. Click the **Netscape Templates** button. Navigator opens the Netscape Web Page Templates page.

3. Scroll down the list, and click on a link for the template you want to use. Navigator opens the template and displays it. (If you don't like the template, click the **Back** button and try a different link.)

235

4. Open the **File** menu and select **Edit Page**. Navigator automatically saves the template and all associated graphics to your hard drive, and opens the template in Composer.

You can start editing the template.

Composer displays the template.

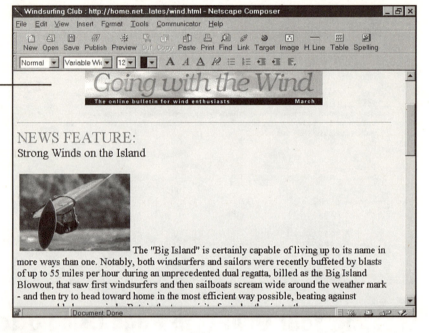

5. Enter your changes and adjust any formatting as desired. See "Making Some Quick Adjustments" later in this chapter, for details.

6. Open the **File** menu and select **Save**. Use the Save As dialog box to save the Web page to your hard drive. You will learn how to place your page on the Web in Chapter 23, "Formatting and Publishing Your Page."

Every Page Is a Template

Don't restrict yourself to using only Netscape's templates. Any page on the Internet can act as a template. If you find a Web page you like while wandering with Navigator, open Navigator's **File** menu and select **Edit Page**. You can then edit the page in Composer, and save the page to your hard drive or to your Web server.

Starting with Your Bookmarks

An easy way to create a Web page that contains links to all of your favorite sites is to start with your bookmarks. In Composer, open the **File** menu and click on **Open Page**. Click the **Choose File** button, and use the Open dialog box to select the file named Bookmark.htm (in Windows 95, the file is in the Program Files/Netscape/Users/*Yourname* folder). Click **Open**. This returns you to the Open Page dialog box. Click on **Composer**, and click the **Open** button.

To ensure that you don't mess up your bookmarks while editing this file, open the **File** menu, select **Save As**, and save the file to a different folder or under another name. You can now edit this file without affecting the bookmark file that Navigator uses as the Bookmarks menu.

Making Some Quick Adjustments

Whether you create your Web page using Netscape's Page Wizard, a template, an existing page, or bookmarks, you're not going to start with a finished page. The page probably has some text and links you want to nuke, some misplaced graphics, or gaps that you want to fill in with your own text.

The following sections provide instructions on how to make some quick and easy changes and use several of Composer's formatting tools. More detailed instructions for working with links, tables, frames, and advanced formatting tools are provided in the remaining chapters in this part.

Deleting and Adding Text

Whether you start with an existing page or open a blank page, Composer displays an insertion point somewhere on the page. The insertion point appears as a blinking vertical line, and it shows you where text will be inserted when you start typing. You can move the insertion point by clicking where you want to place it, or by using the arrow keys on your keyboard.

There are basically two ways to add text to a page: You can just start typing, and then format the text later, or select your formatting options first and start typing. For example, to type a title at the top of the page, you might open the **Paragraph Style** drop-down list and select the **Heading1** style, select **Center** from the **Alignment** drop-down list, and then type your page title.

To add text, start typing.

The Paragraph Style drop-down list

You can select formatting options before you start typing.

The Alignment drop-down list

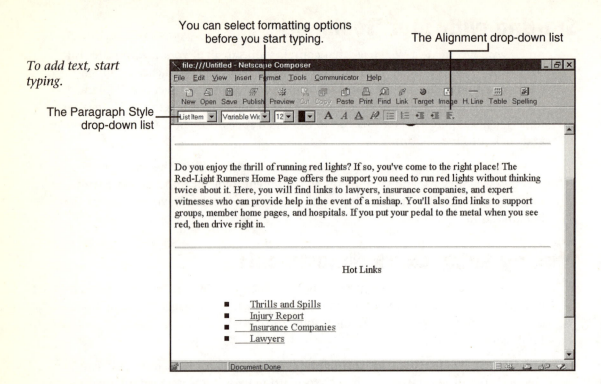

To delete text, drag over it and press the **Delete** key. You can also use the Cut, Copy, and Paste buttons, in the Standard toolbar, to delete, copy, or move text.

Basic Formatting Options

You can do a pretty good job of formatting your Web page without ever opening the **Format** menu. Simply select your formatting options from the Formatting toolbar. The following table explains the purpose of each button. (For more advanced formatting options, see Chapter 23.)

The Formatting toolbar offers two types of formatting tools: text and paragraph. The text formatting tools change the type style, size, and color of text, and apply enhancements—bold, italic, and underline. To apply a text format to existing text, you must first drag over the text. The paragraph formatting tools let you select a paragraph style, indent paragraphs, change their alignment, or transform paragraphs into a bulleted or numbered list. To apply a paragraph format, you must move the insertion point somewhere in the paragraph; you don't have to select all the text.

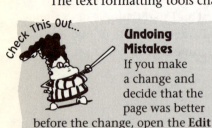

Undoing Mistakes
If you make a change and decide that the page was better before the change, open the **Edit** menu and select **Undo**.

Chapter 20 ➤ *Making a Simple Web Page*

Composer's Formatting Toolbar Buttons

Button	Name	Description
Normal	Paragraph Style	Applies a general style to the entire paragraph. For example, you can click inside a paragraph, and select Heading1 to transform the text into a top-level heading.
Variable W	Font	Changes the type style
12	Font Size	Changes the text size (seven sizes are available)
	Font Color	Changes text color
A	Bold	Makes text thick
A	Italic	Makes text slanted
A	Underline	Underlines text
	Remove All Styles	Removes all formatting you have applied, returning the text to normal
	Bullet List	Transforms selected paragraphs into a bulleted list
	Numbered List	Transforms selected paragraphs into a numbered list
	Decrease Indent	Moves paragraph to the left
	Increase Indent	Moves paragraph to the right
	Alignment	Aligns paragraph left, center, or right

Inserting Graphics and Lines

Most denizens of the Web will quickly skip over your Web page if it doesn't contain some pretty pictures, or at least a couple horizontal lines that divide the text. Fortunately, inserting graphics and lines in Composer is fairly easy.

239

Part 5 ➤ *Publishing Your Own Web Pages*

Check This Out...

New Composer Feature In the previous version of Composer (the Netscape Navigator Gold 3.0 editor), pasted pictures retained their graphic format. This made it difficult for Web browsers to open and display images in unfamiliar formats, such as PCX. In Composer, pasted images are converted into GIF or JPEG format, making them compatible with most systems and browsers.

If you don't have any graphics to insert, you can download sample graphics off the Web, as explained in Chapter 8, "Saving and Printing Your Finds." However, if you plan on lifting and using original artwork, be sure you get permission from the person who created the Web page.

When you have an image to insert, take the following steps to place it on your Web page:

1. Click where you want to insert the image on your Web page. The insertion point moves to the selected position. (It's a good idea to place the image on a blank line.)

2. Click the **Image** button. If you haven't yet saved the page, the Save New Page dialog box appears. Save your file. The Image Properties dialog box then appears, as shown below.

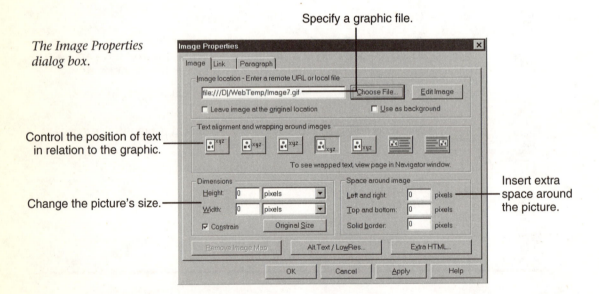

The Image Properties dialog box.

Specify a graphic file.

Control the position of text in relation to the graphic.

Change the picture's size.

Insert extra space around the picture.

3. Click the **Choose File** button next to Image Location text box. The Choose Image File dialog box appears, prompting you to pick a file.

240

4. Change to the drive and folder in which the image file is stored, and click on the file's name. Click **Open**. You're returned to the Properties dialog box.

5. Click on one of the **Text Alignment** buttons to specify how you want text aligned with or wrapped around the graphic. The first five buttons specify vertical alignment (for example, you can align text with the top or bottom of the image). The last two buttons provide text wrapping options.

6. Under **Dimensions**, you can enter settings, but it's easier just to drag the border of the image to resize it once it is on the page.

7. Under **Space Around Image**, you can type entries to insert additional space between the image and surrounding text. (Keep in mind that a pixel is tiny, a screen dot.) The Solid Border option places a black line around the image.

8. Click **OK**. Composer inserts the image. (The text wrapping is not displayed in Composer. Click on the **Preview** button to see how the image will actually appear on the page.)

To change any of the settings you entered, right-click on the image and click on **Image Properties**. You can drag an image to move it, or drag its edge or corner to resize it. You can also use some of Composer's formatting tools to change its position. For example, if the image is on a separate line, you can click the image, and then select Center from the Alignment list to center the image. You can even make the image a bulleted list item, although I can't imagine why anyone would want to do that.

If you have a long page, consider using horizontal lines to divide the page. To insert a horizontal line, move the insertion point to the end of the paragraph below which you want the line inserted. Click the **H. Line** button. You can then drag the middle of the line to make it thicker, or drag an end of the line to make the line longer or shorter. To change any other line properties, right-click on the line, and select **Horizontal Line Properties**. For additional instructions on how to use links, see Chapter 21, "All You Need to Know About Links."

Checking for Misspellings and Typos

Sometime before you place your page on the Web, you should use Composer's new spell-checking tool to check for misspellings and typos. To spell check your page, open it in Composer, and then open the **Tools** menu and select **Check Spelling** (or click the **Spelling** button in the toolbar). The spell checker starts looking through your page, and notifies you of any entries that are not included in its dictionary. You can then choose to correct the entry (assuming it is wrong), or skip it.

The Least You Need to Know

You don't need to know much to create a simple Web page, using the Wizard or a template:

- To create a page with the Wizard, fire up Composer, click the **New** button, click the **From Page Wizard** button, and follow the on-screen instructions.

- To create a page from one of Netscape's templates, click Composer's **New** button, and click on the **From Template** button.

- After creating your page in Navigator, using the Wizard, open Navigator's **File** menu, and select **Edit Page**. Then, use Composer's **File, Save** command to save the page to disk.

- Composer's Formatting toolbar offers most of the tools you need to enhance your text.

- You can use the buttons on the Standard toolbar to quickly insert graphics, horizontal lines, and links.

- If you don't want to mess around with the complexities of Composer, create and publish your Web page at one of the free Web page sites listed in the previous section.

- If you're ready to publish your page, skip over the next two chapters and the first half of Chapter 23, "Formatting and Publishing Your Page," to learn how to place your page on the Web.

Chapter 21

All You Need to Know About Links

In This Chapter

- ➤ Name the two essential parts of a link
- ➤ Link your page to other pages on the Web
- ➤ Make a link that visitors can click on to send you an e-mail message
- ➤ Test your links to make sure they work

Links are the very threads that stitch together the pages, documents, and files that comprise the Web. Without links, you couldn't surf, skip, or even wander the Web. Each page would be a dead end. You would have to type the specific address of each Web page you wanted to visit. Your mouse would be useless. You would have to actually *know* what you were doing. Bummer.

Fortunately, most Web pages have links. These links may point to different areas on the same page, to related pages at the same Web site, to previous pages, to completely unrelated pages, to files or graphics, to audio or video clips, to e-mail addresses, and to any other objects on the Internet. The point is that on the Web, it is polite to point. And in this chapter, you'll learn how to add links that point to stuff on the Web.

Creating a Simple Link

Those little blue underlined text links you have been clicking on are the bread and butter of Web page links. Unlike graphic links, which take forever to travel over a modem connection, these text links slide through without hesitation. They are also very easy to create and maintain. To create a simple text link, take the following steps:

1. Open or start a Web page in Composer, type the text you want to use as the link, and drag over it.

2. Click the **Link** button (or press **Ctrl+Shift+L**). The Character Properties dialog box opens, with the Link tab displayed.

3. In the **Link to a page location or local file** text box, type the URL of the page you want to link to. For example, you might type **http://www.nbc.com** to create a link to NBC Online.

4. Click **OK**. The selected text appears highlighted, and this text points to the specified page.

If you have a graphic that you want to use as a link, first insert the graphic on your Web page. Then, follow the same steps to transform it into a link. Don't worry—it won't turn blue.

Editing and Removing Links

If you transform text or a graphic into a link and then decide later that you do not want the text or graphic acting as a link, you can quickly remove the link property from the object. Simply right-click on the object, and select **Remove Link**.

In most cases, you don't want to remove the link entirely. You just want to change the address of the page or object to which the link points. To do this, right-click on the link, and click on **Link Properties**. The Properties dialog box appears, displaying the Link tab front and center. In the **Link to a page location or local file** text box, type the URL of the Web page you want the link to point to, or click on the **Choose File** button, and pick the name of a file that's on your hard drive.

> **Check This Out...**
>
> **Link Source and Link To**
> Every link consists of two parts: a *link source* and a *link to* (both of which are commonly called *anchors*). The link source is the part that the person clicks on—the blue, underlined text or the graphic. The link to, which the visitor rarely sees, is the address of the page that the link points to.

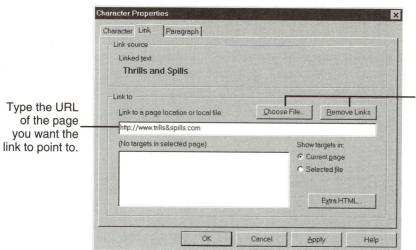

You can change the properties of a link to make it point to something else.

You can point the link to another Web page or file on your hard drive.

Type the URL of the page you want the link to point to.

Understanding Absolute and Relative Links

As you work with links, you should be aware that there are two types of links: *absolute* and *relative*:

➤ The code behind an *absolute* link includes a complete path that describes the exact location of the page or file. For example, a link such as **http://www.iquest.com/~smith/resume.html** tells the name of the server and directory where the file resume.html is stored.

➤ A *relative* link describes the location of the page or file in relation to the folder or directory in which the page containing the link is stored. For example, a link such as resume.html tells only the file name; for the link to work, the file resume.html must be in the same directory as the Web page that contains the link to resume.html.

Relative links are usually shorter and easier to edit than absolute links. However, when you transfer your page to a Web server, to publish it, you must make sure that you place any files that the relative links point to in the same relative locations on the Web server as those files are stored on your hard drive. The easiest way to do this is to store your Web page and all files it points to in the same folder on your hard drive. When you publish the page, place all the files in a single directory on the Web server.

245

Linking Your Page to Other Pages at Your Site

If you are creating a personal home page that's not very long, chances are that you will publish a single page. However, if you have a business or work for a company that has several Web pages (or you just have a lot of important things to say), you can create links to your other Web pages.

To create links to other pages at your Web site, you first need another page to link to. Also, before you start, you have to think about where the two HTML files will be stored on the Web server. You have a few options here:

➤ Store all your Web pages and any related files (such as graphics) in the same folder on your hard drive. To prevent migraines, I strongly recommend this option.

➤ Store the pages in the same folders on your hard disk as those pages will be stored in on the Web server. By doing this, you won't have to edit the links later to point them to the correct directories on the Web server.

➤ Don't worry about it now. This is easy until you find out later that all your links don't work.

When you have another HTML page on your hard drive, take the following steps to create links to these other pages:

1. Drag over the text or select the graphic that you want to act as the link.

2. Right-click on the selected item, and choose **Create Link Using Selected**.... The Properties dialog box appears.

3. Click the **Choose File** button. The Link to File dialog box appears.

4. Use the Link to File dialog box to select the page you want the selected link to point to, and click **Open**. You're returned to the Properties dialog box.

5. Click **OK**. If you selected text as the link, it appears underlined.

6. Click the **Save** button to save the file. Then, to test the link, click the **Preview** button.

7. When Navigator opens, click the link. The linked-to page should appear. Click the **Close** (X) button to close the browser.

Chapter 21 ➤ *All You Need to Know About Links*

Linking to a Specific Place on a Page

If you have a long Web page, you might want to place a table of contents at the top of the page that provides links to various places on the page. This would allow the visitor to quickly navigate your Web page, without wearing out the scroll bar.

To create a link that points to a specific part of a page, you must first mark the destination point as a *target*. You can then create a link that points to the target instead of to a URL. (I usually mark all my targets first.) To mark a target, take the following steps:

1. Click where you want the target placed, or select the target. (If you select text to use as the target, Composer will use that text as the target name, saving you some keystrokes.)

2. Click the **Target** button. The Target Properties dialog box appears, as shown here, prompting you to type a name for it.

Type a name for the target.

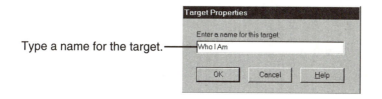

Mark your targets first, so you will have something to link to.

3. Type a brief but descriptive name for the target. When you create a link to the target, you must select the target from a list of marked targets; be sure you type a name you'll remember. (The target name does not appear on the page.)

4. Click **OK**. Composer inserts a small target symbol at the insertion point or to the left of the selected text. This is only an editor's symbol; it won't be seen by visitors who view the page.

Repeat the steps above to mark any additional places on the page as targets. You can quickly edit a target by right-clicking on the target icon and selecting **Target Properties**. Once you have marked at least one target on the page, you can create a link that points to it. Take the following steps:

1. If necessary, type the text that you want to act as the link. Drag over the text to select it. (You can also use an image as a link.)

2. Click the **Link** button. The Character Properties dialog appears, with the Link tab displayed. The "Select a named target in current document" field lists all the targets on the current page, as shown below.

247

Composer lists all the marked targets on the current page.

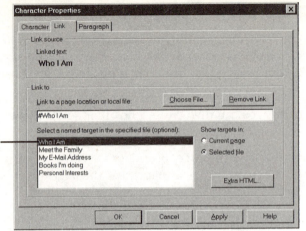

Select the target that you want this link to point to.

3. Click the target name you want to link to. The selected target appears in the Link to a page location or local file text box.

4. Click **OK** to accept this link.

5. Click the **Save** button.

6. Repeat these steps to link to other targets on the page.

The procedure for linking to a targeted location on another page of your site is similar. However, when you make the link, you have to click the **Choose File** button to select the page with the target before you can select the target from the list on the page.

Good Form

If you have a long Web page consisting of several sections, insert a link at the bottom of each section that points to a target at the top of the page, so the user can quickly return to where she started. If you have a Web document consisting of several pages, insert links on the other pages that point to the home page.

Inserting a Link for Your E-Mail Address

If you want people to be able to contact you after reading your Web page, you can insert a link at the bottom of the page that points to your e-mail address. If the user has an e-mail program that's set up properly, he or she can then click on the link. The e-mail program will run automatically and address a new message to you. All the person has to do is type the message and send it.

To insert a link to your e-mail address, first type the text you want to use as the link text (for example, **I Need Mail!**, **E-Mail me**, or your e-mail address). Drag over the text, and click the **Link** button. In the **Link to a page location or local file** text box, type **mailto:** followed by your e-mail address (for example, **mailto:bfink@internet.com**). Click **OK**.

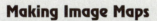

Making Image Maps

In your Web wanderings, you have probably encountered image maps; pictures that contain two or more areas that act as links. Image maps might look like button bars, like actual maps, or simply like big pictures. If you want to add an image map to your page, use a special program for creating image maps. One of the more popular image map programs is LiveView, which you can download at **http://www.mediatec.com/**. Although you can create an image map manually and insert the HTML codes for it, life is too short—get the specialized program.

Drag-and-Drop Web Page Creation

One of the coolest aspects of Composer is that you can drag and drop objects onto a Web page you're creating in Composer. If you have a shortcut on the Windows desktop that points to a Web page or a graphic on your hard drive, or even a document you created, simply drag it into the Composer window, and drop it on the page.

If you open a Web page in Navigator and you want to link to it from your Web page, drag the Location icon from Navigator onto your page in Composer, and release the mouse button. You can even drag and drop graphics from Web pages displayed in Navigator into your Web pages! You might have to reformat them, but it's much easier than typing all those URLs.

You can drag items from the Windows desktop, from documents created in other applications, or from pages on the Web into your Web page.

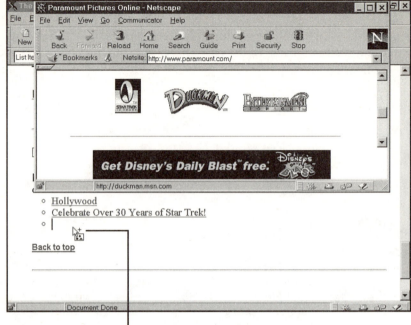

Drag a link from Navigator onto your Web page in Composer.

Testing Your Links

There's nothing worse on a Web page than a link that doesn't work. If your page is full of links that lead only to error messages, your visitors quickly will become disgruntled; they'll back out of your site, and surf off in another direction. So, before you place your page on the Web, and after you place it on the Web, and on a regular basis thereafter, you should check your links.

The easiest way to check your links is to open your page in Navigator, and then start clicking. If you receive an error message, reopen the page in Composer, fix the error, and check the page again.

You can also check links in Composer, but it's kind of a hassle. Whenever you enter the command to follow a link, Composer automatically opens the page in a separate window (a Composer or Navigator window), even if the link points to a target on the same page. For that reason, it is better to check links in Navigator. However, if you want to check a link in Composer, just right-click on the link, and select **Browse to** (to open the linked page in Navigator) or **Open Link in Composer** (to open the linked page in a separate Composer window). Composer or Navigator opens the page.

Chapter 21 ➤ *All You Need to Know About Links*

Check Your Links "Post-Posting"

Don't forget to check your page after placing it on the Web. If the page has any relative links, they can get messed up when your files are transferred to the server. You should make sure that the page works on the Web as well as it works locally.

The Least You Need to Know

Creating links to other pages on the Web is a no-brainer. Here's what you do:

➤ Drag over the link text, click the **Link** button, type the URL of the target page, and click **OK**.

➤ To use an image as a link, first insert the image and select it, then click the **Link** button.

➤ To remove a link, right-click on it, and select **Remove Link**.

➤ To change the URL that a link points to, right-click on the link and select **Link Properties**.

➤ To link to a specific place on a page, you must first mark that place as a target.

➤ You can create a link to your e-mail address by creating a link that points to **mailto:username@internet.service.provider**.

Chapter 22

Working with Tables and Frames

> **In This Chapter**
>
> ➤ Arrange text in columns and rows
>
> ➤ Make a dime store button bar
>
> ➤ Create your very own Web page resume
>
> ➤ Display two Web pages on-screen at the same time with frames

When you create a Web page, you must consider your audience, the people who are going to pull up your page on their 15-inch monitors and try to navigate your site. These folks are going to expect your page to be laid out in some logical way that fits on their screens. Tables and frames are useful tools in achieving a logical, visually appealing page layout.

Tables are especially useful for arranging text in columns and rows. With Composer, you can specify the number of rows and columns you want the table to have, and Composer creates it. All you have to do is type entries into each cell (the box formed by the intersection of a column and row).

Tables make it easy to arrange text in rows and columns.

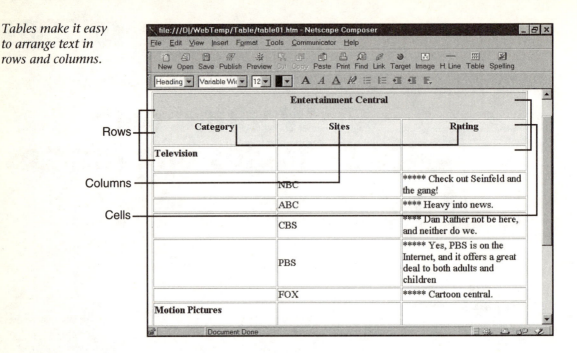

Like tables, frames allow you to arrange text. However, frames are a little more intrusive. Instead of being an actual part of the Web page, frames control the browser window (the viewing area) chopping it into two or more rectangular sections, each of which displays a different Web page. Composer does not offer tools for easily creating frames, but you can create them by typing HTML frame codes, as explained later in this chapter.

Why Not Use Frames?

Frames are difficult to create and manage in Composer. In addition, some older browsers are not capable of displaying frames, so you always have to create an alternative, frameless page (that is, if you want everyone to be able to view your page, regardless of what browser they use). In addition, it's tempting to overuse frames and difficult to design useful frames. Before you work with frames, look around the Web for good and bad examples of frames. Or, visit the I Hate Frames Club at **http://wwwvoice.com/hatefrm.html**.

Chapter 22 ➤ *Working with Tables and Frames*

Inserting a Table

Once you understand the basic concept of tables, you can apply it creatively to your Web page design. For example, create a one-row table with several columns, and insert a link into each cell—instant button bar! Create a three-column table, and use it to make an online résumé—dates in the first column, categories in the second column (Experience, Education, Awards, and so on), and details in the third column. You can even transform your entire Web page into a table, placing a table of contents in the left column and the running text in the right column. The possibilities, although not endless, are certainly numerous.

But before you can make these fancy moves, you need to know the basics. You need to learn how to insert a table and set its properties.

Creating a table in Composer is a breeze. You simply click the **Insert Table** button. The New Table Properties dialog box appears, prompting you to specify the desired number of rows and columns you want the table to have and any other table settings.

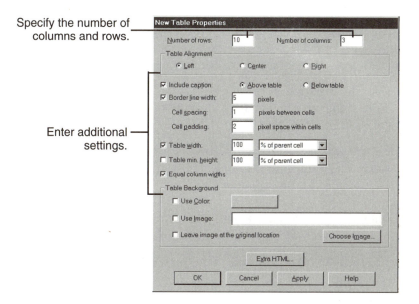

Specify the number of columns and rows.

Enter additional settings.

The New Table Properties dialog box lets you control the look, location, and behavior of the table.

All you really have to do at this point is type the desired number of rows and columns and click **OK**. You can then start typing entries in the cells, and worry about the settings later. However, if you have a clear idea of the table's structure, you can save yourself some time by entering the settings now:

➤ Select an alignment option to control the position of the table in relation to the window: **Left**, **Center**, or **Right**.

- To add a caption above or below the table, click on **Include Caption**, and pick the desired location.

- Type the number of pixels you want to use for the following table attributes (remember, a pixel is an on-screen dot, pretty tiny):

    Border Line Width: This setting controls the width of the lines that make up the table. You can enter 0 (or remove the check mark next to Border Line Width) to have no lines appear.

    Cell Spacing: This setting controls the space between cells.

    Cell Padding: This setting controls the space between the line that defines a cell and the text or object that the cell contains.

- If you don't specify a table width or height, Composer creates a table that's as wide as the page, and inserts rows of a standard height (text wraps automatically inside a cell, and the cell's height expands to accommodate the text). To specify a table width, height, or color, select the following options:

    Table Width: Click on this option to turn it on. You can then use the text box and drop-down list to make the table a certain number of pixels wide or specify the width as a percentage of the window width.

    Table Min Height: This option lets you specify a minimum height for the table. You can set the table height as an absolute number of pixels or as a percentage of the window height.

    Equal Column Widths: Make sure this option is on, so that all columns are the same width. If you turn this off, the columns expand as you type, making it very difficult to control the column width.

- By default, your table is white with black border lines. To change the color of the table or use a graphic background, enter the following Table Background settings:

    Use Color: The table is clear by default. You can choose a color to add some shading to the cells.

    Use Image: Lets you select a graphic image to use as the table background. Click the **Choose Image** button, and select the desired graphic.

    Leave Image at the Original Location: If you choose to use an image that's stored on a Web server, you can choose this option to leave the image on the remote Web server. When a user opens your page, the graphic image loads from the remote server, saving you some storage space. The only trouble is that if the graphic image is moved, your reference to it will no longer work.

You can change these table properties at any time. Right-click anywhere on the table, select **Table Properties**, and click on the **Table** tab. To change the properties of a single row or selected cell(s), see "Restructuring Your Table," later in this chapter.

Typing Entries into Cells

If you did not specify a table width, the table appears as wide as the page, and is divided into the specified number of columns, each equal in width. If you left Equal Column Widths on, the text automatically wraps inside the cell as you type the entries. To make the table (and the columns it contains) wider or narrower, drag the left or right side of the table.

To type an entry into a cell, click inside the cell or use the Tab key or the arrow keys to move from cell to cell. When the insertion point is in the desired cell, start typing. You can also insert links or graphics into cells; the size of the cell automatically adjusts to accommodate whatever object you insert.

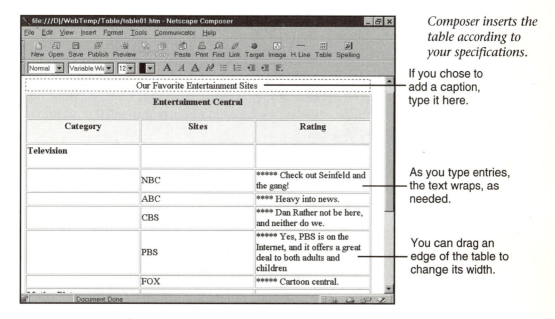

Composer inserts the table according to your specifications.

If you chose to add a caption, type it here.

As you type entries, the text wraps, as needed.

You can drag an edge of the table to change its width.

Restructuring Your Table

The table you created in the previous section is pretty generic. All the columns are the same width, and the rows are the same height. If this works for you, fine, but you probably need something special—maybe you need a cell that spans several columns or rows, or you want to use different colors for each cell in your table. Whatever the case, you can change cell and row properties to create the desired effect.

Let's take the easy, row preferences first. Right-click on any cell in the row whose look you want to change, click on **Table Properties**, and click on the **Row** tab. Then, enter any of the following preferences:

Horizontal Alignment controls the position of text in relation to the left and right borders of the cell. You can choose Default, Left, Right, or Center.

Vertical Alignment controls the position of the text in relation to the top and bottom borders of the cell. You can choose Default, Top, Center, Bottom, or Baselines.

Row Background lets you pick a background color for all the cells in the row. For example, you might want to shade the topmost column green.

You can also change the properties of selected cells, although these options are a little more advanced. First, click inside the cell or drag over the cells whose properties you want to change. Right-click on one of the selected cells, select **Table Properties**, and click on the **Cell** tab. You can then change any of the following settings:

Horizontal and Vertical Alignment options control the horizontal position of the text inside the cell (the position of the text in relation to the left and right sides of the cell) and the vertical position (the position of the text in relation to the top and bottom of the cell).

Cell spans ___ row(s) and ___ column(s) To have a cell span two or more columns, enter the desired number or rows or columns you want the cell to span. For example, if you have a three-column table, and you want a cell at the top that spans all three columns, type 3 in the **column(s)** text box.

Text Style Header Style makes the text bold and centered inside the cell (this is useful if you have a wide cell at the top of the table that spans several columns).

Nonbreaking tells Composer not to wrap the text inside the cell.

Cell Width lets you set the width of the selected cell(s) as a percentage of the table width or as a specific number of pixels.

Cell Min. Height lets you specify the minimum cell height as a percentage of the table height or as a specific number of pixels.

Cell Background allows you to specify a background color for the selected cell(s) (or use a graphic image).

If you chose to make a cell span two or more columns or rows, Composer does not merge the selected cell with the other cells in that row or column, so you may have to delete those cells. If the cells contain entries, use the Cut and Paste buttons to move the entries to other cells. Then, right-click on the extraneous cell, point to **Delete**, and click on **Cell** (repeat to delete additional cells).

Adding and Deleting Rows, Columns, and Cells

When you first create a table, you rarely know how many rows and columns you need. You make your best guess, which is usually wrong, and then you add or delete columns and rows as needed. You can easily add rows, columns, and cells in Composer. When inserting rows or columns, keep in mind that rows are inserted below the selected row, and columns are inserted to the right of the selected column. To add cells, columns, or rows, take any of the following steps:

- ➤ To insert a row, select a cell in the row where you want the new row added. Open the **Insert** menu, point to **Table**, and click on **Row**.

- ➤ To insert a column, select a cell in the column where you want the new column added. Open the **Insert** menu, point to **Table**, and click on **Column**.

- ➤ Right-click on a cell, point to **Insert**, and select the item you want to insert: **Row**, **Column**, or **Cell**. (If you chose Cell, the new cell is inserted to the right of the selected cell.)

To delete rows, columns, or cells, right-click on the row, column, or cell you want to delete, point to **Delete**, and click on **Row**, **Column**, or **Cell**. Or, select the row, column, or cell you want to delete, and select the desired object from the **Edit**, **Delete Table** submenu.

Page Formatting with Tables

You can use tables for more than just grids of data. Because you can create columns in tables, you can use tables to create column-style text layouts. For example, the Web page shown below was created using a table.

To create a similar page, use a wide table. This table has three columns: a column for the titles, a column for the text, and a blank column between them. Using this blank column, you can create a nice amount of space between the titles and the text. Whenever you need to add a new title that you want to line up with the text, just start a new row.

Part 5 ➤ *Publishing Your Own Web Pages*

A table-based page layout at c\net.

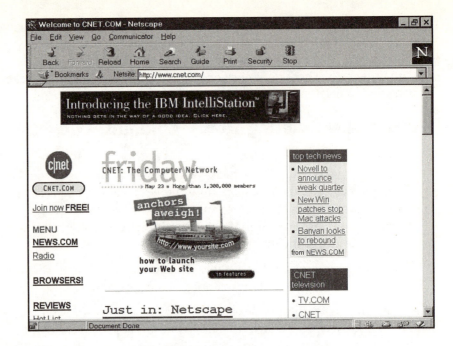

What About that Dime Store Button Bar You Promised?

If you go to Netscape's home page, you'll see an image map at the top of the page that offers buttons labeled Netscape Destinations, Company & Products, and so on. You can create a similar bar using the tables feature. Just insert a one row table at the top of your page, choose a different background color for each cell, and insert a link into each cell. You may also wish to crank up the cell padding and border width and increase the text size.

Framing Your Masterpiece

Used sparingly, frames can help you make your Web site easier to navigate. For instance, you can create a narrow frame on the left that displays a table of contents (complete with links), and use a wide frame on the right to display the contents of the currently selected link. This allows your visitor to easily navigate your web without ever losing site of the table of contents.

Before you create frames, promise me one thing—promise that you will never, ever use more than three frames. Why? Just take a look at the following Web page. It uses so many frames that you really don't know where to start. Too many frames draw your attention away from the main Web page, making it more difficult to navigate the site.

260

Chapter 22 ➤ *Working with Tables and Frames*

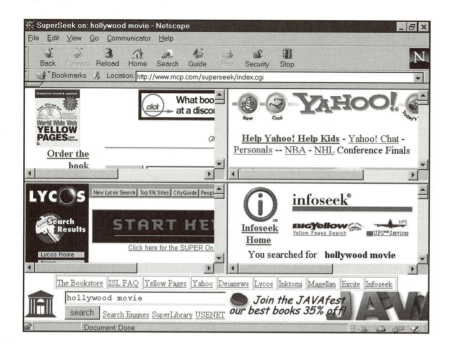

Too many frames are worse than no frames at all.

Composer Doesn't Do Frames

Composer has no Insert Frame command. In fact, Composer can't even display frames after you create them. In order to use frames, you must insert the frame codes manually. Yes, you must open your Web page in a text editor and type the codes yourself. You can use any simple text editor (WordPad or Notepad) or a word processing program that lets you save a file as a text-only file.

The easiest way to edit your page in a text editor is to set up your text editor in Composer. Open the **Edit** menu, point to **Preferences**, and click on **Composer**. Next to **HTML Source**, click the **Choose** button. The Choose HTML Editor Application dialog box appears; use it to select the file that runs your text editor, and click **Open**. (Windows 95 WordPad is in **C:\Program Files\Accessories\Wordpad.exe**.) Click **OK**.

To edit the page that's currently opened in Composer, open Composer's **Edit** menu and select **HTML Source**. Composer runs the text editor, which then opens the HTML coded file. (If you use Notepad, open the Edit menu and select Word Wrap to turn this feature on.)

> **Inserting HTML Codes in Composer**
>
> You can insert HTML codes in Composer. Move the insertion point where you want the code inserted, open the **Insert** menu, and select **HTML Tag**. You can then type the code, and click **OK**. The trouble is that you can enter only one code at a time. You'll actually save time by opening your page in a text editor and typing the codes.

Entering the Frame Codes

To create frames, you insert frame codes into your Web page. These codes tell the visiting Web browser how to divide its window into frames and which page it should load into each frame. You can do all sorts of fancy stuff with these codes, such as nesting a set of frame codes inside another set of frame codes, but we're not going to do that here. Instead, I'm going to give you the codes to enter to create a simple two-frame window. I will then show you how to modify some of the parameters inside the codes to tweak the design. If you want details on how to do the fancy stuff, search the Internet for **html frame**.

> **More About HTML** If you want to know more about working with HTML, as well as making your pages come alive with JavaScript, run back to the bookstore and buy *The Complete Idiot's Guide to Creating an HTML Web Page, Second Edition* and *The Complete Idiot's Guide to JavaScript, Second Edition*.

First, create three Web pages—a file for the framing codes, and two Web pages (one to display in the left pane, and the other for the right pane). To accommodate Web browsers that cannot display frames, you should enter your framing codes at the top of your main Web page file. These codes tell the browser, "If you can handle frames, here's what you do." You can then bracket the rest of the page with <NOFRAME> </NOFRAME> codes that enable a browser that cannot handle frames to display a non-framed page. If your service provider lets you use only one file as your main Web page file, be sure to enter the frame codes in that file.

Now, open your main Web page file in your text editor, and move the insertion point before any <BODY> codes; the framing codes cannot be between the <BODY> and </BODY> codes. Then, enter the following codes, as they are displayed here:

```
<FRAMESET COLS="25%,75%">

<FRAME SRC="index.htm" NAME="index">

<FRAME SRC="main.htm" NAME="main">
```

```
</FRAMESET>

<NOFRAME>

{Insert the Web Page Contents Here}

</NOFRAME>
```

Now, you can go back through and revise the codes to tweak the design and work more effectively for your situation. The following list takes the codes one-by-one, explains what each code does, and shows you how to modify each code:

<FRAMESET COLS="25%,75%"> This turns frames on and divides the window into a left and right pane. The left pane is 25 percent of the window width, leaving 75 percent for the right frame. You can enter different percentages. To divide the window into a top and bottom pane, instead, enter **<FRAMESET Rows="25%,75%">**.

<FRAME SRC="index.htm" NAME="index"> This code tells the browser which Web page to load in the first frame (the left frame, in this case). In place of *index.htm*, type the filename of the Web page that you want to be displayed in the right pane. In place of *index* (after Name=), type a name for the frame, something that will be easy to remember (see the following section for more information).

<FRAME SRC="main.htm" NAME="main"> This code tells the browser which Web page to load in the second frame (the right frame, in this case). In place of *main.htm*, type the filename of the Web page that you want to be displayed in the right pane. In place of *main* (after Name=), type a name for the frame.

</FRAMESET> This code simply says, "We're done with frames."

<NOFRAME> This code essentially tells the Web browser, "If you can't handle frames, then do the following." (Some older Web browsers cannot interpret frame codes.)

{Insert the Web Page Contents Here} This isn't a code. I'm just telling you to insert whatever you want here that provides an alternative for browsers that cannot display frames. You can insert a simple link that points to a non-frame page, or you can insert the codes for an entire Web page.

</NOFRAME> This is the Off code for NOFRAMES.

Check This Out...

Setting Relative Frame Sizes with Asterisks

Instead of entering precise settings for frame sizes, you can use asterisks to set relative sizes. For example, instead of entering <FRAMESET COLS="25%,75%">, you could enter <FRAMESET COLS="*,3*">. This tells the browser to give one share of the window to the left frame and three shares to the right frame.

Holding Your Index Steady in the Left Frame

If you open your framed page up in Navigator, and try to use the index in the left pane to open pages, something very troubling will occur. When you click on a link in the left pane, your index will disappear and be replaced by the page which that link pointed to. The browser doesn't "know" that it's supposed to open the page in the right pane.

To fix this problem you are going to have to add a target code that tells the browser which frame to use for displaying the linked page. For example, the following code

```
<A HREF="http://www.hollywood.com/">Hollywood Online</A>
```

displays **Hollywood Online** as a link that points to **http://www.hollywood.com**. When you click on the link, the browser opens the Hollywood Online page in the current window. To force the browser to open the page in a specific frame, you add a target command, telling the browser which frame to use. The following code tells the browser to open the page in the frame named main (which falls mainly on the plain):

```
<A HREF="http://www.hollywood.com/" target=main>Hollywood Online</A>
```

Where did we get the name "main?" The name comes from the frame codes you entered in the previous section. For example, with the **<FRAME SRC="main.htm" NAME="main">** code, I named the frame on the right "main." If you replaced "main" with some other name, you will have to use that name for the target= command.

The Least You Need to Know

Wow! That last section about frames was a killer, wasn't it? Fortunately, a Web page doesn't require frames. You way want to stick with tables, in which case, there's really not that much to know:

➤ To insert a table, position the insertion point where you want the table inserted, and click on the **Table** button.

- To change the properties of a table, right-click anywhere inside the table, and select **Table Properties**.
- You can change the properties of a selected row or of selected cells to make them appear different from the rest of the table.
- As you type in a cell, the text wraps, and the cell height expands to accommodate the entry.
- You can resize a table by dragging its outer edge.
- Use a really big table to divide your page into sections, so you can avoid having to deal with frames.

Chapter 23

Formatting and Publishing Your Page

In This Chapter

➤ Explain the purpose of all those commands on the Format menu

➤ Make your text blink on and off (ooooh)

➤ Give your page a background color

➤ Stick your page on the Web, so other people can see it

➤ Publicize your page, so it shows up in places like Yahoo!

Now that your page has all the objects required to make it a bona fide Web page, you can fine-tune it and stick it on the Web.

In this chapter, you are going to learn how to add some fancy formatting to your page. You'll learn how to apply additional text formats, change the color scheme of your page, and even add a background images. You'll learn how to add a title, description, and keywords to help users find your page using Internet search tools. And, finally, you will learn how to upload your page to a Web server, making it accessible to anyone in the world who has a computer, an Internet connection, and a Web browser.

Fancy Text Formatting

In Chapter 20, "Making a Simple Web Page," you learned how to use the buttons in Composer's Formatting toolbar to change the type style, size, and color of text, and to add enhancements that make the text bold or italic. However, Composer's toolbar barely scratches the surface of what's available. To access additional text formatting options, open Composer's **Format** menu. Here, you will find the following:

> **Font** displays the Character Properties dialog box, which gives you complete control over the appearance of your text. You can select a type style, size, and color; make a superscript or subscript, and turn on blinking text.
>
> **Size** offers seven different text sizes.
>
> **Style** lets you make text bold, italic, underlined, superscript, subscript, strikethrough, fixed width (a computer font), or blinking.
>
> **Color** palette lets you change the color of selected text.
>
> **Remove All Styles** removes any special text formatting you may have applied, returning the text to normal.

You can apply any text formatting before or after typing your text. To apply formatting after typing the text, first drag over the text to select it.

> **Avoid Blinking Text**
>
> When Netscape introduced blinking text as an HTML extension (an addition to the HTML standard), everyone started placing blinking text on their Web pages, before realizing how annoying it is. If you do choose to use blinking text on your Web page, use it in moderation, and never, ever apply it to link text.

In addition to character formatting, the Format menu offers paragraph formats. You encountered some of these formats in Chapter 20, including indents, alignment, and lists (bulleted and numbered). To access additional paragraph formats, open the **Format** menu and select from the following options:

> **Heading** marks the paragraph as a heading of level 1 to 8. The heading levels are also listed on the Paragraph Style drop-down list in Composer's Formatting toolbar.

Chapter 23 ➤ *Formatting and Publishing Your Page*

Paragraph lets you apply non-heading paragraph to transform a paragraph back to normal text or format text as a block quote, e-mail address, description (definition) title, or description text.

List transforms selected paragraphs into a bulleted or numbered list, a list of descriptions or definitions, a directory list, or a menu.

Align provides the same options you can get more easily from the Alignment button in Composer's Formatting toolbar: Left, Right, and Center.

Increase Indent indents the selected paragraphs farther to the right.

Decrease Indent moves indented paragraphs farther to the left.

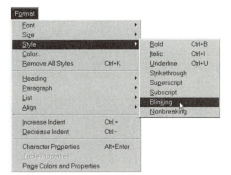

The Format menu offers several options that are not available on the Formatting toolbar.

Changing the Look of Your Graphics

If your page includes graphics (and it should), you can easily change the size of the image by dragging one of its borders, or change its position on the page by dragging it. To change additional properties of the image, including how text wraps around it, right-click on the image, and select Image Properties. This dialog box provides the following options:

Image Location lets you specify the location of the image on the Internet or on your hard drive. You can use the **Choose File** button to easily select a graphic that's stored locally. If you select a graphic from the Internet, you can click on **Leave image at the original location** to save storage space on your Web server. With this option on, your Web page pulls the image from its storage location on the Internet, so you don't have to store the image in a directory on your Web server.

269

Text Alignment and Wrapping options allow you to specify the relative position of neighboring text.

Dimensions allow you to set the height and width of the image. However, you can usually control the size and dimensions of an image more easily by dragging its borders.

Space Around Image lets you increase or decrease the space between the image and surrounding text.

Centering Your Image

You can center your image at the top of the page or push it all the way to the right. With the Image Properties dialog box displayed, click on the **Paragraph** tab, and then click on **Left**, **Right**, or **Center**.

Although Composer does not offer any advanced tools for editing your graphic images, it does allow you to assign a helper application to the task. In the Image Properties dialog box, click on the **Edit Image** button. If no application has been assigned the task of editing graphics, a dialog box appears, prompting you to select a graphics application. Select the application you want to use, and click **OK**. Composer then runs the application and opens the selected graphic. After editing the image, exit your graphics editor. The modified image appears on your Web page. (You can also set up a graphics editor by selecting **Edit/Preferences/Composer**, and clicking the **Choose** button next to **Images**.)

Coloring Your Page

If you don't specify colors for your page background and links, the colors will default to whatever background the person viewing it has configured for his browser. Most browsers use a white or dull gray background with blue, underlined links. If you want to add excitement to the page or if you want to make sure that your colored text will be visible, you should specify a background color. To specify a color scheme, take the following steps:

1. Open the **Format** menu and select **Page Colors and Properties**. The Page Properties dialog box appears.

2. Click the **Colors and Background** tab.

Chapter 23 ➤ Formatting and Publishing Your Page

3. Click the **Use custom colors (Save colors in page)** option button. This tells Composer to insert special background and color codes instead of leaving the choice up to the visitor's Web browser.

4. Open the **Color Schemes** drop-down list, and select a color scheme you want to start with. Each color scheme controls settings for the background, text, and links. The preview area lets you see how the page will look with the current settings.

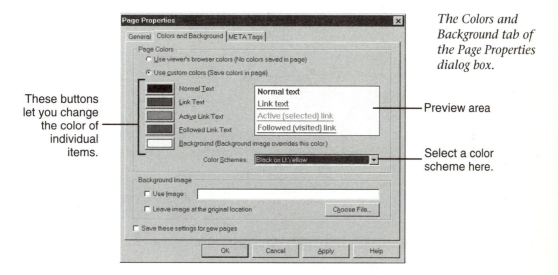

The Colors and Background tab of the Page Properties dialog box.

These buttons let you change the color of individual items.

Preview area

Select a color scheme here.

5. Once you have a color scheme in place, you can change colors for individual items. Click the button for the item whose color you want to change (for example, Background). A color dialog box appears, prompting you to select a color.

6. Select the desired color, and then click **OK** to close the Color dialog box. Repeat Steps 4 and 5 to change the color of any additional items.

7. Click **OK** to save your color settings and close the Page Properties dialog box. Composer redisplays the page in the selected colors.

Using a Background Image

If you want a fancier-looking page, you can select a GIF or JPEG image to go behind the text. If the image isn't big enough to fill the user's browser window, the browser will repeat the image horizontally and vertically to fill the space.

You can use any GIF or JPEG image as a background. If you are wandering the Web and you find a picture you want to use as a background for your own Web page, right-click on it and use the Save As command to save it to your hard drive. Then, take the steps in the following section to use the picture as a page background. (You can find several background images on the CD at the back of this book.)

If you can't find a picture you want to use, go back to Netscape's Template page (**File**, **New**, **Page From Template**), scroll down to the bottom, and click on the link for Web page tools. This takes you to a page with background colors and patterns. Right-click on a link, and click **Save As** to save the graphic to disk.

Finding More Graphics

If you just can't get enough graphics, look to the Web Designer page at http://web.canlink.com/webdesign/. Or, use any of the search described in Chapter 4, "Finding Information and Other Resources," and search for **html web page background**. The Web has many resources where you can pick up useful graphics.

Adding a Background Image to Your Page

Once you have a GIF or JPEG image you want to use as a page background, adding it to your Web page is fairly easy. Take the following steps:

1. With your Web page open, open the **Format** menu, select **Page Colors and Properties**, and click the **Colors and Background** tab.

2. Under Background Image, click the **Use Image** option to place a check in the box.

3. Click on the **Choose File** button. The Select Image File dialog box appears, prompting you to select an image.

4. Select the drive and folder that contains the image you want to use, and click on its file name. Click **Open**. You return to the Page Properties dialog box, and the path to the selected file appears in the Use Image text box.

5. Click **OK**.

Can You Still Read It?

Not all background images or colors are suitable for the text colors you have selected. If you place dark text on a dark background, you and others will have trouble reading the text. If the background image swallows your text, use a different image or use a color instead.

Adding a Title, Description, and Keywords

Before you place your page on the Web, you should add a title, description, and keywords that will help Web search tools find your page and add it to their lists of Web pages. That way, when somebody searches for something that your page contains, the search tool can point them to your page. To add this information, take the following steps:

1. Run Composer and open your Web page.

2. Open the **Format** menu and select **Page Colors and Properties**. The Page Properties dialog box appears.

3. Click on the **General** tab to move it up front.

4. Type a title for the page in the **Title** text box, type your name in the **Author** text box, and type a brief description of the page in the **Description** text box.

5. Under **Other Attributes**, type some unique words that describe your page in the **Keywords** text box. These are words that you think someone might use to search for your page.

6. In the **Classification** text box, type one or more words that describe the category in which your page should be included (for example, Personal Web Page or Fine Art). Some search tools, such as Yahoo!, can use this information to classify your page.

7. Click **OK**.

Where Are My Entries?!

None of the entries you just typed appear on your Web page, but they do appear in the coded HTML file that the Web browser uses to render the page. The title will appear in the browser's title bar when the browser opens your page. It also is used as the bookmark name, should anyone choose to add your page as a bookmark. As for the other entries, they are there just in case someone wants to know that information or search for it.

Part 5 ▸ *Publishing Your Own Web Pages*

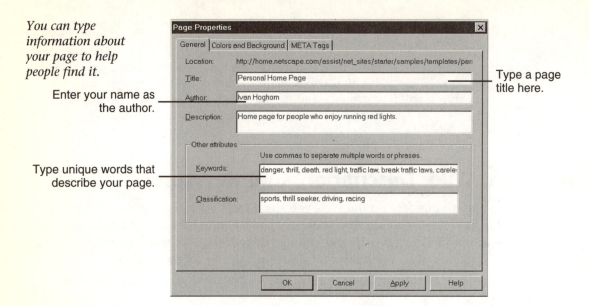

You can type information about your page to help people find it.

Enter your name as the author.

Type unique words that describe your page.

Type a page title here.

Getting Your Page Out on the Web

If you have been working directly on a *Web server* (a computer that stores Web pages), you don't have to do anything to place your page(s) on the Web. When you save your page to a directory on the Web server, you are publishing it. However, if you've been working on pages stored on your computer's hard drive, you will have to upload your page(s) to an FTP or Web server to make them available. Fortunately, Netscape Composer provides a feature that makes publishing your Web page as easy as clicking a button.

Finding a Home for Your Page

Before you start, you need to make sure you have somewhere to place your Web page. The best place to start is to call your Internet service provider. Most providers make some space available on their Web servers for subscribers to store personal Web pages. Call your service provider, and find out the following information:

➤ Does your service provider make Web space available to subscribers? If not, maybe you should change providers.

➤ How much disk space do you get, and how much does it cost, if anything? Some providers give you a limited amount of disk space, which is usually plenty for one or two Web pages.

➤ What is the URL of the server you must connect to in order to upload your files? Write it down.

274

- ➤ What username and password do you need to enter to gain access to the server?

- ➤ In which directory must you place your files? Write it down.

- ➤ What name must you give your Web page. In many cases, the service lets you post a single Web page, and you must call it **index.html**.

- ➤ Are there any other specific instructions you must follow to post your Web page?

- ➤ After posting your page, what will its address (URL) be? You'll want to open it in Navigator as soon as you post it.

Now, if your service provider does not offer Web page service, fire up Navigator, connect to your favorite search page, and search for places that allow you to post your Web page for free. These services vary greatly. Some services require you to fill out a form, and then the service creates a generic Web page for you (you can't use the page you created in Composer). At others, you can copy the HTML-coded document (in Notepad or Wordpad) and paste it in a text box at the site. A couple other places will let you send them your HTML file and associated files. Find out what's involved.

Configuring Composer's Publisher

In order to publish your page, the Composer needs to know your user name, your password, and your FTP or Web site address. Once you have that information, follow these steps to configure the publisher:

1. Open Composer's **Edit** menu, and select **Preferences**. The Preferences dialog box appears.

2. Click the plus sign next to Composer, and click on **Publishing**.

3. Maintain Links and Keep Images with Page are both on by default. Leave them on to ensure that your page's links will work and that any associated graphic files will be shipped along with your page.

4. In the first text box under Default Publishing Location, type the address of the FTP or HTTP (Web site) to which you want to upload your file(s). This address consists of the URL of the server plus the path to the directory. Here's an example:

   ```
   ftp://ftp.internet.com/pub/users/webpages/
   ```

5. If you are uploading your page to an FTP server, click inside the second text box under Default Publishing Location, and type the URL you must use to open the page in a Web browser.

6. Click **OK**.

Tell the publisher where you want the page sent, as well as your user name and password.

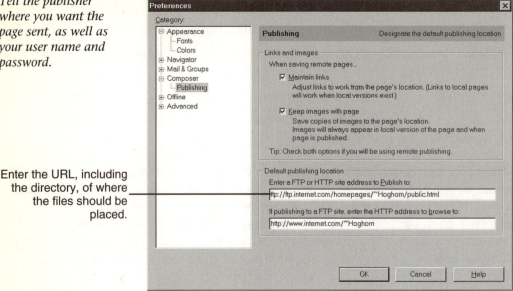

Enter the URL, including the directory, of where the files should be placed.

Publishing Your Pages

You can use the Composer to publish any pages you have, whether they were created with the Web page editor or with any other tool. You can even mix pages from different sources. Just make sure that all of the pages you want to publish are in the same directory on your hard drive before you begin. To publish your pages, follow these steps:

1. Establish your Internet connection, run Composer, and open the page you want to place on the Web.

2. Click the **Publish** button (or open the **File** menu and select **Publish**). The Publish Files dialog box appears, and the first two text boxes are filled in for you.

3. If the **HTTP or FTP Location to Publish to** is blank, open the drop-down list, and select the desired location, or click the **Use Default** button to insert the address you entered under Preferences.

4. If this is the first time you are publishing a page, enter your user name and password in the appropriate text boxes. To have Composer save this information (for the next time you publish a page), click **Save Password**.

Chapter 23 ➤ *Formatting and Publishing Your Page*

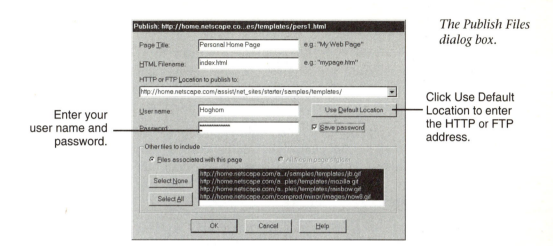

The Publish Files dialog box.

Enter your user name and password.

Click Use Default Location to enter the HTTP or FTP address.

5. To publish just this one page, click the **Files Associated with This Page** option button, which will upload the HTML file for this page, along with all of the files for graphics, sounds, and video clips on the page. To publish all the pages in the current directory, click the **All files in page's folder** option button.

6. Click **OK** to start the publishing process. Composer connects to the Internet if you were not already connected. The Publishing Page dialog box appears, listing the name of each file as it is uploaded, and showing the number of files that have been uploaded in relation to the total number to be uploaded. When all the files have been uploaded, this box disappears. Congratulations! Your material is now out on the Web!

Test It Again

Once you have your page on the Web, open it, and check it again to make sure it was not corrupted during transfer, that all the graphics and lines are positioned correctly, and that your links work. If you have a different Web browser or a friend who uses a different browser, check it out in a different browser.

Publicizing Your Page

Now that your page is on the Web, you probably have this strange idea that people are going to flock to your Web site just to check out what the new kid has to offer. Don't fool yourself. Your puny, little Web page is tucked away in a dark corner of the Web where few search engines will look for it, and few Web surfers will catch a glimpse of it.

If you want people to visit your page, you need to publicize it. You have already taken one important step earlier in this chapter, by adding a title, classifying your page, and adding key words. This information will help search engines find your page and add it to their indices. But that's not enough. You need to actively promote your Web page by registering it with various search engines.

If you want to register with a search tool, go to that tool's Web site, and look for a link that points to a registration form. For example, at the bottom of Yahoo!'s opening screen (**http://www.yahoo.com**) is a link called **How to Include Your Site**. At Lycos (**http://www.lycos.com**), look for the following link at the bottom of the page: **Add Your Page to Lycos**. (AltaVista has a link called Add URL, which provides a pay service that can add your page to 100 search tool directories!) Following is a list of other places where you can register your page:

> HotBot at **http://www.hotbot.com**
>
> Infoseek at **http://www.infoseek.com**
>
> WebCrawler at **http://www.webcrawler.com**
>
> YelloWWWeb Pages at **http://yellowwweb.com/freyel.html**

Click on the link for registering your page, and then enter the requested information. You may be asked to type your Web page's title, enter keywords that will help people find your page, and enter your e-mail address. At Yahoo, you also have to specify a category for your Web page, as shown below.

To register your page for free with 20 popular Internet directories, connect to Submit-It at **http://www.submit-it.com**. Fill out the form, and... er... submit it. To register with an additional 300 directories, you can submit 60 bucks.

Chapter 23 ➤ *Formatting and Publishing Your Page*

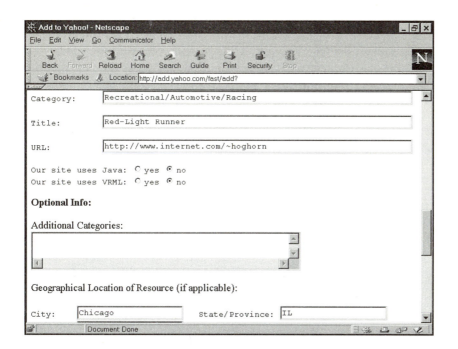

You can register your page with various Internet directories.

The Least You Need to Know

Now that your page is on the Web, and it's being registered with hundreds of search engines, you don't really need to know anything. However, if you plan on creating and publishing another page (it is addictive), keep the following essentials handy:

➤ If Composer's Formatting toolbar does not offer the formatting tool you need, poke around on the Format menu to find it.

➤ To change the look and behavior of a graphic image, right-click on the image, and select **Image Properties**.

➤ You can change the color scheme for your page by opening the **Format** menu and selecting **Page Colors and Properties**.

➤ Before placing your page on the Web, open the **Format** menu, select **Page Colors and Properties**, click on the **General** tab, and type the requested information. This will help search engines find your page later.

- Before you attempt to publish your Web page, get instructions from your service provider.
- You have to tell Composer where to place your Web page file. Open the **Edit** menu, select **Preferences**, and click on **Publishing** (below Composer). Enter the requested URLs.
- Once Composer is properly set up, publishing pages is easy; just click the **Publish** button, and respond to the Publish dialog box.

Speak Like a Geek: The Complete Archive

absolute reference   In a Web document, a link that refers to a specific document regardless of the current document's address. Think of it like this: If you give a person an absolute reference, it's sort of like telling her to go to a specific address. A relative reference would be like saying, "It's two blocks west of the Village Pantry."

ActiveX   A relatively new technology that makes it easy to embed animated objects, data, and computer code on Web pages. With ActiveX controls and the right plug-in, Navigator can play ActiveX components and open documents that support ActiveX.

address   A text string that designates a specific page, resource, or mailbox on the Internet.

anchor   The part of a link that causes the mouse pointer to turn into a pointing finger. See also *links*.

anonymous login   The process of connecting to a system incognito. Many FTP sites (places where you can get files) allow users to connect anonymously and access public areas. Anonymous login privileges usually do not allow you to place files on the server or change anything.

Archie   An Internet search tool that helps you find files. In most cases, you need to know the exact name of the file or a partial file name. See also *Jughead* and *Veronica*.

associate   To establish a connection between a given file type and the helper application needed to view or play that file type. In Navigator, you must create file associations so Navigator will "know" which application to run when you choose to view, watch, or listen to a file. For example, you might associate movie files that end in .mpg with an MPEG movie player.

Auto Load Images   An option in Navigator that tells it whether it should display the pictures on a Web page. When this option is on, Navigator automatically loads and displays pictures on a Web page. You can turn this option off to prevent pictures from appearing, and speed up Navigator.

BBS Short for *bulletin board system*, a BBS is a computer that's set up to automatically answer the phone and allow callers to exchange messages, files, and information. Special interest groups, professional organizations, and software companies commonly set up BBSs.

bookmark A Navigator tool that lets you mark your favorite Web pages so you can quickly return to them later.

Boolean operators Conjunctions, including "and" and "or," used to separate search terms. For example, if you search for "Clinton and Whitewater," you get a list of all resources that relate to both "Clinton" and "Whitewater." If you use "or" the search is much broader, finding anything that relates to either "Clinton" or "Whitewater."

bps Short for *bits per second*, this is a unit used to measure the speed of data transfer between two computers.

browser See *Web browser*.

cache A temporary storage area that Navigator creates both in RAM and on your hard disk. Navigator stores Web pages in the cache, so it can quickly load these pages if you decide to return to them.

censor To prevent access to specific Web pages, Internet features, or Internet content. Internet censoring programs are designed to help you control what comes into your computer from the Internet, so the government won't have to do it for you.

channel A Web page which you subscribe to in order to have Netscape Netcaster automatically download an updated page on a regular basis. With Netcaster, you can subscribe to any Web page and set it up as a *channel*. You can then use Netcaster as a channel changer, to tune into your favorite Web pages.

chat To "talk" to another person by typing at your computer. What you type appears on the other person's screen, and what the other person types appears on your screen. Communicator's Conference component allows you to chat online with other people.

client Of two computers, the one that's being served. Whenever you connect to a Web site, the computer at that site is the *server*, and you are the *client*. Think of yourself as the *customer*.

Collabra The Component formerly known as Netscape News (TCFKANN), Collabra allows you to read and post messages in Internet newsgroups and in intranet discussion groups.

Communicator Netscape's Internet suite. Communicator consists of several integrated components, including Netscape Navigator (a Web browser), Messenger (for e-mail), Collabra (for reading and posting newsgroup messages), Composer (for creating and publishing Web pages), and Conference (an Internet phone program).

Component bar A button bar that appears in the status bar of all the Communicator components, and allows you to quickly switch to Navigator, Messenger, Collabra, or Composer.

Composer   Communicator's Web page creation and editing program. Collabra works like a word processing or desktop publishing program for the Web. As you type, insert graphics, and format your page, Composer inserts the necessary Web page codes (HTML tags) that instruct a Web browser on how to display the page.

compressed file   A file that's been squished so it takes up less disk space and travels faster through network and modem connections. Before you can use the file, you must *decompress* (or expand) it using a special program. Popular decompression programs include PKZip (for DOS) and WinZip (for Windows).

Conference   Formerly known as CoolTalk, Conference allows you to place phone calls over the Internet without having to use AT&T, Sprint, or MCI. Conference allows you to carry on voice conversations, type messages back and forth, leave voicemail messages, doodle on a whiteboard, and exchange files with friends and colleagues.

cookie   A piece of information that a server can attach to Navigator, so the server can recognize you if you come back later.

Cosmo Player   A Netscape plug-in for Navigator which allows you to explore interactive, three-dimensional, virtual worlds on the Web. This type of program is called a VRML browser.

cyberspace   The universe created by the connection of thousands of computers. Computer users can use modems to enter cyberspace and converse with other users. This term was first used by William Gibson in his novel *Neuromancer*. In the novel, people plugged their brains into cyberspace. If you've ever seen the glazed look people get when they're wired to the Web, you know that Gibson's notion is not too far from the truth.

decompress   To unsquish a squished file and make it usable.

Dial-Up Networking   A program that comes with Windows 95 that establishes the Internet connection you need in order to run Navigator and access the World Wide Web.

digital certificate   An electronic ID badge that you can use in Navigator to identify yourself on the Internet. This badge passes your username, password, and personal information to a certified server, so you can gain access to the server without manually entering a password.

discussion group   Netscape's warm and fuzzy name for a USENET newsgroup. (See *newsgroup* and *Collabra*.)

document   On the Web, this could be anything: an index of topics, several screenfuls of text, or even a page full of pictures.

document source   The coded document that controls the way Web pages appear.

domain name   A unique identification for an Internet site. Each computer on the Internet has a domain name that distinguishes it from other computers on the Internet. Domain names usually provide some vague indication of the establishment that runs the server. For example, here's the domain name of the Whitehouse server: **www.whitehouse.gov**.

domain name server (DNS) A computer that matches a site's name to a number that identifies that site. All servers on the Internet have a domain name, for example ncsa.uiuc.edu. Each server also has a unique IP (Internet Protocol) number, such as 128.252.135.4. Your Internet service provider has an electronic database, called a *DNS (Domain Name Server)* that matches the domain to the IP number to find the server that has the requested data. As you innocently click links, the DNS is matching domain names and IP numbers to make sure you get where you're supposed to be.

download To copy a file from another computer (usually an FTP server) to your computer.

e-mail Mail that requires no postage and usually gets there on time. E-mail is a system in which people can send and receive messages through their computers, on a network or using modems. Each person has a designated mail box that stores messages sent by other users. He can then retrieve and read messages from the mail box.

e-zine Pronounced "ee-zeen," this is an electronic rendition of a *zine*, a noncommercial magazine that leans toward the bizarre, twisted, or edgy side. One person or a small group of people typically put together zines, which rarely contain advertisements.

FAQ Pronounced "fack," short for *frequently asked questions*, this is a list of answers to the most-often-asked questions at a particular Internet site. Good Internet etiquette demands that you read the FAQ at a site before you post any questions. That way, you won't risk getting flamed. See *flame*.

finger A special UNIX command that pokes around through the directory of users and finds information about that person, including the person's e-mail address, and whether or not that person has read her mail recently or even logged in.

firewall A security feature that prevents unauthorized access to a network. Businesses and universities commonly set up firewalls to prevent evil hackers from breaking into their networks and accessing sensitive data. See also *proxy*.

flame To verbally abuse another user during an online discussion, via e-mail, or in a newsgroup. Common flaming techniques include name-calling, abusive innuendos about one's parents, and other puerile gems of wit.

form A fill-in-the-blank Web document. Sites commonly use forms to take credit card orders, ask for your password, or let you enter search instructions.

frame A Web feature that divides the Web browser window into two or more sections, each of which can display a separate Web page. For example, a Web site may divide your window into a left and right pane. The left pane may contain an index or table of contents. When you click on a heading in the left pane, the right pane shows the contents of that heading.

FTP Short for *File Transfer Protocol*, a set of rules that govern the transfer of files between computers. True geeks use this acronym as a verb. For example, "I FTPed to ftp-dot-netscape-dot-com to nab the latest Navigator beta."

geek   1. An overly obsessive computer user who will sacrifice food, sleep, sex, and other pleasantries of life to spend more time at the keyboard. 2. A carnival performer whose act usually includes biting off the head of a live snake or chicken.

GIF file   Pronounced "giff file" or "jiff file," a picture file, commonly a photograph or painting. GIF is short for *Graphic Interchange Format*, a format developed by CompuServe for transferring graphic files. The format stores lots of graphic information in little space.

Gopher   An indexing system that allows you to access various Internet services by selecting menu options. Whenever you connect to a Gopher site, it presents you with an opening menu. When you select a menu item, the server presents you with another submenu containing additional options and files. These options may kick you out to another Gopher server, an FTP server, a newsgroup, or other Internet servers. You proceed through the menus until you find the information you want... or reach a dead end.

handle   A user's computerized nickname or ID number. When you look for a person using Whois, you might find the person's handle. You can often find out more about a person by performing the search again using the person's handle.

helper application   A program that performs a specialized job that Navigator is unfit to manage. Whenever you click a link that Navigator can't play, Navigator loads the file to disk and then summons (spawns) the helper application associated with that file. The helper application loads the file and plays it.

history list   A directory of all the Web sites you visited since you connected. You can view the history list in Navigator by opening the **Window** menu and clicking **History**.

hits   In a WAIS search, the number of times a search word was found in an article. The higher the number, the more likely it is that the article contains the information you're looking for. See also *score*.

home page   The page that greets you when you first start Navigator or first connect to a Web site. No relation to "home boy."

host   In biology, the being that is leeched on by a parasite. On the Internet, it pretty much means the same thing. The host is the computer that has the information. Your computer is the client, sucking the lifeblood out of the host.

HTML   Short for *HyperText Markup Language*, the code used to create Web documents. These codes tell the Navigator how to display the text (titles, headings, lists, and so on), insert anchors that link this document to other documents, and control character formatting (by making it bold or italic).

HTML editor   A program designed to make it easier to create Web pages. Instead of typing codes, you format the document as if you were using a desktop publishing program. The HTML editor inserts the codes for you. Communicator comes with its own HTML editor, Netscape Composer.

HTTP Short for *HyperText Transfer Protocol*, a set of rules that govern the exchange of data between a Web host and a client (your computer). The address for every Web server starts with **http**. If you see an address that starts with different letters (for example, **ftp** or **gopher**) the address is for a different type of server: Gopher (**gopher**), FTP (**ftp**), WAIS (**wais**), Usenet (**news**), or Telnet (**telnet**).

hyperdocument A Web page that contains links connecting it to other pages. On the Web, a hyperdocument might contain links to other text, graphics, sounds, or movies.

hyperlinks Icons, pictures, or highlighted chunks of text that connect two documents. For example, a document about pork might contain a link for sausage. If you click the link, Navigator displays a document about how to make sausage. Sausage is the link, although it's not actually a sausage link.

hypermedia A dynamic computerized soup that contains movie clips, graphics, sound files, text, and anything else that can be stored in a digitized form. That's the "media" part, anyway. The "hyper" part deals with the fact that these ingredients are interlinked, so you can jump quickly from one to another.

HYTELNET A phone book for other telnet hosts. It contains addresses and login information for hundreds of online library catalogs, bulletin board systems (BBSs), Freenets (free online systems), and other information resources. See also *telnet*.

image map A graphical tool used to navigate some Web sites. An image map is typically a large graphic that appears on the top or bottom of the opening Web page. It is divided into several areas, each of which provides a link to a different Web page.

inline image A graphic that appears inside a Web document. You can tell Navigator not to display these images… if you can't stand waiting for them to load.

interactive A user-controlled program, document, or game. Interactive programs commonly display on-screen *prompts* asking the user for input so he can decide how to carry out a particular task. These programs are popular in education, allowing children to follow their natural curiosity to solve problems and gather information.

Internet The world's largest system of interconnected networks. The Internet was originally named ARPAnet after the Advanced Research Projects Agency in the Defense Department. The agency developed the ARPAnet in the mid-1970s as an experimental project to allow various university and military sources to continue to communicate in a state of national emergency. Nowadays, the Internet is used mostly by private citizens for connecting to databases, exchanging electronic mail, and wasting loads of productive time.

Internet Phone A program that lets you place voice phone calls over the Internet using a sound card and speakers rather than your phone. Because the voice signals travel over the Internet rather than over phone company lines, you can avoid long-distance charges. Communicator features its own Internet phone program, Netscape Conference.

IP address A unique number assigned to each computer on the Internet. Most of the time, you work with domain names, such as nasa.uiuc.edu. Behind the scenes, whenever you enter a domain name, your service provider matches that name to the site's IP number (for example 128.252.135.4), and then calls that site. The idea here is that it's easier for you to remember names and easier for computers to remember numbers. The domain name/IP number link makes everyone happy.

IRC Short for *Internet Relay Chat*, this is a technology that allows users to type messages back and forth using their keyboards. It's sort of like talking on the phone, but less expensive and much slower.

Java Coffee. Also, a relatively new technology that allows you (or at least someone who knows how to use Java) to create animations and other moving video clips and embed them in Web pages. All you need to know about Java is that if you click a link for a Java applet (application), Navigator will play it.

JPG Short for *Joint Photograph Group*, a file-compression format used for storing graphic files. If you come across a file that ends in .JPG, you can view it in Netscape Navigator, or you can have one of your helper applications display it.

Jughead An Internet search tool used to find resources at a specific site. Archie, Veronica, and Jughead (all Internet search tools) are related. Archie searches for FTP servers that contain the files you want to download. Veronica searches all Gopher sites to find the ones that store various resources. Jughead searches only the current Gopher site to find the specified resources.

links A.k.a. *hyperlinks*, these are icons, pictures, or highlighted chunks of text that connect the current page to other pages, Internet sites, graphics, movies, or sounds.

log in To connect to another computer on a network or on the Internet so you can use that computer's resources. The login procedure usually requires you to enter your username (or user ID) and a password.

log out To disconnect from another computer on a network or on the Internet.

logical codes In a Web document, codes that provide general directions on how to display text. For example, <em> stands for emphasis, which might mean bold or italic. Physical codes give more precise instructions. For example, <b> means bold.

lurk When you read newsgroup messages posted by other people but don't respond to them or post any messages of your own.

map A graphical navigational tool used on many Web pages. Think of it as one of those mall maps with the **YOU ARE HERE** arrow on it, but with a Web map, you can actually go places by clicking on different areas of the map.

Messenger   Communicator's e-mail program. Messenger allows you to send and receive e-mail messages, attach files to outgoing messages, and, with the help of Composer, create fancy e-mail messages complete with graphics.

MIME   Short for *Multi-purpose Internet Mail Extensions*, a protocol that controls all file transfers on the Web. Navigator uses MIME to recognize different file types. If an HTML document arrives, Navigator "knows" to play that file itself. If an .MPG file arrives, Navigator calls the associated helper application. MIME was originally developed to attach different types of files (usually multimedia files) to e-mail messages.

mirror site   A server that contains the same files as the original site. Why the redundancy? Because some sites are so busy that users might have trouble connecting during peak hours.

MOO   Acronym for *MUD Object-Oriented*, another type of hip interactive computer game that involves several players. MOOs are written in a more dynamic programming language than the one used for MUDs.

MPEG   Short for *Moving Pictures Expert Group*, a video-compression and movie presentation standard used for most video clips stored on the Web. The only thing that matters is that if you encounter a file that ends in .MPG, you need an MPG or MPEG player to watch it.

MUD   Short for *Multi-User Dimensions* (or *Dungeons* or *Dialogues*), hip interactive computer games that usually involve several players.

Navigator   A navigational program for the World Wide Web. Navigator transforms Web documents (which consist of boring codes) into exciting multimedia documents, complete with sounds, pictures, and movies.

Netcaster   A component of Netscape Communicator that allows you to subscribe to Web sites and have updated pages delivered to your Windows desktop. In addition, Netcaster transforms your PC into a channel changer for the Web!

newbie   Derogatory term for a new user on the Internet. Newbies are often the target of obnoxious Internet junkies who are bitter because their little secret is not so little nor so secret as it once was.

newsgroup   An Internet bulletin board for users who share common interests. There are thousands of newsgroups ranging from body arts to pets (to body art with pets). Newsgroups let you post messages and read messages from other users.

news server   An Internet computer that gives users access to newsgroups, where they can read and post messages.

pane   A portion of a window. Netscape Mail uses panes to divide its window into logical areas.

physical codes   In a Web document, codes that provide specific directions on how to display text. For example, <bold> stands for bold. *Logical codes* give less precise instructions. For example, <em> means emphasis, which might mean bold or italic.

plan   A file that a user might attach to her finger file that includes more information. A plan might include the person's address, phone number, job interests, and anything else that person wants to make publicly accessible.

plug-in   A program that becomes a part of Navigator and increases its capabilities. Compare it to a helper application, which is an independent program that works with Navigator. You can get plug-ins for displaying graphics, playing audio and video clips, and for exploring virtual worlds.

port   A sweet, robust wine that has a rich taste and aroma. Also, the hardware connection through which a computer sends and/or receives data. And one more thing; a port can be an application that's set up on a server. When you specify the server's port, you're actually telling it to run one of its applications.

post   To tack up a message in a bulletin board or newsgroup for all to see.

postmaster   The person at a given site who is in charge of assigning users their e-mail addresses. You can usually send a message to the postmaster by addressing it to *postmaster@sitename*.

PPP   Short for *Point-to-Point Protocol*, which probably means as little to me as it does to you. What's important is that when you choose an Internet service provider, you get the right connection: SLIP or PPP; otherwise, you won't be able to use Navigator.

protocol   A set of rules that govern the transfer of data between two computers.

proxy   A special connection that allows two incompatible networks to communicate. For example, say you're on the Web with Navigator and you decide to use WAIS to search for a list of articles. You can't use WAIS directly from Navigator, so you have to work through a Web/WAIS proxy. The proxy acts as a middleman, ensuring that the data transfer goes smoothly.

push content   A relatively recent Web browser innovation that allows Web sites to deliver content to your computer at regularly scheduled times. This allows Netcaster to automatically load pages while you are working on something else or sleeping. You can then view the pages at your convenience by loading them from your hard drive. Netscape Netcaster is designed to take full advantage of push technology, cutting down on the time you have to spend waiting for pages to download from the Internet.

relative reference   In a Web document, a link that refers to the location of another page or file in relation to the address of the current page. For example, if the page is in the /PUB directory, and a linked page is in /PUB/HOME, a relative reference might specify /HOME. An absolute reference would have to give the complete path: /PUB/HOME.

score   In WAIS searches, a number that indicates the relative likelihood that an article will contain the information you need. The topmost article gets a score of 1,000. Subsequent scores are relative to 1,000, so 500 would mean that the article had half as many occurrences of the search term as the top article.

server In the politically incorrect world of the Internet, the computer that serves up all the data. The other computer, the client, acts as a customer, demanding specific information.

service provider The company that you pay in order to connect to its computer and get on the Internet.

shareware Computer programs you can use for free and then pay for if you decide to continue using them. Many programmers use the Internet to distribute their programs, relying on the honesty and goodwill of Internet users for their income. That's why most of these programmers have day jobs.

Shockwave A multimedia player that can play Macromedia Director, Freehand, and Authorware files. These files are cool, interactive, multimedia presentations, tutorials, or games.

SLIP Short for *Serial Line Internet Protocol*, a type of Internet connection that allows you to connect directly to the Internet without having to run programs off your Internet service provider's computer.

spam To post the same announcement to multiple newsgroups, usually for the purpose of advertising a product or service. Spamming is considered bad form in most newsgroups.

SSL Short for *Secure Sockets Layer*, this is Netscape's new security technology. Web pages protected with SSL prevent misanthropic hackers from nabbing personal information that you might enter on the page (including your credit card number).

status bar The area at the bottom of the Navigator window that shows you what's going on as you work. The little key in the status bar indicates whether a document is or is not secure; if the key looks broken, the document is not secure.

stop word In a search, any word that is excluded from the search. For example, if you are searching a computer database, the database may refuse to look for common words, such as "and" and "computer."

tags HTML codes that work behind the scenes to tell Navigator how to display a document and how to open other linked documents. Tags can control the look of text (as in titles and headings), insert anchors that link this document to other documents, and control character formatting (by making it bold or italic).

TCP/IP Acronym for *Transmission Control Protocol/Internet Protocol*, the preferred method of data transfer over the Internet. With TCP/IP, the sending computer stuffs data into packets and sends it. The receiving computer unstuffs the packets and assembles them into some meaningful and useful form. The most famous TCP/IP program is Winsock.

telnet The process of connecting to a server and using it to run programs, just as if you were sitting at its keyboard (or sitting at the keyboard of a terminal that's connected to the server). Think of it as using the computerized card catalog at the local library.

terminal connection The type of connection you don't want to have if you're using Navigator. A terminal connection makes your computer act like one of your service provider's workstations. You run programs on the service provider's computer, and connect to the Internet indirectly through that computer. With a SLIP or PPP connection, you connect through the service provider's computer, but you use software on your computer to do all your work.

terminal emulation A technique used to make one computer act like another so the two computers can carry on a conversation. Some mainframe computers will interact with only a specific type of terminal. If you want to connect to that mainframe computer using your personal computer, you must make your computer act like the required terminal.

thread In newsgroups and e-mail, a way of grouping messages, so that you can quickly tell that they belong to the same topic of conversation.

UNIX shell The equivalent of a DOS prompt for computers that are running the UNIX operating system. You type commands at the prompt, just as if you were using a PC.

upload To copy a file from your computer to another computer. You usually upload files to share them with other users.

URL Short for *Uniform Resource Locator* (or *Unreliable Resource Location*, depending on the URL), an address for an Internet site. The Web uses URLs to specify the addresses of the various servers on the Internet and the documents on each server. For example, the URL for the Whitehouse server is **http://www.whitehouse.gov**. The **http** stands for HyperText Transfer Protocol, which means this is a Web document. **www** stands for World Wide Web. **whitehouse** stands for Whitehouse. And **gov** stands for Government.

USENET Short for *USEr's NETwork*, USENET sets the standards by which the various newsgroups swap information. See also *newsgroup*.

Veronica One of many Internet search tools, this one finds Gopher sites that have what you're looking for. For a comparison of popular search tools, see *Jughead*.

viewer A program that Navigator uses to play movie clips, sound clips, PostScript files, graphics, and any other file Navigator itself cannot handle. See also *helper application*.

virtual memory Disk storage that is treated as RAM. Why am I including it in this glossary? Because Navigator uses so much memory that you'll need some virtual memory just to use it.

voice mail A feature that allows you to leave a voice recording, so the other person doesn't have to talk to you right away. Conference allows you to leave voice-mail messages when the person you want to talk to is unavailable or is just ignoring you.

VRML Pronounced "vermal," VRML stands for Virtual Modeling Language, a programming language used to place interactive, three-dimensional worlds on the Web. With a VRML player, such as Netscape's Live3D, you can explore these worlds.

WAIS Pronounced "ways," short for Wide Area Information Server, a system that allows you to search various databases on the Internet for specific articles and other resources.

Web browser Any of several programs you can use to navigate the World Wide Web. The Web browser controls the look of the Web documents and provides additional tools for jumping from one Web document to another. Navigator is a Web browser.

Web page A specially coded file that acts as an electronic page on the World Wide Web. Most Web pages contain links that connect the page to other Web pages. They also commonly contain pictures, sounds, video clips, and other multimedia files that you can play.

Web robot A search tool that regularly searches the Internet for Web sites and indexes the Web documents it finds. The robot then allows you to search its indexes for Web sites that contain the resources you need.

Web server A specialized computer on the Internet devoted to storing and serving up Web documents.

Webmaster The person who created and maintains a Web document. If you find an error in a Web document, you should notify the Webmaster (in a nice way).

Webtop An innovative concept that allows you to place automatically updating Web pages right on your desktop. The Webtop keeps you abreast of the latest information from your favorite Web sites and transforms your desktop into an information center.

whiteboard A work area in Conference that allows you and your colleagues to collaborate online. When any member in the discussion chooses to open a picture on the Whiteboard, that picture pops up on everyone's screen. Conference participants can then draw on the screen and type messages back and forth to share their insights and ideas.

Whois Just another UNIX command that you can use to find out a person's e-mail address, mailing address, phone number, or other information, if you know the person's last name and the location of the server that person logs in to.

World Wide Web A collection of interconnected documents stored on computers all over the world. These documents can contain text, pictures, movie clips, sounds, and links to other documents. You move from one document to another by clicking links.

zine A noncommercial magazine that leans toward the bizarre, twisted, or edgy side. Zines started on paper but soon moved to the Internet in the form of e-zines. See also *e-zine*.

zip The process of compressing a file so that it takes up less space and transfers more quickly. If you have a zipped file, you must unzip it before you can use it.

Index

Symbols

& (ampersands), Web
    searches, 39-40
+ (plus signs)
    Collabra, 203
    Web searches, 39-40
> (right angle brackets),
    e-mail, 177

A

absolute links, 245, 281
ActiveX, 11, 121-122,
    127-128, 136-137
    advantages, 128
    downloading plug-ins,
        136-137
    security, 121-122
    Web sites, 136-137
    see also helper
        applications; plug-ins
ActiveX Gallery Web site,
    136
addresses
    address books, 191
        adding addresses,
            192-194
        Conference, 219-220
        deleting addresses,
            192
        editing entries, 193
        electronic business
            cards, 197
        importing, 194
        mailing lists, 196

Conference phone calls,
    see Conference, phone
    numbers (addresses)
defined, 281
e-mail, 166
    anonymous FTP
        passwords, 95
    addressing messages,
        168-169
    Cc (carbon copies),
        173
    inserting addresses
        from address books,
        194-195
    mailing lists, 196
    multiple recipients,
        172-173
    placing long-distance
        calls, 217
    specifying for
        identification
        (Navigator), 95
IP (Internet Protocol)
    addresses, 219, 287
newsgroups, 202-203
searching the Web,
    193-194
servers, 167-168
see also URLs
.aif files, see audio
alerts, Navigator security,
    115-116
    cookies, 118
AltaVista search tool Web
    site, 43
    publicizing Web pages,
        278
    see also searching the
        Web

ampersands (&), Web
    searches, 39-40
anchors, 281
anonymous (public) FTP
    servers, connecting to, 95
applets, see Java
Archie search tool, 281
ASCII files, sending
    (Conference), 225
associating file types, 281
    helper applications/
        plug-ins, 141-144
        MIME types, 142-144
        saving Web files to
            disks, 85
attached files
    e-mail, 169-170
        viewing, 176
    newsgroup postings,
        210-211
.au files, see audio
audio
    file types, 129
    helper applications,
        mapping files, 141-144
    links, 145
    LiveAudio player, 129
    Netcaster, see Netcaster
    quality, 146
    saving audio files from
        Web, 84-85
    sound cards, 146
        Conference, 214-216
    telephone calls, see
        Conference
    Web sites, 145
    see also ActiveX
        controls; helper
        applications; plug-ins

AutoAdmin component (Professional edition), 4
Automatically Load Images option (Navigator), 105
.avi files, *see* video

B

Back button, Navigator, 27-28, 59
backgrounds, Web pages, 271-273
BBS (bulletin board systems), 282
binary files, sending (Conference), 225
blinking text, Web pages, 268
Blue Skies Web site (Java), 152-153
<BODY> HTML tag, 262
bold text, Web pages, 239
    see also formatting
bookmark.htm file, *see* bookmarks, files
bookmarks (Navigator), 59-61
    adding to Personal toolbar, 68-69
    closing bookmark lists, 64
    creating, 59-60, 65-66
    deleting, 62
    editing bookmark lists, 61-66
        separators/submenus, 63-65
    files, 64
        creating multiple files, 66
        importing/exporting, 67
        opening, 66
        saving bookmark lists as Navigator home pages, 67-68
        saving bookmark lists as Web pages (Composer), 237
    links, 61
    moving, 62, 65
    renaming bookmarks, 62
    updating URLs, 66

Boolean operators (AND, NOT, and OR), Web searches, 39-40, 282
bps (bits per second), 282
browsers
    default browser, 59
    defined, 292
    downloading Communicator from Internet, 15-16
        Macintosh version, 20
    VRML browsers, 156-158, 160
        Cosmo Player, 156-158
browsing the Web offline (Netcaster), 81
bugs, 52
bulleted lists, Web pages, 239
business cards, Conference, 215-216
buying Communicator, 14, 16-17

C

cache (Navigator), 110-111, 282
Café del Sol Web site (Java), 152
Calendar (Professional edition), 4
calls (telephone), *see* Conference
cascading Navigator windows, 35
Channel Properties dialog box (Netcaster), 75
channels (Netcaster), 72, 74-77, 282
    adding
        from Channel Finder, 75-76
        from Web sites, 77
    default opening channel, setting, 80
    deleting, 77
    displaying channels as Webtops, 78
    right-click menus, 77

updating
    automatically, 75
    manually, 77
    viewing, 76, 81
    see also Webtops
Character Properties dialog box (Composer), 245, 248
chat, 282
    Conference Chat Tool, 222
    IRC (Internet Relay Chat), 287
clients, 282
codes, Web pages, *see* HTML (HyperText Markup Language)
Collabra, 7-8, 200
    attachments, sending/receiving, 210-211
    commands
        Attachments (View menu), 211
        Go Offline (File menu), 211
        Go Online (File menu), 212
        Preferences (Edit menu), *see* Collabra, preferences
        Search Messages (Edit menu), 207
    connecting to newsgroups, 202
    downloading messages, 211-212
    listing newsgroups, 203
    opening, 200-201
    posting messages
        attachments, 210-211
        replying to postings, 208-209
        starting discussions, 210
    preferences (Mail & Groups)
        groups server, 201
    starting Communicator with Collabra, 201
    reading messages, 205-206
        offline, 211-212
        threads, 207
        viewing replies, 207

294

Index

searching messages, 207
server setup, 201-202
sorting messages, 207
spell check, 210
starting, 200-201
subscribing to newsgroups, 204-205
toolbar
  Expand All button, 203
  Get Groups button, 203
  New Msg button, 210
  Reply button, 208
  Spelling button, 210
  Subscribe button, 203
unsubscribing to newsgroups, 205
color
  links, 28, 108-109
  Navigator preferences, 108-109
  Web pages, 270-272
    background color compatibility, 273
commands
  Collabra
    Attachments (View menu), 211
    Go Offline (File menu), 211
    Go Online (File menu), 212
    Search Messages (Edit menu), 207
    History (Communicator menu), 30, 58
  Composer
    Check Spelling (Tools menu), 241
    HTML Source (Edit menu), 261
    HTML Tag (Insert menu), 262
    Open Page (File menu), 237
    Page Colors and Properties (Format menu), 270, 272-273
    Publish (File menu), 276
    Table (Insert menu), 259
  Conference
    Auto Answer (Call menu), 222
    Do Not Disturb (Call menu), 222
    Hang Up (Call menu), 217
    Save (Chat Tool), 222
  Messenger
    Compress Folders (File menu), 186
    Empty Trash Folder (File menu), 186
    Flag (Message menu), 185
    Font (Format menu), 171
    Import (File menu), 194
    Mail Filters (Edit menu), 186
    New Folder (File menu), 184
    Search Messages (Edit menu), 188
    Send Later (File menu), 170, 174
    Send Now (File menu), 170, 174
    Send Page (File menu), 168
  Navigator
    About Plug-ins (Help menu), 132
    Add Bookmark (Bookmarks menu), 60, 65
    Blank Page (File menu), 232
    Bookmark Properties (Edit menu), 66
    Close (File menu), 64
    Delete (Edit menu), 62
    Edit Bookmarks (Bookmarks menu), 61, 65-67, 69
    Edit Page (File menu), 232-233, 236
    Hide (View menu), 104
    Home (Go menu), 30
    Import (File menu), 67
    New Bookmark (File menu), 66
    New Folder (File menu), 63
    New Navigator Window (File menu), 35
    New Separator (File menu), 63
    Open Bookmarks Folder (File menu), 66
    Open File (File menu), 64
    Open Page (File menu), 32, 87, 232
    Page From Template (File menu), 232
    Page From Wizard (File menu), 232
    Page Info (View menu), 117
    Page Setup (File menu), 88
    Page Source (View menu), 85-86
    Preferences (Edit menu), *see* Navigator, preferences
    Print Preview (File menu), 89
    Reload (View menu), 30, 36
    Save As (File menu), 66, 86
    Set as Bookmark Menu (View menu), 65
    Set as New Bookmarks Folder (View menu), 65
    Set As Wallpaper, 90
    Show (View menu), 104
    Show Personal Toolbar (View menu), 68
    Update Bookmarks (View menu), 66
    Upload File (File menu), 99

295

Communicator, 3-4, 10-11
  buying, *see*
    downloading
  components, 3-4
    AutoAdmin
      (Professional
      edition), 4
    Calendar
      (Professional
      edition), 4
    Collabra, *see* Collabra
    Component bar, 21
    Composer, *see*
      Composer
    Conference, *see*
      Conference
    IBM Host-On-
      Demand
      (Professional
      edition), 4
    interaction, 10
    Messenger, *see*
      Messenger
    Navigator, *see*
      Navigator
    Netcaster, *see*
      Netcaster
    switching between
      components, 10, 21
  downloading from
    Internet, 14-19
    cost, 14
    FTP programs, 17-19
    Macintosh version,
      20
    subscriptions/upgrade
      certificates, 16-17
    Web browsers, 15-16
  FTP site, 17-18
  icons/Programs menu,
    20
  installing, 19-20
  Macintosh version, 20
  Professional edition, 4
  running, 20-21
  Web site, 15
Composer, 8, 229-231
  blinking text, 268
  commands
    Check Spelling (Tools
      menu), 241
    HTML Source (Edit
      menu), 261
    HTML Tag (Insert
      menu), 262
    Open Page (File
      menu), 237
    Page Colors and
      Properties (Format
      menu), 270,
      272-273
    Preferences (Edit
      menu), *see*
      Composer,
      preferences
    Publish (File menu),
      276
    Save As (File menu),
      87
    Table (Insert menu),
      259
  creating Web pages
    adding/deleting text,
      237-238
    bookmarks, 237
    existing pages, 236
    formatting text,
      238-239
    graphics, 239-241
    horizontal lines, 241
    spell check, 241
    templates, 235-236
    Wizard, 233-234
  dragging/dropping
    objects, 249
  formatting e-mail,
    170-172
  formatting pages, 267
    backgrounds, 271-273
    color, 270-273
    Format menu,
      268-269
    graphics, 269-270
  frames, 253-254,
    260-264
    accommodating
      non-frame browsers,
      262
    HTML tags, 262-264
    relative sizing, 264
    specifying HTML
      editor applications,
      261
    targets, 264
  graphics, 269-270
  HTML tags,
    inserting, 262
  image maps, 249
  keyboard shortcuts
    Link, 244
    open Composer, 231
  links, 244-245
    absolute/relative, 245
    creating, 244, 246
    deleting (removing),
      244
    e-mail addresses, 249
    editing, 244-245
    linking to specific
      parts of pages,
      247-248
    targets, 247
    testing, 250-251
  opening
    Composer, 231-232
    Web pages, 232
  preferences
    graphics editor, 270
    HTML Editor
      Application, 261
    Publishing, 275
  previewing pages, 234
  publishing pages,
    274-277
    configuring publisher
      feature, 275
    finding Web servers,
      274-275
    testing pages, 277
    uploading pages,
      276-277
  saving Web pages,
    233-234
  starting, 231-232
  tables, 253-254
    adding cells/columns/
      rows, 259
    cell preferences,
      258-259
    inserting into Web
      pages, 255-257
    page formatting, 259
    row preferences, 258
    typing cell entries,
      257
  titles, 273
  toolbars
    Formatting toolbar,
      170-171, 238-239
    Image button, 240

Index

Insert Table button, 255
New button, 233, 235
Publish button, 276
Spelling button, 241
Web page classifications, 273
compressing
  files
    defined, 283
    FTP sites, 98-99
    GZip compression utility (VRML files), 157
  folders, Messenger, 186
Conference, 9-10, 213-214
  Address Book button, 218-219
  answering calls, 222
  browsing the Web (collaborative browsing), 225
  business cards, 215-216
  Chat Tool, 222
  commands
    Auto Answer (Call menu), 222
    Do Not Disturb (Call menu), 222
    Hang Up (Call menu), 217
    Preferences (Edit menu), *see* Conference, preferences
    Save (Chat Tool), 222
  Dial button, 217-218
  hanging up, 217
  help, 222
  keyboard shortcuts
    opening Conference, 215
    Send, 222, 225
  modem speed, 10
  opening, 215
  phone numbers (addresses), 217
    Address Book, 219-220
    Speed Dial, 220
    Web phonebook, 218
  placing calls, 217
    from Address Book, 220
  preferences
    answering options, 222
    business cards, 216
    List my name in phonebook, 218
    requirements, 214-215
    sending files, 225-226
    setting up, 215-216
    Silence Sensor, 216
    sound quality, 214
    Speed Dial buttons, 220
    starting, 215
  toolbar
    Chat button, 222
    Collaborative Browsing button, 225
    File Exchange button, 225
    Whiteboard button, 223
  troubleshooting, 221-222
  voicemail, 221
  volume, adjusting, 217-218
    troubleshooting, 221
  Web Phonebook button, 218-219
  Whiteboard, 223-224
cookies (Internet), 117-118
CoolTalk, 9
  see also Conference
Corel WordPerfect, 11
Cosmo Player VRML browser, 129, 156-158
credit-card transactions, *see* security
Cyber Patrol Web site, 123
CYBERsitter Web site, 123
cyberspace, defined, 283

D

decompressing
  defined, 283
  helper applications, 140
deleting
  addresses (address books), 192
  bookmarks, 62
  channels, 77
  digital certificates, 120
  e-mail messages, 178, 186-187
    automatically, 187
    Trash folder, 186
  links, 244
  table items, 259
Dial-Up Networking, 283
dialog boxes
  Channel Properties (Netcaster), 75
  Character Properties (Composer), 245, 248
  Filter Rules (Messenger), 187
  Font (Messenger), 172
  Image Properties (Composer), 240
  Save As (Navigator), 87
  New Table Properties (Composer), 255
  Page Properties (Composer), 274
  Target Properties (Composer), 247
digital certificates (Internet), 118-120
discussion groups, *see* newsgroups
DLS (Dynamic Lookup Services), 218-219
DNS (Domain Name Server), 284
  Failed DNS Lookup error message (Web), 52-53
docking Component bar, 21
Document Not Found error message (Web), 53-54
documents, *see* Web pages
domain names, URLs, 31, 283
  see also DNS (Domain Name Server)
downloading
  Communicator from Internet, 14-19
    FTP sites 17-19
    Macintosh version, 20
    subscriptions/upgrade certificates, 16-17
    Web site, 15
  FTP, 17-19, 98-99

297

Gopher sites, 100
graphics, 84-85
   setting as wallpaper, 90-91
newsgroup messages, 211-212
plug-ins, 129-133
   ActiveX plug-ins, 136-137
   Stroud's List Web site, 130-133
   Tucows Web site, 130
Shockwave, 154
viruses, 121-122
   see also Navigator, security features
Web pages
   channels, 81
   source code, 85-87
Dynamic Lookup Services (DLS), 218-219

E

e-mail (Messenger), 6, 165
   > (right angle brackets), 177
   address books, 191
      adding addresses, 192-194
      deleting addresses, 192
      editing entries, 193
      electronic business cards, 197
      importing, 194
      inserting addresses into messages, 194-195
      mailing lists, 196
      searching, 195
   addresses, 166, 168-169
      address as anonymous FTP password (Navigator), 95
      Cc (carbon copy), 173
      inserting addresses from address books, 194-195
      mailing lists, 196
      multiple recipients, 172-173
      placing long-distance calls, 217
      specifying for identification (Navigator), 95
   attaching files, 169-170
      viewing attachments, 176
   deleting, 178, 186
      automatically, 187
      Trash folder, 186
   encoding, 173
   folders
      compressing, 186
      creating, 184
      deleting messages, 186
      selecting/moving messages, 184-185
   Followup-To option, 173
   formatting messages, 170-171
      message format, 174
   identities, 167
   incoming mail
      automatically retrieving, 189
      filtering, 186-187
   inserting graphics, 172
   junk mail, deleting automatically, 187
   Message Center, 182-183
   Message window (Inbox), 182-183
   opening new messages, 168
   postmasters, 289
   replying, 176-178
      quoting messages, 177-178
      Reply-To option, 173
   retrieving/reading messages, 175
      viewing attachments, 176
   return receipts, 173
   searching for messages, 188
   sending, 170
      composing messages offline, 174
      message sending options, 173-174
      sending Web pages, 168-169
   servers, 167-168
   signatures, 173
   sorting messages, 187-188
   threads, 291
   see also Messenger
e-zines, 284
electronic mail, *see* e-mail
encryption, e-mail, 173
error messages, 51-54
   Access Denied (anonymous FTP sites), 95
   bugs, 52
   Document Not Found, 53-54
   Failed DNS Lookup, 52-53
   File Contains No Data, 54
etiquette, newsgroups, 209
Excite! search tool, 45
   see also searching the Web
exporting bookmark files (Navigator), 67
external viewers, *see* helper applications

F

Failed DNS Lookup error message (Web), 52-53
FAQs (frequently asked questions), 284
File Contains No Data error message (Web), 54
File Exchange program (Conference), 225-226
File Transfer Protocol, *see* FTP
files
   associating, *see* associating file types
   attachments
      e-mail, 169-170, 176
      newsgroup postings, 210-211
   bookmark.htm (Navigator), *see* bookmarks, files
   downloading, *see* downloading

Index

FTP sites, 97-99
sending
    attachments, *see* files, attachments
    Conference, 225-226
filters, Messenger, 186-187
finger search tool, 48-49
    plans, 289
firewalls, Internet, 111, 284
flags, Messenger
    selecting messages, 185
    sorting messages, 188
flaming, 284
folders, Messenger
    compressing, 186
    creating, 184
    deleting messages, 186
    selecting/moving messages, 184-185
Font dialog box, 172
fonts
    e-mail, 171-172
    Navigator preferences, 107-108
    Web pages, creating, 239
    see also formatting
formatting
    e-mail, 170-171
    tables, 259
    Web pages, 267
        backgrounds, 271-273
        color, 270-273
        Format menu (Composer), 268-269
        graphics, 269-270
forms, 114
Forward button, Navigator, 27-28, 59
<FRAME> HTML tag, 262-263
frames (Web pages), 35-36, 253-254, 260-264
    accommodating non-frame browsers, 262
    HTML tags, 262-264
    I Hate Frames Club Web site, 254
    relative sizing, 264
    specifying HTML editor applications, 261
    targets, 264
<FRAMESET> HTML tag, 262-264

FTP (File Transfer Protocol), 14-19, 93-94
    Access Denied error messages, 95
    changing directories, 97
    compressed files, 98-99
    downloading files, 98-99
    Communicator, 15-20
    finding files, 97
    Netscape FTP site, 17
    Communicator directory, 18
    servers, connecting to, 95-99
        private servers, 96
        public (anonymous) servers, 95
    uploading files, 99

G

games
    MOOs (MUD Object-Oriented), 288
    MUDs (Multi-User Dimensions), 288
geeks, defined, 285
GIF (Graphic Interchange Format) files, 285
    see also graphics
Go menu, Navigator, 30, 58
Gopher, 93-94, 100-101, 285
    downloading files, 100
    University of Minnesota Gopher site, 100
    Veronica search tool, 100-101
    Whois search tool, 50
graphics
    cache (Navigator), 110-111
    Conference business cards, 215-216
    e-mail, 172
    finding, 272
    newsgroup messages, 211
    sending with Whiteboard (Conference), 223-224

Web pages
    backgrounds, 271-273
    creating pages, 239-241
    disabling image loading, 54-55, 105
    editing, 270
    formatting, 269-270
    saving, 84-85, 87
    setting as wallpaper, 90-91
Guide button, Navigator, 28
.gz files, *see* virtual reality
GZip compression utility, 157

H

help
    Conference, 222
    Navigator plug-ins, 132, 136
    technical support (World Wide Web), 50
helper applications, 127-128, 139-140
    advantages, 128
    decompressing, 140
    defined, 285
    installing, 141
    mapping files (associating file types), 85, 141-144
        MIME types, 142-144
    opening saved files, 85
    saving Web files, 85
    see also ActiveX; plug-ins
hiding Navigator toolbars, 104
Hollywood Online Web site, 145
Home button, Navigator, 30
home pages
    creating, *see* Composer
    defined, 285
horizontal lines, Web pages, 241
hosts (Internet), defined, 285
HotBot search tool, publicizing Web pages, 278

299

HotJava, 151
.HQX files, decompressing, 140
HTML (HyperText Markup Language), 230, 262, 285
   editors, 285
      specifying editor applications, 261
   hyperlinks, *see* links
   source code, Web pages
      editing, 261
      saving, 86-87
      viewing, 85-86
   style sheets, 122
   tags
      defined, 290
      inserting, 262
      frames, 262-264
   URLs, *see* URLs
HTTP (HyperText Transfer Protocol)
   defined, 286
   URLs, 31
hyperlinks, *see* links
hypermedia, 286
HyperText Markup Language, *see* HTML
HyperText Transfer Protocol, *see* HTTP
HYTELNET, 286

I

I Hate Frames Club Web site, 254
IBM Host-On-Demand (Professional edition), 4
IBM Web site, 50
Image Properties dialog box (Composer), 240
imagemaps (Web pages), 34, 249
   see also links
images, *see* graphics
importing
   address books, 194
   bookmark files (Navigator), 67
InfoSeek search tool, 45
   publicizing Web pages, 278
   see also searching the Web

inline images
newsgroup messages, 211
Web pages, disabling loading, 54-55
see also graphics
installing
   Communicator, 19-20
      Macintosh version, 20
   helper applications, 141
   INSTALL.TXT/ SETUP.EXE files, 141
   plug-ins, 134
   Shockwave, 154
Internet, 4, 286
   Archie search tool, 281
   BBS (bulletin board systems), 282
   chat, 282
      Conference Chat Tool, 222
      IRC (Internet Relay Chat), 287
   connecting to Internet with Navigator, 20
   downloading Communicator, 14-19
   etiquette, newsgroups, 209
   firewalls, 111
   FTP, *see* FTP (File Transfer Protocol)
   Gopher, 93-94, 100-101
      Whois search tool, 50
   hosts, 285
   Java, 149
      HotJava, 151
      playing applets, 150-152
      security, 121-122, 150-151
   Jughead search tool, 287
   newbies, 288
   newsgroups, *see* newsgroups
   security, 113-114
      ActiveX, 121-122
      censoring adult sites, 122-123
      cookies, 117-118
      digital certificates, 118-120

      Java, 121-122, 150-151
      Navigator security features, 114-117
      viruses, 121-122
   Shockwave, 149
   TCP/IP (Transmission Control Protocol/ Internet Protocol), 290
   telnet, 290
   terminal connections, 291
   URLs, *see* URLs
   virtual reality, *see* virtual reality
   WAIS (Wide Area Information Server), 292
   see also World Wide Web
Internet Explorer, downloading Communicator, 15-16
Internet Movie Database Browser Web site, 32
Internet Phone program, 286
Internet service providers, 274-275
intranets, 7
IP addresses, 219, 287
IRC (Internet Relay Chat), 287
italic text, Web pages, 239
   see also formatting
IUMA (Internet Underground Music Archive) Web site, 145

J

JARS (Java Applet Rating Service) Web site, 152-153
Java, 121-122, 149
   applets, 150
      playing, 150-152
   defined, 287
   disabling/enabling, 122
   HotJava, 151
   security, 121-122, 150-151
   Web sites, 151-152

Index

JavaScript, disabling/
  enabling, 122
.jpg files, *see* graphics
Jughead search tool, 287
junk e-mail, deleting
  automatically, 187

K

keyboard shortcuts
  Composer
    Link, 244
    open Composer, 231
  Conference
    open Conference, 215
    Send, 222, 225
  Messenger
    Address Book, 192
    Forward, 177
    Get Messages, 175
    Message Center, 183
    New Message, 168
    Reply, 177
  Navigator, 33-34, 105
    Add Bookmark, 60
    ahead to next page, 34
    back to previous page, 34
    bottom of Web page, 34
    Close Bookmark List, 64
    Copy, 86
    Edit Bookmarks, 61
    following links, 33
    History, 58
    New Navigator Window, 35
    Open, 87
    Open Page, 32
    Paste, 86
    Reload, 30
    Save, 86
    stop loading page, 34
    switching between multiple windows, 35
    top of Web page, 34
  Netcaster, starting Netcaster, 73
Kid's Corner Web site, 145

L

.la files, *see* audio
links (World Wide Web), 26, 243, 287
  absolute/relative references, 245, 281
  bookmarking, 61
  color, 28, 108-109
  creating, 244
    e-mail addresses, 249
    linking pages, 246
    linking to specific parts of pages, 247-248
  deleting (removing), 244
  editing, 244-245
  following with keyboard, 33
  maps, 34
  multimedia links, 145
  newsgroups, 202
    attachments, 210-211
  preferences, setting, 28
  properties, 244-245
  saving, 84
  shortcuts, creating (Windows 95), 59
  targets, 247-248
  testing, 250-251
lists, Web pages, 239
LiveAudio player, 129
.lma files, *see* audio
lock icon, Navigator, 116-117
log in/out 287
logical codes, Web pages, 287
long-distance calling, *see* Conference
lurking, 287
Lycos search tool, 46
  Lycos Top 5% Web site, 33
  publicizing Web pages, 278
  see also searching the Web

M

Macintosh Communicator version, 20
Macmillan
  SuperSeek search tool, 44
  WWW Yellow Pages Web site, 44
  see also searching the Web
Macromedia Shockwave, 154-155
mail, *see* e-mail; Messenger
mailing lists, e-mail, 196
mapping files to helper applications, 141-144
maps (Web pages), 34, 249
  see also links
McAfee VirusScan Web site, 121
Media Player, 129
Message Center, 182-183
  newsgroups (discussion groups), 204-205
  see also Messenger
messages, *see* e-mail; newsgroups, messages
Messenger, 6, 166
  address books, 191
    adding addresses, 192-194
    deleting addresses, 192
    editing entries, 193
    electronic business cards, 197
    importing, 194
    inserting addresses into messages, 194-195
    mailing lists, 196
    searching, 195
  addressing e-mail, 168-169
    Cc (carbon copy), 173
    inserting addresses from address books, 194-195
    mailing lists, 196
    multiple recipients, 172-173

301

attaching files, 169-170
  viewing attachments, 176
commands
  Compress Folders (File menu), 186
  Empty Trash Folder (File menu), 186
  Flag (Message menu), 185
  Font (Format menu), 171
  Import (File menu), 194
  Mail Filters (Edit menu), 186
  New Folder (File menu), 184
  Search Messages (Edit menu), 188
  Send Later (File menu), 170, 174
  Send Now (File menu), 170, 174
customizing, see Messenger, preferences
deleting messages, 178, 186-187
encoding messages, 173
flagging messages
  selecting messages, 185
  sorting messages, 188
folders, 184-186
formatting messages, 170-171
  message format, 174
incoming messages
  automatically retrieving, 189
  filters, 186-187
inserting graphics, 172
junk mail, deleting automatically, 187
keyboard shortcuts
  Address Book, 192
  Forward, 177
  Get Messages, 175
  Message Center, 183
  Reply, 177
Message center, 182-183
  newsgroups (discussion groups), 204-205

Message window (Inbox), 182-183
  sorting messages, 187-188
opening
  Messenger, 166
  new messages, 168
personal cards, 197
preferences (Mail & Groups), 178-180
  identity, 167
  message display options, 179
  outgoing mail, 179-180
  quoting original message when replying, 177
  server information, 167-168
replying to messages, 176-178
  quoting messages, 177-178
  Reply-To option, 173
retrieving/reading e-mail, 175
  viewing attachments, 176
return receipts, 173
searching for messages, 188
sending e-mail, 170
  composing messages offline, 174
  message sending options, 173-174
sending Web pages, 168-169
setting up, 166-168
signatures, 173
threads
  selecting messages, 185
  sorting messages, 188
toolbar
  Attach button, 169
  New Msg button, 168
Trash folder, 186
Microsoft Internet Explorer, downloading Communicator, 15-16
midi files, see audio

MIME (Multi-purpose Internet Mail Extensions), 144, 288
  helper applications, 142-144
mirror sites, 288
modems, Conference call sound quality, 10, 214
monitors, 146
MOOs (MUD Object-Oriented), 288
.mov files, see video
.mpeg files, see video
MPEG (Moving Pictures Expert Group), 288
  see also video
MUDs (Multi-User Dimensions), 288
multimedia
  audio, see audio
  file types, 128-129
  Gopher sites, 100
  helper applications, mapping files, 141-144
  Java, see Java
  links, 145
  quality, 146
  Shockwave, 154-155
  video, see video
  virtual reality, see virtual reality
  Web sites, 145
  see also ActiveX controls; helper applications; plug-ins
My Channels list (Netcaster), 73
  adding channels, 75-77
  right-click menus, 77
  updating channels, 75, 77
  viewing channels, 76, 81

N

NASA Web site, 33
Navigator, 4-5
  ActiveX, 127-128, 136-137
    advantages, 128
    downloading plug-ins, 136-137
    security, 121-122
    Web sites, 136-137

Index

Back/Forward buttons, 27-28, 59
bookmarks, 59-61
   adding to Personal toolbar, 68-69
   arranging bookmark lists, 62-65
   closing bookmark lists, 64
   creating, 59-60, 65-66
   deleting, 62
   importing/exporting bookmark files, 67
   links, 61
   opening bookmark files, 66
   renaming, 62
   saving bookmark lists as home pages, 67-68
   updating URLs, 66
cache, 110-111, 282
collaborative browsing (Conference), 225
commands
   About Plug-ins (Help menu), 132
   Add Bookmark (Bookmarks menu), 60, 65
   Blank Page (File menu), 232
   Bookmark Properties (Edit menu), 66
   Close (File menu), 64
   Delete (Edit menu), 62
   Edit Bookmarks (Bookmarks menu), 61, 65-67, 69
   Edit Page (File menu), 232-233, 236
   Hide (View menu), 104
   Import (File menu), 67
   New Bookmark (File menu), 66
   New Folder (File menu), 63
   New Navigator Window (File menu), 35
   New Separator (File menu), 63
   Open Bookmarks Folder (File menu), 66
   Open File (File menu), 64
   Open Page (File menu), 32, 87, 232
   Page From Template (File menu), 232
   Page From Wizard (File menu), 232
   Page Info (View menu), 117
   Page Setup (File menu), 88
   Page Source (View menu), 85-86
   Preferences (Edit menu), *see* Navigator, preferences
   Print Preview (File menu), 89
   Reload (View menu), 30, 36
   Save As (File menu), 66, 86
   Set as Bookmark Menu (View menu), 65
   Set as New Bookmarks Folder (View menu), 65
   Set As Wallpaper, 90
   Show (View menu), 104
   Show Personal Toolbar (View menu), 68
   Update Bookmarks (View menu), 66
   Upload File (File menu), 99
Communicator component interactions, 10
connecting to Internet, 20
customizing, 112
   color, 108-109
   fonts, 107-108
   history options, 109
   home page, 109
   security options, 115-116
   speed, 105, 111
   startup program, 107
   toolbars, 104-105, 107
   see also Navigator, preferences
default browser, 59
Document Info window, security, 117
downloading
   Communicator, 15-16
   plug-ins, 129-130
finger, 48-49
Forward button, 27-28
frames (Web pages), 35-36
FTP sites, *see* FTP
Go menu, 30, 58
   Home command, 30
Gopher sites, 100-101
graphics
   disabling, 54-55
   saving, 84-85, 87
   setting as wallpaper, 90-91
Guide button, 28
help, plug-ins, 132, 136
helper applications, 127-128, 139-140
   advantages, 128
   decompressing, 140
   installing, 141
   mapping files, 141-144
   MIME types, 142-144
history, 28, 30, 58
   Back/Forward buttons, 27-28, 59
   clearing, 28
   customizing history options, 109
   Go menu, 30, 58
   Home, 30
   keyboard shortcuts, 34
home page, 109
   bookmark lists, 67-68
   defined, 285
   Home button, 30

303

Java
    HotJava, 151
    playing applets,
      150-152
    security, 121-122,
      150-151
keyboard shortcuts,
  33-34, 105
    Add Bookmark, 60
    ahead to next page,
      34
    back to previous
      page, 34
    bottom of Web page,
      34
    Close Bookmark List,
      64
    Copy, 86
    Edit Bookmarks, 61
    following links, 33
    History, 58
    New Navigator
      Window, 35
    Open, 87
    Open Page, 32
    Paste, 86
    Reload, 30
    Save, 86
    stop loading page, 34
    switching between
      multiple windows,
      35
    top of Web page, 34
links, 26
    color, 28
    following with
      keyboard, 33
    Location text box, 33
    drop-down list, 58
    entering URLs, 27, 33
maps, 34
multimedia
    file types, 128-129
    see also plug-ins
N icon, 26
newsgroups, connecting
  to, 202-203
offline/online work
    modes, 109-110
opening Web pages,
  32-33
    multiple pages, 35

Personal toolbar, 68-69
plug-ins, 127-128
    advantages, 128
    downloading,
      129-133, 136-137
    file types playable,
      128-129
    finding, 129-132,
      136-137
    help, 132, 136
    installing, 134
    uninstalling, 134-136
preferences, 106, 112
    automatically loading
      images, 54, 105
    color, 108-109
    cookies, 118
    digital certificates,
      119
    email address for
      identification/
      anonymous FTP
      password, 95
    fonts, 107-108
    helper applications,
      141-143
    history options, 109
    home page, 68, 109
    Java, 150-151
    Java/JavaScript, 122
    links, 28
    offline/online work
      modes, 109-110
    on startup launch
      option, 107
    proxies, 111
    save to disk option,
      85
    security, 115-116
    show toolbar as, 107
    startup program, 73,
      201
printing Web docu-
  ments, 88-90
    page setup, 88
    print preview, 89-90
reloading pages, 30
saving Web files
    automatically, 85
    Save As dialog box,
      87
screen (window), 26

Search button, 40-41
security features,
  114-117
    ActiveX, 121-122
    censoring adult sites,
      122-123
    cookies, 117-118
    digital certificates,
      118-120
    Java, 121-122,
      150-151
    secured site
      indicators, 116-117
    viruses, 121-122
    warnings, 115-116,
      118
Shockwave, 154-155
speed
    cache comparison
      options, 111
    disabling image
      loading, 54-55, 105
status bar, 290
stopping page loading,
  55
style sheets, 122
switching between
  multiple windows, 35
toolbars, 27-28
    customizing, 104-105,
      107
    playing Java applets,
      151
    Print button, 88
    Reload button, 30
    smart buttons, 27-28
    Stop button, 55
URLs, entering, 32-33
virtual reality, see virtual
  reality
Warning dialog box,
  38-39
see also World Wide
  Web
NCompass Web site, 137
Net Nanny Web site, 123
Netcaster, 6, 71-72
    button bar, 73-74
    Channel Finder, 73-76
        adding channels to
          My Channels list,
          75-77
        deleting channels, 77

Index

Channel Properties
  dialog box, 75
closing, 73
control bar, 73-74
  Add button, 77
  Options button, *see*
    Netcaster, options
default opening
  channel, setting, 80
displaying channels as
  Webtops, 78
keyboard shortcuts,
  starting Netcaster, 73
My Channels list, 73
  adding channels,
    75-77
  right-click menus, 77
  viewing channels, 76,
    81
opening Netcaster, 73
options
  deleting channels, 77
  displaying channels
    as Webtops, 78
  layout, 79
  updating Web pages,
    77
preferences, startup with
  Netcaster, 73
starting, 73
updating channels
  automatically, 75
  manually, 77
Webtops, 72, 74
  control buttons, 78
  moving, 79
window, 73
  customizing, 79-80
Netscape
  Collabra, *see* Collabra
  Communicator, *see*
    Communicator
  Composer, *see* Composer
  Conference, *see*
    Conference
  CoolTalk, 9
    see also Conference
  File Exchange, 225-226
  FTP site, 17
    Communicator
      directory, 18
  history, 5
  Mail, *see* Messenger

Media Player, 129
Messenger, *see*
  Messenger
Navigator, *see* Navigator
Netcaster, *see* Netcaster
News, *see* Collabra
Web site, 15
network proxies
  (Navigator), 111
news tickers (Web), 200
newsgroups (discussion
  groups), 199-200, 283
  addresses (URLs),
    202-203
  attachments, sending/
    receiving, 210-211
  Collabra, 7-8
  connecting to, 202
  etiquette, 209
  links
    attachments, 210-211
    Web links, 202
  listing available
    newsgroups, 203
  lurking, 287
  messages
    downloading, 211
    posting new
      messages, 210
    reading, 205-206
    replying to, 208-209
    searching, 207
    sorting, 207
    spell check, 210
    threads, 207
    viewing replies, 207
  names (titles), 202-203
  searching, InfoSeek
    search tool, 45
  servers, 201-202
  spamming, 290
  starting Collabra,
    200-201
  subscribing, 204-205
  threads, 291
  unsubscribing, 205
  USENET, 200, 291
  see also Collabra
<NOFRAME> HTML tag,
  262-263
NPAVI32 DLL video player,
  129

O

Open File command
  (Navigator File menu), 64
opening
  Collabra, 200-201
  Composer, 231-232
  Conference, 215
  helper applications, 85
  Messenger, 166
  Netcaster, 73
  Web pages
    from hard disks,
      87-88
    from hard drive, 81
    in Composer, 232

P

Page Properties dialog box
  (Composer), 274
Page Setup command,
  Navigator File menu, 88
passwords
  digital certificates,
    118-120
  FTP sites
    private, 96-98
    public (anonymous),
      95
people searches, 47-50
  finger, 48-49
  Netscape people finder
    links, 47
  Web phone directories,
    48
Perry-Castaneda Library
  Map Collection Web site,
    145
phone calls, *see* Conference
physical codes, Web pages,
  288
Pioneer VRML browser, 160
Planet 9 Web site (VRML),
  159
plug-ins, 11, 127-128
  ActiveX, *see* ActiveX
  associating file types, 85
  downloading, 129-133
    ActiveX plug-ins,
      136-137
    Stroud's List Web site,
      130-133

305

file types, 128-129
finding, 129-132
    Netscape plug-ins page, 132
    Stroud's List Web site, 130-133
    Tucows Web site, 130
help, 132, 136
installing, 134
opening saved files, 85
saving Web files to disks, 85
uninstalling, 134-136
see also ActiveX; helper applications
plus signs (+)
    Collabra, 203
    Web searches, 39-40
pornography (World Wide Web), censoring, 122-123
ports, 289
postmasters, 289
PPP (Point-to-Point Protocol), 289
printing, Navigator, 88-90
    page setup, 88
    print preview, 89-90
Professional edition, 4
proxies, Navigator, 111
    defined, 289
publishing Web pages (Composer), 274-277
push content (Web), 6, 72, 289
    browsing Web pages offline, 81

Q-R

quoting e-mail messages in replies, 177-178

reading
    e-mail (Messenger), 175-176
    newsgroup messages (Collabra), 205-206
        offline, 211-212
        viewing replies, 207
README.TXT files, 141
reloading Web pages, 30
    frames, 36
replying to e-mail, 176-178
    Reply-To option, 173

return receipts, e-mail, 173
right angle brackets (>), e-mail, 177

S

saving
    e-mail attachments, 176
    files
        FTP sites, 98
        Gopher sites, 100
        Web, 84-85
    graphics
        setting as wallpaper, 90-91
        with page source code, 87
    links, 84
    Web pages, 85-87
        Composer, 233-234
screen captures, sending (Whiteboard), 224
ScriptActive plug-in, 137
searching the Web, 37
    addresses, 193-194
    Boolean operators, 282
    case-sensitivity, 39
    Channel Finder, 74-76
        adding channels, 75-77
        deleting channels, 77
        viewing channels, 76, 81
    composing search strings, 39-40
    hits, 285
    Navigator Search button, 40-41
    people searches, 47-50
        Finger, 48-49
        Netscape people finder links, 47
        Web phone directories, 48
    publicizing Web pages, 278
    scores, 289
    search tools, 42-46
        AltaVista, 43
        Excite!, 45
        Finger, 48-49
        InfoSeek, 45
        Lycos, 46

SuperSeek, 44
WebCrawler, 45
Whois search tool, 50
Yahoo!, 42-43, 145
spamdexing, 41
stop words, 290
technical support, 50
Web page keywords, entering, 273
see also Internet, search tools
Secure Sockets Layer (SSL), 115-116
    defined, 290
security, 113-114
    firewalls, 284
    Java, 121-122, 150-151
    Navigator security features, 114-117
        ActiveX, 121-122
        censoring adult sites, 122-123
        cookies, 117-118
        digital certificates, 118-120
        Java, 121-122
        secured site indicators, 116-117
        viruses, 121-122
        warnings, 115-116, 118
    passwords
        digital certificates, 118-120
        FTP sites, 95-98
        see also digital certificates
    SSL (Secure Sockets Layer), 115-116
        defined, 290
Send Page command (File menu), 168
sending
    e-mail, 170
        composing messages offline, 174
        message sending options, 173-174
        see also e-mail
    files, Conference, 225-226
servers
    addresses, 167-168
    defined, 290

Index

entering server information into Messenger, 167-168
FTP (File Transfer Protocol), 95-99
   downloading files, 98-99
   finding files, 97
   uploading files, 99
Gopher, 100-101
news servers (newsgroups), 201-202
Web servers, 274-275
setting up Communicator, 19-20
SETUP.EXE files, 141
shareware, 290
Shockwave, 149, 154-155
   downloading/installing, 154
shortcuts
   keyboards, *see* keyboard shortcuts
   Web pages shortcut (Windows 95), 59
signatures, e-mail, 173
   personal cards, 197
Silence Sensor, Conference, 216
SLIP (Serial Line Internet Protocol), 290
smart buttons, Navigator toolbars, 27-28
sorting newsgroups messages (Collabra), 207
sound cards, 146
   Conference requirements, 214-215
   Silence Sensor, 216
   troubleshooting, 221
   see also audio
source code, Web pages
   editing, 261
   saving, 86-87
   viewing, 85-86
spamming, 41, 290
spell check
   newsgroups, 210
   Web pages, 241
SSL (Secure Sockets Layer)
   defined, 290
   Navigator, 115-116
startup program, choosing
   Collabra, 201
   Navigator, 107
   Netcaster, 73
status bar, Navigator, 290
Steve's Tequila Race Web site (Shockwave), 155
Stop button, Navigator, 55
Stroud's List Web site, 99
   plug-ins, 130-133
StuffIt Expander utility, 140
style sheets, Navigator, 122
Submit-It Web site, publicizing Web pages, 278
subscribing
   newsgroups, 204-205
      unsubscribing, 205
   Web sites, 6
      push content, 72, 81
      see also channels
SuperSeek Web site, 44-45
   see also searching the Web
support, technical, 50
Surf Watch Web site, 123

T

tables (Web pages), 253-254
   cells
      adding/deleting, 259
      preferences, 258-259
   columns, 259
   inserting tables, 255-257
   page formatting, 259
   rows
      adding/deleting, 259
      preferences, 258
   typing cell entries, 257
tags (HTML)
   inserting, 262
   defined, 290
   frames, 262-264
Target Properties dialog box (Composer), 247
targets
   frames, 264
   links, 247-248
TCP/IP (Transmission Control Protocol/Internet Protocol), 290
technical support, 50
telephone
   telephone calls, *see* Conference
   Web phone directories, 48
telnet, 290
   HYTELNET, 286
templates, Web pages (Composer), 235-236
terminal emulation, 291
Terminal Reality Web site (VRML), 157-158
text
   e-mail messages, 170-171
   Navigator preferences, 108-109
      color, 108-109
      fonts, 107-108
   Web pages
      adding/deleting, 237-238
      alignment around images, 241
      blinking (Web pages), 268
      formatting, 238-239
      graphics, 269-270
threads
   defined, 291
   Messenger
      selecting messages, 185
      sorting messages, 188
   newsgroup messages (Collabra), 207
tiling
   multiple Navigator windows, 35
   wallpaper images, 91
toolbars
   Address Book toolbar, New Card button, 192
   Collabra
      Expand All button, 203
      Get Groups button, 203
      New Msg button, 210
      Reply button, 208
      Spelling button, 210
      Subscribe button, 203

Composer
  formatting e-mail, 170-171
  Formatting toolbar, 238-239
  Image button, 240
  Insert Table button, 255
  New button, 233, 235
  Publish button, 276
  Spelling button, 241
Conference
  Chat button, 222
  Collaborative Browsing button, 225
  File Exchange button, 225
  Whiteboard button, 223
Messenger
  Attach button, 169
  New Msg button, 168
Navigator, 27-28
  customizing, 104-105, 107
  Guide button, People, 47
  Personal toolbar, 68-69
  playing Java applets, 151
  Security button, *see* Navigator, security features
  smart buttons, 27-28
Netcaster, 73-74
Trash folder, Messenger, 186
Tucows Web site, 99
  plug-ins, 130

U

UFO Information Center Web site, 33
Uniform Resource Locators, *see* URLs
uninstalling plug-ins, 134-136
UNIX shell, 291

unsubscribing to newsgroups, 205
updating Web pages
  automatically, 75
  manually, 77
upgrading Communicator, 16-17
uploading
  files to FTP sites, 99
  Web pages, 275-277
    see also publishing Web pages
URLs (Uniform Resource Locators), 31-34
  absolute/relative links, 245
  bookmarks
    creating bookmarks, 59-61, 65-66
    updating, 66
  defined, 291
  domain names, 31
  entering in Navigator, 32-33
    Location text box, 27, 33
  HTTP (HyperText Transfer Protocol), 31, 286
  links, creating, 244
  Location text box, 33
  newsgroups, 202-203
  server types, 31
  uploading Web pages, 275-276
  see also Web sites
USENET, 200, 291
  see also newsgroups; Collabra
Uuencode, e-mail, 173

V

VDO Live video player, *see* plug-ins
VeriSign Web site, 119
Veronica search tool (Gopher), 100-101
video
  file types, 129
  helper applications, mapping files, 141-144

  links, 145
  MPEG (Moving Pictures Expert Group), 288
  quality, 146
  QuickTime player, 129
  saving video files from Web, 84-85
  Web sites, 145
  see also ActiveX controls; helper applications; plug-ins
viewing source code, 85-86
virtual memory, 291
virtual reality, 149, 155-160
  browsers, 160
    Cosmo Player, 129, 156-158
  VRML (Virtual Reality Modeling Language), 155-156
    GZip compression utility, 157
    VRML worlds, 157-159
viruses, 121-122
voicemail, Conference, 221
VR Scout VRML browser, 160
VRealm VRML browser, 160
VRML (Virtual Reality Modeling Language), *see* virtual reality, VRML
VRML Mall Web site, 159

W

WAIS (Wide Area Information Server), 292
wallpaper, setting Web graphics as wallpaper, 90-91
Warning dialog box, Navigator, 38-39
warnings, Navigator security, 115-116
  cookies, 118
.wav files, *see* audio
Web Designer Web site, 272

Index

Web pages
  backgrounds, 271-273
  blinking text, 268
  bookmarking, 59-61
    see also bookmarks
  classifications, 273
  creating, see Composer
  defined, 292
  e-mailing pages, 168-169
  frames, see frames
  graphics, see graphics,
    Web pages
  image maps, 249
  keywords, 273
  links, see links
  opening
    from hard disks,
      87-88
    from hard drive, 81
    in Composer, 232
  printing, 88-90
  publicizing, 278
  saving
    graphics, 87
    source code, 85-87
  shortcuts (Windows 95),
    59
  source code
    editing, 261
    saving, 86-87
    viewing, 85-86
  tables, see tables
  titles, 273
  updating
    automatically, 75
    manually, 77
  uploading, 275-277
    see also publishing
      Web pages; World
      Wide Web
Web sites
  ActiveX Gallery, 136
  AltaVista search tool, 43
  Blue Skies (Java),
    152-153
  Café del Sol (Java), 152
  channels, 282
  Cyber Patrol, 123
  CYBERsitter, 123
  Excite! search tool, 45
  finger gateways, 49
  Hollywood Online, 145

I Hate Frames Club, 254
IBM, 50
InfoSeek search tool, 45
Internet Movie Database
  Browser, 32
IUMA (Internet
  Underground Music
  Archive), 145
JARS (Java Applet Rating
  Service), 152-153
Kid's Corner, 145
Lycos search tool, 46
Lycos Top 5% Web
  sites, 33
Macromedia, 154
McAfee VirusScan, 121
NASA, 33
NCompass, 137
Net Nanny, 123
Netscape, 15
news tickers, 200
Perry-Castaneda Library
  Map Collection, 145
phone directories, 48
Pioneer VRML browser,
  160
Planet 9 (VRML), 159
Shockwave, 154
Steve's Tequila Race
  (Shockwave), 155
Stroud's List, 99
Stroud's List (plug-ins),
  130-133
    downloading files,
      132-133
Submit-It, 278
subscribing, 6
  push content, 72, 81
  see also channels
SuperSeek search tool,
  44-45
Surf Watch, 123
Terminal Reality
  (VRML), 157-158
Tucows, 99
  plug-ins, 130
UFO Information
  Center, 33
VeriSign, 119
VRML Mall, 159
Web Designer, 272
Whois search tool
  (Gopher), 50

WinZip utility, 140
WIRL VRML browser,
  160
WWW Virtual Library,
  33
WWW Yellow Pages
  search tool, 44
Yahoo! search tool,
  42-43, 145
ZD3D Terminal Reality
  (VRML), 157-158
WebCrawler search tool, 45
  publicizing Web pages,
    278
  see also World Wide
    Web, searching
WebSpace VRML browser,
  160
Webtops (Netcaster), 72, 74
  control buttons, 78
  moving, 79
  see also channels
whiteboards (Conference),
  223-224, 292
Whois search tool, 50
windows
  cascading/tiling
    (Navigator), 35
  see also dialog boxes;
    warnings
WinZip utility, 140
WIRL VRML browser, 160
wizards, creating Web
  pages (Composer),
  233-234
WordPerfect, 11
World Wide Web (WWW),
  4-5, 25
  ActiveX, see ActiveX
  addresses, see URLs
  browsers
    default browser, 59
    downloading
      Communicator
      from Internet,
      15-16, 20
    Internet Explorer,
      15-16
    Navigator, see
      Navigator
  browsing offline
    (Netcaster), 81

309

bugs, 52
chat, 282
collaborative browsing, Conference, 225
connecting to Web (Navigator), 20
creating Web pages, *see* Composer
defined, 292
DNS (Domain Name Servers), 52-53
downloading Communicator, 15-16
error messages, 51
  Document Not Found, 53-54
  Failed DNS Lookup, 52-53
  File Contains No Data, 54
forms, 114
frames, *see* frames
graphics, *see* graphics
HTML (HyperText Markup Language), *see* HTML
HTTP (HyperText Transfer Protocol)
  defined, 286
  URLs, 31
indexes, *see* World Wide Web, searching
Java
  HotJava, 151
  playing applets, 150-152
  security, 121-122, 150-151
links, *see* links
maps, 34
pages, *see* Web pages
push content, 6, 72, 289
  browsing Web pages offline, 81
searching, 37
  addresses, 193-194
  AltaVista search tool, 43
  Boolean operators (AND, NOT, and OR), 39-40, 282

case-sensitivity, 39
Channel Finder, 74-76
composing search strings, 39
Excite! search tool, 45
finger, 48-49
hits, 285
InfoSeek search tool, 45
Lycos search tool, 46
Navigator Search button, 40-41
Netscape people finder links, 47
publicizing Web pages, 278
scores, 289
spamdexing, 41
stop words, 290
SuperSeek search tool, 44-45
technical support, 50
Web page keywords, entering, 273
Web phone directories, 48
WWW Yellow Pages, 44
Yahoo! search tool, 42-43, 145
security, 113-114
ActiveX, 121-122
censoring adult sites, 122-123
cookies, 117-118
digital certificates, 118-120
Java, 121-122, 150-151
Navigator security features, 114-117
viruses, 121-122
servers, 274
defined, 292
finding, 274-275
Shockwave, 149, 154-155
sites, *see* Web sites

speed
  disabling image loading, 54-55, 105
  long-distance call sound quality, 214
style sheets, 122
URLs, *see* URLs
WorldView VRML browser, 160
.wrl files, *see* virtual reality
.wrz files, *see* virtual reality
WWW, *see* World Wide Web
WWW Virtual Library Web site, 33
WWW Yellow Pages Web site, 44

X-Y-Z

Yahoo! Web site, 42-43, 145
  publicizing Web pages, 278
  see also searching the Web
ZD3D Terminal Reality Web site (VRML), 157-158
zines, 292
zipped files (.zip), 292
  decompressing, 140
zooming, Navigator print preview, 89-90

Complete and Return this Card for a *FREE* Computer Book Catalog

Thank you for purchasing this book! You have purchased a superior computer book written expressly for your needs. To continue to provide the kind of up-to-date, pertinent coverage you've come to expect from us, we need to hear from you. Please take a minute to complete and return this self-addressed, postage-paid form. In return, we'll send you a free catalog of all our computer books on topics ranging from word processing to programming and the internet.

Mr. ☐   Mrs. ☐   Ms. ☐   Dr. ☐

Name (first) _____ (M.I.) __ (last) _____
Address _____
_____
City _____ State __ Zip _____
Phone _____ Fax _____
Company Name _____
E-mail address _____

Please check at least (3) influencing factors for purchasing this book.

Front or back cover information on book .... ☐
Special approach to the content .... ☐
Completeness of content .... ☐
Author's reputation .... ☐
Publisher's reputation .... ☐
Book cover design or layout .... ☐
Index or table of contents of book .... ☐
Price of book .... ☐
Special effects, graphics, illustrations .... ☐
Other (Please specify): _____ ☐

How did you first learn about this book?

Saw in Macmillan Computer Publishing catalog .... ☐
Recommended by store personnel .... ☐
Saw the book on bookshelf at store .... ☐
Recommended by a friend .... ☐
Received advertisement in the mail .... ☐
Saw an advertisement in: _____ ☐
Read book review in: _____ ☐
Other (Please specify): _____ ☐

How many computer books have you purchased in the last six months?

This book only .... ☐   3 to 5 books .... ☐
2 books .... ☐   More than 5 .... ☐

4. Where did you purchase this book?

Bookstore .... ☐
Computer Store .... ☐
Consumer Electronics Store .... ☐
Department Store .... ☐
Office Club .... ☐
Warehouse Club .... ☐
Mail Order .... ☐
Direct from Publisher .... ☐
Internet site .... ☐
Other (Please specify): _____ ☐

5. How long have you been using a computer?

☐ Less than 6 months   ☐ 6 months to a year
☐ 1 to 3 years   ☐ More than 3 years

6. What is your level of experience with personal computers and with the subject of this book?

	With PCs	With subject of book
New	☐	☐
Casual	☐	☐
Accomplished	☐	☐
Expert	☐	☐

Source Code ISBN: 0-7897-1029-3

7. Which of the following best describes your job title?
- Administrative Assistant ☐
- Coordinator ☐
- Manager/Supervisor ☐
- Director ☐
- Vice President ☐
- President/CEO/COO ☐
- Lawyer/Doctor/Medical Professional ☐
- Teacher/Educator/Trainer ☐
- Engineer/Technician ☐
- Consultant ☐
- Not employed/Student/Retired ☐
- Other (Please specify): _____ ☐

8. Which of the following best describes the area of the company your job title falls under?
- Accounting ☐
- Engineering ☐
- Manufacturing ☐
- Operations ☐
- Marketing ☐
- Sales ☐
- Other (Please specify): _____ ☐

9. What is your age?
- Under 20 ☐
- 21-29 ☐
- 30-39 ☐
- 40-49 ☐
- 50-59 ☐
- 60-over ☐

10. Are you:
- Male ☐
- Female ☐

11. Which computer publications do you read regularly? (Please list)

_____
_____
_____
_____
_____
_____
_____
_____

Comments: _____

Fold here and scotch-tape to ma

BUSINESS REPLY MAIL
FIRST-CLASS MAIL PERMIT NO. 9918 INDIANAPOLIS IN

POSTAGE WILL BE PAID BY THE ADDRESSEE

ATTN MARKETING
MACMILLAN COMPUTER PUBLISHING
MACMILLAN PUBLISHING USA
201 W 103RD ST
INDIANAPOLIS IN 46290-9042

NO POSTAGE
NECESSARY
IF MAILED
IN THE
UNITED STATES

Check out Que® Books on the World Wide Web
http://www.quecorp.com

As the biggest software release in computer history, Windows 95 continues to redefine the computer industry. Click here for the latest info on our Windows 95 books

Make computing quick and easy with these products designed exclusively for new and casual users

Examine the latest releases in word processing, spreadsheets, operating systems, and suites

The Internet, The World Wide Web, CompuServe®, America Online®, Prodigy® —it's a world of ever-changing information. Don't get left behind!

Find out about new additions to our site, new bestsellers and hot topics

In-depth information on high-end topics: find the best reference books for databases, programming, networking, and client/server technologies

A recent addition to Que, Ziff-Davis Press publishes the highly-successful *How It Works* and *How to Use* series of books, as well as *PC Learning Labs Teaches* and *PC Magazine* series of book/disc packages

Stay on the cutting edge of Macintosh® technologies and visual communications

Find out which titles are making headlines

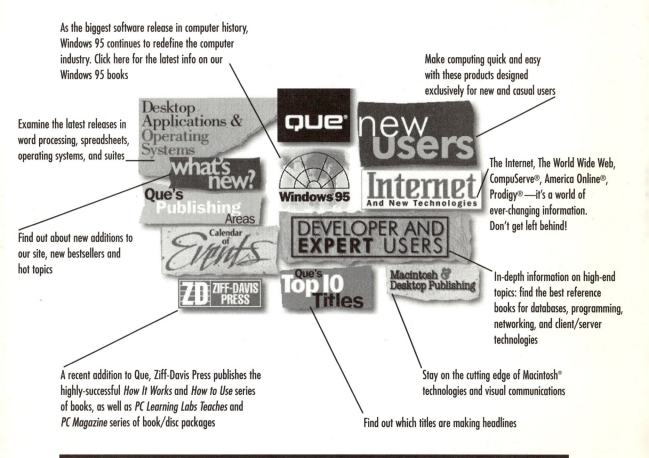

With 6 separate publishing groups, Que develops products for many specific market segments and areas of computer technology. Explore our Web Site and you'll find information on best-selling titles, newly published titles, upcoming products, authors, and much more.

- Stay informed on the latest industry trends and products available
- Visit our online bookstore for the latest information and editions
- Download software from Que's library of the best shareware and freeware

Copyright © 1997, Macmillan Computer Publishing-USA, A Viacom Company

Technical Support:

If you need assistance with the information in this book or with a CD/Disk accompanying the book, please access the Knowledge Base on our Web site at **http://www.superlibrary.com/general/support**. Our most Frequently Asked Questions are answered there. If you do not find the answer to your questions on our Web site, you may contact Macmillan Technical Support **(317) 581-3833** or e-mail us at **support@mcp.com**.